THE
NORWICH
BOOK
OF
DAYS

CAROL TWINCH

For Silas, Willow and Christian

First published 2012

The History Press
The Mill, Brimscombe Port
Stroud, Gloucestershire, GL5 2QG
www.thehistorypress.co.uk

© Carol Twinch, 2012

The right of Carol Twinch to be identified as the Author
of this work has been asserted in accordance with the
Copyrights, Designs and Patents Act 1988.

British Library Cataloguing in Publication Data.
A catalogue record for this book is available from the British Library.

ISBN 978 0 7524 6589 0

Typesetting and origination by The History Press
Printed in India
Manufacturing managed by Jellyfish Print Solutions Ltd

JANUARY 1ST

2000: On this day 40,000 revellers crowded into Norwich for the City of Light Festival to welcome in the new millennium. The Walk, Haymarket and the Market Place were packed solid and on Tombland there were jugglers, fire-eaters and acrobats. The city centre was buzzing, and the crowd were in party mood as they watched a millennium countdown beamed on to the castle as part of a laser and light show. There was dancing as the classical music from earlier in the evening gave way to the likes of Pulp, Oasis and Madonna. In the city there were bangs and flashes from fireworks as others enjoyed private parties. At midnight the illuminations were accompanied by the sound of Emerson, Lake and Palmer's 'Fanfare for the Common Man' as green beams shot from lasers mounted high on City Hall, fanning across the castle opposite. But there was no disguising the disappointment of many who felt that the fifteen-minute show was not worthy of such a momentous night. Despite widespread publicity that there would be no public fireworks, many believed there would be. However, thousands thronged into the city pubs before stepping out into the street to welcome in the special New Year in time-honoured fashion. (*Eastern Daily Press*, 1 January 2000)

JANUARY 2ND

1946: On this day 'The Boy John' (Sidney Grapes) sent his first letter to the *Eastern Daily Press*, written in 'broad Norfolk' dialect.

Dear Sar, yow did print a message in yar pearper, a wishin all yar readers a happy Christmas. Well, me and Arnt Agatha, an granfar, thort as how we wud be sum o' the fust to rite an wish yow, an yar staff an orl, a werry happy New Year ... We had a quiet Christmas. Arnt Agatha, she went up to Norwich for shoppin a few days afore, an she stood in a que for an hour and a half to git a harf bottle of rum, wot she wanted for her Christmas pudden. Well, bor, she cort the marster cold threw a waitin in that que. When she got home, she put her feet straight inter a barth of mustid an hot warter, and had a good tot of hot rum. Grandfar, he had a bit of a tissic, too, when he see that rum, an I'm blowed if her an granfar dint finish up that rum so we had no rum in our pudden.

(Grapes, S., *The Boy John*; The Norfolk News Co. Ltd., undated)

January 3rd

1899: On this day Gilbert's Circus of Varieties was enjoying a successful run at the Agricultural Hall, which 'opened with a bumper house, and the interest centred in this popular place of entertainment seems in no way to have fallen off after the Christmas holidays.' Norwich-born George Gilbert was a famous equestrian and, with his wife Jennie O'Brien, established a long tradition of circus entertainment in Norwich and Yarmouth (where he built the famous and extant Hippodrome). Gilbert's ground-breaking showing of 'The Royal Cinematographe – The Animated Photographs – Presenting with Marvellous Accuracy Scenes of Everyday Life' was a miscellany of images featuring jugglers, horsemanship, clowns and performing dogs which both amazed and thrilled the Norwich audiences. Equally popular were the performing parrots and cockatoos which were 'a source of wonderment and amusement ... the feathered performers, besides indulging in all kinds of pleasing tricks, appear to great advantage as firemen, and the intrepid manner in which one member of the brigade enters the burning house and clears out the contents meets with a hearty outburst of applause.' Exhibitions of equestrianism were given by the Clarke family, Mr C.A. Clarke billed as 'the unchallenged champion rider of the universe.' (*Eastern Daily Press*, 3 January 1899)

January 4th

1928: On this day serious flooding took place in Norwich as the Wensum overflowed at Lenwade and the rising water rushed through the city at 'a great pace.' Made worse by melting snow and heavy rain, the water reached a small under-line bridge on the railway line which collapsed just after the Norwich mail train had passed. Considerable anxiety had been felt in the city the previous night when it was ascertained that the high tide at Norwich was due at about 8.30 a.m. Luckily, although the wind had veered to the north-west, a direction with which extra high tides are usually associated, it was very light. One veteran waterman with many years acquaintance with the river stated that because of reduced wind, 'the water at St Martin's bridge was a foot lower than it had been during the afternoon and that it was passing through the New Mills at a rate of about 8 miles an hour.' He felt that the water was under control but the city authorities were taking every precaution in their power to minimise the situation. Many people who lived in the Oak Street neighbourhood were anxiously watching the water as it went 'whirling through the city.' (*Eastern Daily Press*, 4 January 1928)

JANUARY 5TH

1941: On this day, New Year's Eve had come and gone, and it was five days into 1941 when the siren's piercing wail was heard in the city at 10.38 a.m. and a single enemy aircraft came in from the south-west. Its bombs fell on the outskirts of the city and its machine guns pumped bullets along Ampthill Street and Unthank Road causing surprisingly little damage. The pilot released his bombs after diving down to 100ft and they fell on the City of Norwich School's playing fields and the Eaton Golf Course. There were sixteen in all, evenly spaced, between 20–100 yards apart, causing craters 6ft deep. No doubt the golfers in no way appreciated these additional German-made bunkers. The last bomb fell 30 yards from the east end of the City of Norwich School, the only damage being broken windows. During 1940 there had been a total of 580 alerts lasting in all 640 hours and 19 minutes ... still, the January sales were on and there were some good bargains in the shops. One store had a good supply of winter coats for £1 and a number of dresses at 10s. (Banger, J., *Norwich at War*, Wensum Books, 1974)

January 6th

1956: On this day it was full speed ahead for the centenary celebrations of the founding of the Norwich YMCA. with a Twelfth Night Party. Numerous events were to take place throughout the year including concerts, talks, film showings, foreign trips, sporting tournaments, the Open Gardens Scheme and more besides. The formation of the Association was first discussed in 1859; nine years after the movement had begun in London. It began in a single room over a tobacconist's shop called Newbegin in the Market Place and grew rapidly, moving several times to larger premises. A hostel was opened after the First World War and between 1939 and 1945, 'everything was subservient to the needs of the young men in uniform. The whole premises were turned over to sleeping and feeding troops, and providing for their leisure. Thousands of young men were accommodated during those years.' After the building of the City College the Association turned its attention to the large number of students and trainees who needed lodgings in the city: 'They need simple accommodation and good food at a modest price, and somewhere to study in quiet and comfort.' (Norwich YMCA., *A Century of Service 1856 to 1956*, City of Norwich Young Men's Christian Association Programme, 1956)

JANUARY 7TH

1896: On this day the tightrope walker Menotti the Stockholm Wonder gave a thrilling and sensational performance on a lofty telephone wire stretched across the Agricultural Hall. He entered the ring dressed in faultless evening attire and after tripping gently along his 'slender means of support' pretended he had been drinking. He rocked along his 'airy perch', lighting a cigarette as he went to round after round of applause. Without leaving the wire he divested himself of his evening attire and continued his act in tights. With his eyes securely bandaged and his head enveloped in a sack he walked the tightrope and then made the return journey on skates. A brave member of the audience volunteered to be carried across the wire by Menotti, which drew gasps from the audience and applause when accomplished. After more varied acts, including a troupe of circus dogs, the evening was pronounced 'the best of its kind ever placed before a Norwich audience'. The performance was put on by George Gilbert, who 'provided a bill of fare for his patrons which met with hearty approbation from the audience for the good things that the energetic proprietor had presented for their entertainment.' (*Eastern Daily Press*, 7 January 1896)

January 8th

1774: On this day the *Norwich Mercury* reported an incident that had taken place in the normally peaceful parish of Eaton, 'A few nights ago some villains stole and carried away all the poultry belonging to Mr Blyth. They also took away a horse with a bridle and saddle, which horse has not since been heard of.' The *Mercury* had occasion to report more wrongdoing in the area:

> On Wednesday night, about 8 o'clock as Mr James Esdriss, of Larlingford, farmer, was coming to the city [he] was attacked on Eaton Hill by two footpads, who presented a pistol to his breast and robbed him of 1 guinea, 2 half-guineas, and some silver. They used him in an inhuman manner, one of them beating him very cruelly with a large stick.

The traditional trade of the village was horticulture, growing fruit trees and roses. The proprietor of Ewing's Nurseries became 'so prosperous that in 1836 he is called in the directory W.E. Ewing, Esq., and I am told he lived in a big house near the Church.' (Rye, W., *History of the Parish of Eaton in the City of Norwich*, Roberts & Co., 1915)

January 9th

1923: On this day the teacher and educationist, David Holbrook, was born in Norwich. He was to carve out a career as a prolific novelist, poet and critic of literature and society, one of his formative influences being the adolescent experience of working and acting under Nugent Monck at the Maddermarket Theatre. In *A Play of Passion*, Holbrook's fictionalised persona, Paul Grimmer, is sent by his headmaster to help at the theatre. Set in 1940, Holbrook used Monck's real name 'because it would be absurd to try and disguise him.' On arrival Paul and the other pupils stood awkwardly, embarrassed, listening to Nugent proclaim, 'I built the theatre in 1908, and it was the first theatre to be designed on the lines of the Elizabethan Globe, with an apron stage and a simple fixed set ... as you see, it has no proscenium arch.' None of the boys knew what a proscenium arch was. They had been to the Theatre Royal (pronounced 'thee-etter') and to the Haymarket, but were unacquainted with the technicalities so they looked blank. 'The sensitive little man was immediately aware of their discomfort and ignorance and turned fatherly rather than spinsterish.' (Holbrook, D., *A Play of Passion*, W. H. Allen & Co., 1978)

JANUARY 10TH

1644: On this day, in a wave of Puritan fervour, committees were appointed to search the city churches for 'idolatrous images'. Sheriff Toft, Aldermen Lindsey, Puckle, Sherwood and Greenwood, together with Mr Kett, John Knight and others met from time to time to visit:

> ... the several churches in this city and view the same, and take notice of such scandalous pictures, crucifixes, and images, as are yet remaining ... and demolish or cause them to be demolished, and also to take the names of all such persons as can give any information of any misdemeanours of scandalous ministers, and to certifye from time to time their doings therein to the mayor.

The mayor and deputy lieutenants would sit in the council chamber every Tuesday and Thursday to receive information and thereafter to proceed further, 'as the cause shall require'. These newly constituted reformers began thereafter to 'deface the monuments, break the windows, file the bells, dash in pieces the carved works, and reave the brasses off the stones and monuments.' Little escaped the felonious hands of Toft, ringleader of the rabble, once he had a taste of the value of the brasses he pulled off, the cathedral affording him above a hundred. (Blomefield, *The History of Norfolk*, 1805-10)

January 11th

1664: On this day Henry Howard (later 6th Duke of Norfolk) was at the ducal palace in Norwich celebrating his son's birthday. He had spent Christmas there, on which occasion the entertainments were of considerable splendour. He established good relations with the mayor and corporation, dining in public with them and making rich presents of plate, one year a basin and ewer, another 'a noble mace of silver gilt'. Edward Browne described the jollifications in his journal: 'I was at Mr Howard's ... who kept his Christmas this year at the Duke's palace in Norwich, so magnificently that the like hath scarce been seen.' They had dancing every night, offering entertainment to all that would come:

> ... he built up a room on purpose to dance in, very large, and hung with the bravest hangings I ever saw; his candlesticks, snuffers, tongues, fire shovel and andirons were silver; a banquet was given every night after dancing ... I have seen his pictures, which are admirable, he hath prints and draughts, done by most of the great masters' own hands. Stones and jewels, such as onyxes, sardonyxes, jacinths, jaspers, amethysts, etc., more and better than any prince in Europe.

(Robinson, J.M., *The Dukes of Norfolk: A Quincentennial History*, Oxford University Press, 1982)

JANUARY 12TH

1843: On this day Mr Farnell announced the forthcoming term for pupils to his Theatre Street House Establishment, who were to reassemble on the twenty-first instant after the Christmas break. Mr Farnell's standards were high and he awarded himself fulsome praise: 'At this School the inculcation of good Habits, Manners, and Disposition, and the formation of correct Moral Feelings are made earnest objects of a faithful regard, while an ardent and unceasing energy is directed in studying the best methods of imparting solid and useful instruction.' Mr Farnell offered thirty years' experience of a 'system of Mercantile and Mathematical Tuition, unequalled in its practical adaption' and was pleased to say that many excellent teachers and accountants in the city had been educated at his establishment, thus proving the success of his endeavours. Greek, Latin, French and English Classics were also taught. In addition to study, pupils were offered boarding facilities and 'domestic enjoyments', a private playground and 'many advantages conducive to health, recreation, and general comfort'. Terms for boarders were moderate and at the request of parents only one charge was made, inclusive of books, stationery, washing and all extra, excepting 'disbursements made for the pupil'. (*Norwich Mercury*, 12 January 1843)

January 13th

1942: On this day Miss Mabel Mary Field wrote on her diary, 'Snow, snow, snow, snow all day long! I went to the city in a.m. and got an accumulator for wireless … Cecil Goodhill arrived 2 p.m. and we had lunch and did not go out again as it snowed all day.' The world had turned into a 'white world and was very cold.' Mabel was an elderly single lady of independent means, living at No.105 Newmarket Road. She had moved there with her oldest sister, Edith, in June 1941 to be near their married sister, Hilda Skoulding. Mabel's father, Sidney Field, was an architect and the family's existence was one of relative wealth. Even by 1942, all three sisters kept large households of servants. The snow did not let up for the rest of January and 'Snow!' appears at the start of all her diary entries well into February. On 16 January she wrote, 'Very cold, stayed in all day' and the following day, 'Snow still lying … very cold, still snow … went down to bank to cash a cheque … very cold.' Edith had died at the beginning of January, only a short time after their move, and the funeral took place as the snow fell fast and with no respite. (Mabel Mary Field's Appointment Diary (1942) unpublished, Norfolk Record Office, MC2705)

JANUARY 14TH

1824: On this day an account of a ball was noted in the Assembly Room records:

> The ball was opened by the Hon. Mrs Miles and Mr Jerningham with the Russian Dance which was succeeded by quadrilles; these were performed with more than usual animation, in numerous sets, forming large and small circles from the top of the room to the bottom. These graceful dances were kept up with great spirit till three in the morning.

There is also an earlier note (1802) of the dresses worn by the ladies, which were 'elegant and highly becoming, chiefly of fine worked muslin. Feathers were very generally worn, with fancy caps and Spanish hats'. Traffic could be a problem, even in the 1800s. Advertisements were placed for those attending a Norwich First Subscription Ball in November 1784, to the effect that, 'Ladies who intend dancing minuets are requested to place themselves on the Front Seats. Many inconveniences having arisen from the obstruction of carriages at the door, gentlemen are requested to order their servants to drive off, when informed by the Porter.' The minuet was a popular dance, as was the waltz introduced in 1827. (Stephenson, A., *The Assembly House Norwich*, H.J. Sexton Norwich Arts Trust, undated)

JANUARY 15TH

1898: On this day 'Old Mortality', writing in the *Norfolk Chronicle*, revealed new research pointing to St Peter Mancroft churchyard having been the usual burial place of actors dying in Norwich. The White Swan playhouse formerly stood beside the church, as did a subsequent theatre in the immediate locality, and performers had their lodgings in the neighbouring lanes and streets. Only two stones could be found marking the burial of Norwich Company members. One is inscribed to 'Ann the wife of Thomas Jackson, comedian, who died March 22, 1784'. Near the north-west gate is a tomb which records the death of Nathaniel Bolingbroke and has an inscription to the memory of Miss Sophia Ann Goddard, a favourite actress on the Norwich circuit:

> This Stone is dedicated to the Talents and Virtues of Sophia Ann Goddard, who died March 15 1801, aged 25. The former shone with superior Lustre and Effect in the Great School of Morals, the theatre while the latter informed the private Circle of Life with Sentiment, Taste and Manners that still live in the Memory of Friendships and Affection.

Memorials also existed to William West, a member of the White Swan Company, and Henrietta Maria Bray, 'a popular actress'. (*Norfolk Chronicle*, 1 January 1898)

JANUARY 16TH

1841: On this day the Theatre Royal's new season opened but with some dispute as to the dramatic value of the productions. One critic wrote:

> We constantly see surrounding the mighty Shakespeare the names of Knowles, Bulwer, Colman and Talfourd, and others of those whose dramas (though smothered for a time by the invasion of stage monstrosities, filled with the most pernicious innuendo, dressed with nothing and void of any plot or sense) will surely find a home upon the English stage again … but 'Geishas' (or any girl of any occupation) are only a peg on which to hang gaudy mounting, the most elaborate undress permissible, a few catchy and in many cases, I must admit, melodious numbers, some dances more than a trifle risky – and there you have the making of a huge success in the theatre of today. A total absence of plot is no bar at all, but rather a recommendation to the absurdity in question … one has really nothing to think about; the whole thing is as free from any tinge of intellectuality as the turns in a travelling Circus.

(Harcourt, B., *Theatre Royal Norfolk: The Chronicles of an Old Playhouse*, Norfolk News Co., 1903)

January 17th

1887: On this day Charles Mowbray and Frederick Henderson, described as 'Socialists', together with two labourers named Hall and Hurrell, were brought up in custody before the mayor and other magistrates at Norwich Guildhall. The charge was 'riotously and tumultuously assembling to disturb the public peace, and with doing damage to the windows of the bank of Messrs Lacon, to the shop window of Mr Bonser, and to the shop of Mr Ladell.' They were further charged with rioting to the terror and alarm of Her Majesty's subjects. Evidence was given showing that at a political meeting in the Haymarket, Mowbray and Henderson had incited the unemployed to attack the bakers' shops, telling them it was no crime to get food if they wanted it. Mowbray led a deputation to the Guildhall, 'on the steps of which he used strong language and hinted at window breaking.' Both prisoners were committed for trial but the magistrates were willing to accept bail – Mowbray, Hall and Henderson £100 each, with two sureties of £50 each, and Hurrell £50 with two sureties of £50 each. Bail was not forthcoming and under a strong escort of police the prisoners were removed to the castle gaol. (*The Times*, 17 January 1887)

JANUARY 18TH

1834: On this day an advertisement appeared in the *Norwich Mercury* on behalf of the London, Lowestoft, Norwich & Beccles Shipping & Trading Co. announcing that Norwich was officially a modern port. The age of the coach was drawing to its close and it seemed imperative for the city's commerce to improve access to the London wharves. Accordingly, the city commissioned the Norwich & Lowestoft Navigation scheme, built to bypass Yarmouth, which opened in September 1833. Two schooners were built expressly for the accommodation of the shippers in Norwich, one of which would load every Wednesday at Griffin's Wharf in London and on the same day the second vessel would load at R. & S. Rudrum's Wharf, King Street, Norwich. But the venture was short-lived – it was overtaken by the railways in 1846. Norwich and Yarmouth, at each end of the navigable river Yare, often engaged in a tug of war over trade, with frequent associated trickery and arguments over Yarmouth's income from cargoes being unloaded from coasters onto river craft. The original canal basin was filled in and is now the car park in front of Thorpe Station. (*Norwich Mercury*, 18 January 1834; King, C., *The River Gateway to Norwich*, Norwich Rivers Heritage Group, 2004)

JANUARY 19TH

1963: On this day Her Majesty, Queen Elizabeth the Queen Mother, opened the new Norwich Central Library and the Norwich Record Office. It was noted that, 'Her Majesty has far more than a formal interest in libraries and archives. Since 1953 she has been Patron of the British Records Association and of the Norfolk Record Society.' Norwich had been the first city to adopt the Public Libraries Act of 1850 and the old library in St Andrew's Street (opened in 1857), was the first building specially designed for its purpose. However, Norwich had had a municipal library in St Andrew's Hall since 1608 and many of the books from that old library were moved to the latest building. The reference library had shelf footage of 1,746ft which equated to around 14,000 volumes. An American memorial room was opened in the new library funded by the 2nd Air Division, USAAF, to commemorate those officers and men who, flying from East Anglian bases, lost their lives in combat or died in the line of duty. Unfortunately, this library was destroyed in a disastrous fire in 1999, but is reborn in the Forum. (Norwich Central Library, Norwich Libraries Committee, 1963)

JANUARY 20TH

1911: On this day Dr Mary Bell addressed a women's suffrage meeting to consider a question that was, 'no new question ... that of the enfranchisement of women.' Norwich was not a hotbed of the suffrage movement, although an office of Millicent Fawcett's National Union of Womens' Suffrage Societies (NUWSS) had been opened in Brigg Street in 1909, and Mrs Pankhurst's Women's Social and Political Union (WSPU) in London Street. Dr Bell pointed out that women were still thought of as 'the weaker sex', and 'not fit to vote ... men were not put under any examination before they were given the vote, therefore, why were not women equally as competent to vote?' She exampled medical women, who had waged a long struggle for professional recognition: 'at last the doors were opened to them, but look at the waste of time, the waste of brains and energy that all that lapse of time necessitated.' She demonstrated the inconsistency of the law in that she was thought incompetent to vote but as a doctor she could, with another female doctor, certify a man insane and unfit to vote. Her audience applauded and shouted, 'Hear, Hear!' (*Eastern Daily Press*, 20 January 1911)

January 21st

1841: On this day a meeting was convened in Norwich to decide how to put Norwich on the railway map. It was clear to the Norwich burgesses that the directors of the Eastern Counties Railway had no immediate intention of trying to get anywhere nearer than Colchester. ECR rejected all proposals and the city became frustrated in the extreme. Eventually it was agreed that their best hope for reviving the city's flagging economy lay with the relatively simple route along the Yare Valley, connecting Norwich with the Port of Yarmouth; a fashionable watering place which served as the port for Norwich. Construction was fairly rapid and a special train was given a trial run along the line, single throughout, during April, carrying the government inspector and distinguished guests, among them the Bishop of Norwich, together with representatives of the press. The formal opening took place on 30 April and the line opened for business on 1 May 1844. It was the occasion both for rejoicing and feasting 'on a Lucullan scale'. The fourteen-coach special train, carrying 200 guests, left Norwich at 10.30 a.m. with a brass band in the coach next along from the engine. The journey took 50 minutes. (Allen, C. J., *The Great Eastern Railway*, Ian Allan, 1967)

JANUARY 22ND

1821: On this day John Thurtell advertised that he had been in Chapel Field at 9 p.m. when three men had knocked him down and robbed him of £1,508. The cash was in his pocketbook: 'In notes, 13 of which were of the Bank of England, value £100 each and the name "John Thurtell" is indorsed on them.' A reward of £100 was offered to whoever might give information 'which may lead to the apprehension and conviction of the persons concerned in this robbery.' It sounded an incredible sum of money to be carrying and before long it was discovered to be a scam. Thurtell's bombazine firm had been declared bankrupt and he was hoping to enjoy a public subscription. In 1923 another John Thurtell was accused of murdering a notorious swindler, William Wear. John's father, a Norwich alderman, created a stir by refusing to pay for a lawyer to cross-examine the prosecution witnesses. John Thurtell was hanged for the murder in 1924 but his father survived the scandal and became mayor of Norwich in 1828. Many in the family felt the Thurtell name so tarnished that they changed their name to Turner and others to Murray. (Meeres, F., *A History of Norwich*, Phillimore, 1998)

JANUARY 23RD

1901: On this day the *Eastern Daily Press* carried its first editorial page, announcing at length the news of the death of Queen Victoria. The story continued over several pages and included reaction from various Norfolk locations. The Queen had died the previous day at Osborne House on the Isle of Wight and the county was plunged into deep mourning. When Victoria visited Norwich in her Golden Jubilee year of 1887 the city welcomed her enthusiastically. The city had not been visited by a reigning monarch for 216 years, since Charles II came in 1671. Edward VII came in 1909 and it was he who made Norfolk a Royal county, as he based himself at Sandringham during his years as Prince of Wales. As was usual at that time – and up until 1940 – the story did not appear on the front page, which was devoted to advertising and public notices. In 1901 there was a milestone in the paper's history for other reasons, as the paper's length increased to twelve pages. New premises had been acquired in London Street and during 1898 and thereafter sales continued to rise. (*Eastern Daily Press*, 23 January 1901)

JANUARY 24TH

1559: On this day Norwich-born physician and academic, John Caius, accepted the office as warden of Caius Court, Cambridge. His true name appears to have been 'Keye' and he was born in the city in 1510 in the parish of St Etheldreda. He received his schooling in Norwich and was admitted whilst very young as a student of Gonville Hall where he afterwards became a Fellow. He returned to Norwich and practised as a physician here until 1551, the year in which the 'sweating disease' broke out and killed 960 people in Norwich alone. He treated the disease with uncommon success, which gained him a high reputation and brought him to the attention of Edward VI who appointed him as his own physician. In 1556, Caius published his history of the 'sweating disease' (in Latin) and in 1557 became physician to Queen Mary, who 'possessed the greatest regard for him.' He became Master of Gonville Hall, but his Catholicism upset the Fellows, who were mainly Protestants. Norwich maintains links with Gonville and Caius and a number of Norfolk men have been College Masters. (*The History of the City and County of Norwich from the Earliest Accounts to the Present Time*, printed by John Crouse, 1768)

JANUARY 25TH

1589: On this day a message arrived from Sir Francis Drake that he wished five Norwich 'waits' to accompany him on his forthcoming voyage round the coasts of Spain and Portugal. 'Three new howboyes and one treble recorder' and a 'saquebut' (sackbut) were supplied for their use on-board. Peter Spratt was the sackbut player and requested a new case for his instrument which cost 10s. They were given 'cloakes of Stamell cloath' and a wagon (which the city was to pay for) to transport them to Plymouth where Drake had assembled eight naval ships, armed merchantmen and sixty Dutch flyboats. Norwich waits were musicians who acted as city watchmen and each town had a 'signature' tune. The Norwich waits played a large part in the musical entertainment of Elizabeth I during her royal progress to Norwich in 1578. Norwich waits were reckoned to be the best in the kingdom. William Kemp, who earned national fame by dancing a morris dance from London to Norwich, said there were 'fewe Citties in our Realme have the like, none better.' Only two of the waits returned from the expedition and the city compensated the widows. (Day, J.W., *Norwich Through the Ages*, The East Anglian Magazine Ltd, 1976)

January 26th

1820: On this day *The Times* reported on the Norwich Fox Dinner, held annually to celebrate the birthday of the Whig politician, Charles James Fox (1749–1806). It was held at St Andrew's Hall and 460 tickets were issued. As no room in the city was capable of entertaining such a large number of guests, the mayor allowed them the use of the Town Hall for the meeting. The offer was 'joyfully accepted and for some days previous to that on which the dinner was held, the stewards were employed in superintending the boarding and matting of the hall.' The Duke of Suffolk, Earl of Albemarle, Sir R. Ferguson, Mr Coke of Holkham, and others, arrived for the event and on the day of the grand dinner 'strangers kept pouring into Norwich from various quarters of the county.' The evening began with 'the shouting of the multitude without, and the striking up of the music within the hall.' When the Duke of Sussex made his appearance there were loud cheers and the band struck up God Save the King. After dinner *Non nobis Domine* was sung by some musical amateurs, toasts given and drunk, and then the speeches began. (*The Times*, 26 January, 1820)

JANUARY 27TH

2012: On this day an independent documentary film was premiered in London that celebrated the University of East Anglia lecturer and celebrated writer W.G. Sebald. Sebald, who was known to friends as Max, taught at the UEA for more than thirty years, until his death in a car accident in 2001. *Patience (After Sebald)* was made to coincide with the 10th anniversary of his death on the A146 near Norwich. In it, Grammy nominated film maker and director Grant Gee follows the journey taken by the author through East Anglia in his book, *The Rings of Saturn.* Grant Gee said the book was unclassifiable, with elements of travel writing, local history, memoirs and fiction all combined: 'What starts off as an everyday summer holiday walk becomes a very moving, very strange story about the end of all things.' Contributors include former Poet Laureate and UEA colleague Andrew Motion and novelist Rick Moody. Sebald was born in Germany but moved to Norfolk in 1970 to take up the position of German lecturer at the UEA. Dr Jo Catling was one of Sebald's UEA colleagues and thought him 'an inspiration to generations of students, colleagues and readers.' (*Eastern Daily Press*, 30 January, 2012)

JANUARY 28TH

1404: On this day Henry IV granted a Charter to Norwich, allowing it more power to govern itself and giving the city the right to elect a mayor and two sheriffs. It gained autonomy as the County of the City of Norwich within the county of Norfolk. The mayor was granted the right to have a sword carried erect before him in presence of all magnates and lords, except kings. The sergeants at mace of the mayor and the two sheriffs were allowed to carry gifts or silver maces bearing the king's arms, even before the king within the liberty. The first office holder was William Appleyard (1403–04) who lived in what is now the Bridewell Museum. The Guildhall was built to house the councils and courts that flowed from these appointments and mayor 'making' was on the first of May. The mayor was both ceremonial and executive head of the city, a powerful position needing a substantial private income, necessary to maintain the office and the high cost of entertainment. This system changed after the Municipal Reform Act of 1835 and the role became increasingly ceremonial, with the title becoming Lord mayor rather than just mayor in 1909. (*Norwich, a Fine City*, Norwich City Council, 1992)

JANUARY 29TH

1876: On this day the half-yearly general meeting of the shareholders of the Norwich Water Works Co. took place. Top of the agenda was the proposal that 'in the interests of the Company ... the accounts should be printed and circulated amongst the shareholders previces to the half-yearly meetings.' In a bid to show that the directors 'had nothing to conceal' it was thought that 'by this means alone would shareholders ... be made acquainted with the management of the business of the company.' They would then be able to compare one half-year with another 'and could then see whether the company was prospering or the reverse.' Not everyone was in agreement, however, a Mr Ayres pointing out that 'it would be impossible to have the accounts printed and circulated before the meetings, unless the meetings were postponed, the consequence of which would be about three weeks delay in the payment of the dividend.' After lengthy discussion it was agreed that a resolution be drawn up to the effect that the board would convene a special meeting 'to consider the advisability of publishing the half-yearly accounts.' The board promised that the directors would give the matter their 'best consideration.' (*Norwich Mercury*, 29 January, 1876)

JANUARY 30TH

1864: On this day the religious zealot and self-styled 'Father' Ignatius moved into No.14 Elm Hill, declaring it the monastery of the Third Order of the Order of St Benedict. It was a bitterly cold day. The streets were deep in snow. The premises had once been a Dominican Priory but had lately been used as a ragman's warehouse. No fires had been lit in the warehouse for years. Doors were without locks and most windows without glass. Snowflakes flurried in and mice scampered off as Ignatius and Brother Dunstan began the conversion of the old place into the Priory of St Mary and St Dunstan. Elm Hill was a poor district, but no one was as poor as the monks. Human pity cut across all prejudice of creed and garb. The locals could not bear to see their fellow creatures in such an awful place. Carpenters, masons, plasterers, glaziers all gave their skills to keep the worst of the weather out of the new monastery. Women volunteered to act as laundresses and brought small contributions of food, wood and fuel. A doctor, called to attend a brother attacked by rheumatism, offered future services free to the order. (Calder-Marshall, A., *The Enthusiast*, Faber & Faber, 1962)

JANUARY 31ST

1758: On this day Thomas Ivory's New Theatre opened with *The Way of the World* by William Congreve. It was built on land adjoining the present Theatre Royal site. Together with Goldsmith and later Sheridan, Congreve was providing the country with badly needed 'good new plays'. Sheridan's *School for Scandal* was first performed in Norwich in 1779, only two years after its London debut. The following week a presentation of Shakespeare's *Henry V* was enjoyed by a loudly patriotic audience. It was during the Seven Years War between England and France and the play was subtitled: 'The victory of the English over the French'. It is easy to imagine the blood being stirred in that auditorium by Shakespeare's immortal words: 'Once more unto the breach dear friends ...' A year later the building was described as 'The Grand New Concert Hall', although no theatre licence had been granted. This was rectified in 1768 when the Act of Parliament for licensing the theatre received royal assent. Plays were performed during each year's season, from Christmas to July. Out of season, it also opened during Assize week, an important social event when crowds flocked into the city from the surrounding countryside. (Howard, V., *The Show Must Go On*, Wensum Books, 1977)

FEBRUARY 1ST

1961: On this day Norwich-based Anglia TV's award-winning *Survival* series made its ITV debut. The team went on to make well over 1,000 wildlife programmes, shown in 112 countries, and its films and film-makers won more than 250 awards worldwide, including four Emmy Awards and a BAFTA. It began in the summer of 1960 when Aubrey Buxton, a founding director of Anglia TV and lifelong naturalist, introduced a 15 minute regional nature programme called *Countryman* and after a few months, he saw the opportunity to offer ITV a new natural history strand. The pilot programme was a film about coypus, the South American rodents that had been introduced into the Norfolk Broads where they caused great damage to riverbanks and vegetation. The London ITV company agreed to back an on-going project with the first broadcast featuring the wildlife of London. From there *Survival* went on to explore and record wildlife and nature across the globe, becoming ITV's premier wildlife strand and one of British television's trailblazing programmes. In 1989 the *Survival* unit moved to its own premises in Queen Street, close to Anglia TV's headquarters. It was disbanded in 2001. (*A Knight on the Box, 40 Years of Anglia Television*, Anglia Television Ltd., 1999)

FEBRUARY 2ND

1820: On this day the accession of George IV was proclaimed on the Castle Hill by Sir William Windham Dalling, High sheriff of the county of Norfolk, accompanied by Edmond Wodehouse, MP, who gave three cheers for his Majesty. In accordance with a writ the proclamation was made in the city with due formality. The corporation assembled at the Guildhall and the 14th Light Dragoons paraded in the Market Place. From the leads of the Guildhall, after a flourish of trumpets, the Town Clerk read the proclamation amid loud cheers. A procession was formed and passed through the city. At the upper gate of The Close the Under Chamberlain advanced and demanded the gates be opened in pursuance of the king's writ. The Chapter Clerk then answered from within, 'In obedience to his Majesty's commands the gates shall be opened.' After the proclamation was made in The Close the procession returned to the Guildhall where refreshments were served. Two weeks later all the shops in Norwich were closed for the funeral day of the late king, and 'almost every person appeared in deep mourning.' Officials of the corporation wore black scarves over their robes and processed solemnly to the cathedral. (Mackie, C., *Norfolk Annals Vol. I*, 1901)

FEBRUARY 3RD

1722: On this day the *Norwich Gazette* published verses 'made by one Mr Henry Least' in praise of Edmund Roe, one of the city's minstrels (or Waits) who was an excellent violinist. They were set to music by Mr Charles Lulman:

WHEN the Ingenious ROE
Directs his Nimble BOW,
And Artful Graces give the Smallest String,
I think Ten Thousand Nymphs and Syrens sing,
To banish my Fatigue of Grief and Cares,
With Wat'y murmurs and Aethereal Airs:
And if he does the Larger touch,
The charming Melody is such,
I think APOLLO wakes his Sacred Lyre,
Or that I hear the bright Celestial Choir,
But when upon them all he Rolls and Ranges,
Runs such Divisions, such delightful Changes,
Such Sounds salute my more than ravisht Ears,
As parallel the Musick of the Spheres.

Mr Least had ample opportunity to hear the 'nimble bow' as in the first half of the eighteenth century the minstrels performed regularly at the assemblies which were held during Assize week and Sessions week at Chapel Field House. Organised by Abraham Catherall they were continued by his wife after his death in 1731. (Stephen, G.A., *The Waits of the City of Norwich though four centuries to 1790*, Goode, 1933)

FEBRUARY 4TH

1810: On this day John Fransham, known as Hornbutton Jack, was buried in the churchyard of St George Colegate where his father had been clerk of the parish and where he had been baptised in 1730. Although clever, John was denied proper education when his patron died, but he retained his love of classical antiquity. He put himself under the instruction of a journeyman weaver and fellow freethinker, Daniel Wright, and the two sat facing each other, so that they could carry on discussions amid the rattle of their looms. John had a brief spell in London and took to wearing a plaid – a green jacket with large horn buttons, a broad hat, drab shorts, coarse worsted stockings and large shoes earning him the nickname 'old horn-buttoned Jack'. Hornbutton Jack was penniless for most of his life but put his education to good use by taking tutoring jobs to make ends meet. On one occasion he reduced his daily food allowance to a farthing's worth of potatoes and to save on lodgings experimented with sleeping on Mousehold Heath in his plaid. Unfortunately the latter resulted in a violent cold and was not repeated. (Jewson, C.B., *Jacobin City: A Portrait of Norwich 1788-1802*, Blackie & Son, 1975)

FEBRUARY 5TH

1974: On this day Norwich City Council accepted proposals drafted by the Bowthorpe Development Committee for a master plan that would result in planning permission for residential and ancillary development of the parish of Bowthorpe, or 'Boethorp' as it was named in Domesday Book. Part of the village had been transferred to the City of Norwich in 1968:

> Bowthorpe is to be a pleasant place in which to live. Not for any one particular sector of society but for everyone ... to encourage a feeling of identity and character to a comprehensible area the housing has been designed into three related 'villages' and it is hoped that the detailed design of the individual layouts within each village will contribute to this character.

The village is on the western periphery of Norwich and about 3 miles from the city centre bounded to the south by the river Yare. The ruins of the fourteenth-century church were to be retained in the Master Plan as they were 'of architectural or historic interest ... Records of the Church of St Michael, of which only some of the walls remain, date back to 1304 and show that it was originally allowed to fall into disrepair in the mid-16th century.' (Bowthorpe Master Plan, City of Norwich, 1974)

February 6th

1962: On this day the writer and columnist Adrian Bell wrote:

I was walking between Tombland and Elm Hill, and had just passed Augustine Steward's sixteenth-century home, when I heard a loud whistling above the noise of the traffic. I thought at first it must be some industrial noise – chirrup of pulley-belt on shiny metal – which my ear was pleased to imagine bird-like. Then I came to Elm Hill, and it was louder, echoing. I looked around.

Was some Ludwig Koch's nature disc, much amplified, sounding from a window? Or perhaps it was a canary-seed advertisement, or maybe a children's toy? Then he noticed a group of people looking up:

… and there on the topmost branch of the great tree which stands near the Briton's Arms was a thrush singing as loud as any carolling bell. Even then I wondered, could he be real … But he was no puppet bird with a transistor in his abdomen, for as the wind swung his bough through an arc and back again, his neck undulated on his balancing body and his feathers fluttered: he was real and alive and singing in the midst of the city.

(*Eastern Daily Press*, 21 January, 2012)

FEBRUARY 7TH

2009: On this day Norwich Cathedral was full for Sir Bernard Feilden's memorial service. He was a big, lovable man and the warmth with which he was remembered by so many was palpable. He had a huge zest for everything and, above all, for everyone. The Norwich Society still runs substantially on the lines that he introduced in 1959 and his influence on the surviving face of Norwich cannot be overstated. In 1962, Sir Bernard was asked for his opinion about the spire and roofs of Norwich Cathedral, which were in danger of collapse. There was even a suggestion that the spire be demolished and rebuilt. 'Not on your life,' retorted Bernard! He consulted a French architect, Bertrand Monnet, who interrogated him for two days 'like an opposing barrister.' Monnet advised adding rings of stainless steel wire as a 'belt and braces' measure and together they devised a way to strengthen the spire by inserting the stainless steel wires into its horizontal joists. With no safety equipment, Bernard climbed the outside of the spire many times (feeling sick as it swayed in the wind) to demonstrate the success of the enterprise. (Lady Tina Feilden; RIBA Journal, 2009; *The Times*, 2 December 2008)

FEBRUARY 8TH

1808: On this day Richard Bullard was born in the parish of St John Maddermarket. When he was twenty he married and went to live at the top end of Oak Street where he was Overseer of the Parish. After several more moves he took on the old dye office near St Miles' Bridge where, in partnership with James Watts, he founded the Anchor Brewery. Mr Watts soon lost interest but Richard Bullard was a good brewer and before long business had increased at such an extraordinary rate that more buildings were needed, surrounding properties purchased and new premises erected. When he died in 1864 his obituary said:

> The deceased, well known as a brewer and merchant, of extensive business, sprang from very humble life. By industry and constant application, he made the best use of the good intellect he was gifted with, and steadily raised himself to a foremost position amongst the traders of this city ... young men [should know] that it is possible for energy, industry, and business talent to force their way even now-a-days through the greatest obstacles.

Bullards went on to own over 1,000 public houses but, unable to compete against the big national brewers, brewing ceased at the Anchor in 1966. (Gurney-Read, J., *Trades & Industries of Norwich*, Gliddon Books, 1988)

FEBRUARY 9TH

1819: On this day the Norwich Paving Act Commissioners met to discuss a plan submitted for lighting the city streets with gas. Supported by 26 votes to 17, it was agreed that 'it is expedient to light such parts of the city with gas on the plan suggested.' It was not until the end of September that another meeting was held 'for the purpose of receiving information relative to the proposed introduction of oil gas.' The mayor decided a public meeting was called for and it was another month before contractors began breaking up the streets so that the pipes could be laid down to the satisfaction of the City Surveyor. Almost overnight two separate bodies came into existence, both hoping to gain the lighting contract. After prolonged negotiation the two companies 'adjusted their differences' and by the start of the following year the first of the iron gas pipes was laid in the Market Place. In May 1820 street lamps were lit for the first time. 'It produced a strong and steady light as far as it extended, and before Messrs Bignold's house and office in Surrey Street, where there were three lamps, the effect was brilliant.' (Mackie, C., *Norfolk Annals*, 1901)

February 10th

1788: On this day Henry Cabell and Susannah Holmes were married in Australia, the first wedding ceremony in the new colony. They had met in Norwich gaol, both destined for transportation, and begun a life-long relationship that was to take them to the other side of the world and establish a long line of descendants who still return to Norwich retracing their family's ignoble beginnings. Henry Cabell, his father and uncle were arrested in 1783 for burglary. The two older men were hanged but Henry was imprisoned in Norwich Castle. Here he encountered Susannah, also convicted of theft, and they somehow contrived to become lovers, their son Henry being born in the prison. Henry was refused permission to marry Susannah who was taken to Plymouth and put aboard the First Fleet's *Dunkirk* bound for Botany Bay. Her baby was refused passage but a guard took pity on them and petitioned the Home Secretary. Two weeks later the keeper of the Castle was instructed to allow Henry to join Susannah and their baby on-board the *Dunkirk*. After their marriage they in due course prospered and had many more children. (*History and Guide: The Castle as a Prison*, Norwich Castle Museum & Art Gallery)

FEBRUARY 11TH

1996: On this day Bishop Peter was nearing the end of his year-long diocesan pilgrimage to mark the 900th anniversary of Norwich Cathedral. He wrote:

> On my way to St George's, Tombland, I took a shortcut through the cathedral, dressed as usual for the pilgrimage in my increasingly tatty old cassock, shoulder bag and stick. People were arriving for the cathedral Eucharist and gave me very odd looks, no doubt thinking I was some peculiar kind of tramp. I said hello to them but many still averted their eyes. At St George's I dedicated the new tower and conducted an old-fashioned High Mass with all the trimmings which I much enjoyed ... After lunch Paul drove me to the Earlham estate where I boarded a bus, driven by a parishioner, who at his own expense, hires a bus every Sunday to tour the estate and take parishioners to church. We had a jolly ride and I had fun being a kind of bus conductor dishing out badges instead of tickets. A big congregation gathered in the small church of St Mary's, Earlham, near the university ... This has been a good week, very full and tiring but immensely varied and rewarding.

(Nott, The Rt Revd Peter, *Bishop Peter's Pilgrimage*, The Canterbury Press, 1996)

FEBRUARY 12TH

1285: On this day a local man named Walter Eghe was found in possession of stolen goods. Although he claimed he had bought them honestly from a man in a pub, he was arrested and charged. The evidence against him was flimsy in the extreme, but the fact that he was found in possession was enough for the local magistrates to find him guilty. Walter was sentenced to hang and despite appeals from his friends and family the sentence was carried out. His body was cut down and taken to St George's Church where it was laid on a slab while the burial men went to fetch his coffin. In their absence, Walter fully regained consciousness and declared that he had been spared 'by the grace of God'. He escaped and ran across Tombland, straight into the cathedral where he claimed sanctuary. He remained there until King Edward visited the city in March whereupon the king decided to grant Walter a full pardon. He lived the rest of his life peacefully, the only person to have been hanged at the castle who lived to tell the tale. (Hudson, W. (ed), *Records of the City of Norwich Vol. I*, 1906; Chisnell, D., *Haunted Norwich*, Tempus Publishing, 2005)

February 13th

1853: On this day Susan Madders recorded the traditions of St Valentine's eve in Norwich:

The streets swarm with carriers and baskets laden with treasures. Bang go the knockers, and away rushes the banger, depositing first upon the doorstep some package from the basket ... then the next ... till the baskets are empty. Anonymously St Valentine presents his gifts, labelled only with 'St. Valentine's love'. Within the houses of destination – the screams, the shouts ... the flushed faces, sparkling eyes, rushing feet to pick up the fairy gifts ... inscriptions to be interpreted, mysteries to be unravelled, hoaxes to be found out, and great hampers to be unpacked, out of which jump live little boys with St Valentine's love to the ladies fair.

There are also the mock parcels that vanish from the doorstep by invisible strings when the door opens ... Happy is he who expects nothing, and he will not be disappointed! It is a glorious night ... its mirth, its smiles and mysteries of loving kindness, its tender reverential tributes to old age, and time-tried friendship, that mark the season in our hearths and homes, so true, and holy, that good St Valentine himself may feel justly proud.

(Madders, S.S., *Rambles in an Old City*, 1853)

February 14th

1340: On this St Valentine's Day a jousting tournament was held in a part of the Gildencroft known as the Jousting Acre. Edward III appointed the tournament to be held in Norwich and prohibited all such events from being held elsewhere in the realm on that day. The king and Queen Phillipa brought their son Edward Prince of Wales (the Black Prince), and stayed for two weeks. The Acre was the city's place for knights and men-at-arms to practice martial skills, such as tilting at quintains with lances on horseback, and archery. A small hill, known as Tut Hill (possibly meaning 'look-out hill') once stood to the west of the Acre near the modern junction of Bakers Road and St Martins. It was here that the archery 'butts' were set up for the compulsory archery and crossbow practice that young men performed in the Middle Ages. It is thought that Tut Hill was also the viewing area for the arenas below. The Black Prince was renowned for his enthusiastic participation in jousts. He had gained a reputation as a fearless soldier at Crecy and Poitiers and brought prestige to the Norwich Joust. (Blake, M.M., *The Glory and Sorrow of Norwich*, Jarrolds, 1899)

FEBRUARY 15TH

1952: On this day King George VI was laid to rest in London, his body having left Sandringham Church a few days earlier, borne on a gun carriage to Wolferton Station drawn by horses of the Queen's Troop of the Royal Horse Artillery. The event was felt most keenly in Norwich, the Royal Family having been regular visitors to the city.

A crowd filled St Peter's Street and Guildhall Hill in Norwich to see the Lord mayor, Eric Hinde, proclaim the city's loyalty to the new monarch from the steps of City Hall. Speaking at a meeting of the city council on the same day, the Lord mayor also reflected George VI's relationship with Norfolk. He was indeed a king greatly loved and it is natural that those of us who live in the county in which he was born and where he had his family home should feel a sense of keen personal loss. Within the memory of most of us the late king made four official visits to our city and in October, 1938, accompanied by his queen, he opened this building in which we are now met.

(*Eastern Daily Press*, 9 & 16 February, 1952)

FEBRUARY 16TH

2010: On this day a blue plaque was unveiled to Pablo Fanque (1810–1871), Britain's first black circus proprietor, who is commemorated in a Beatles' song lyric. Born William Darby at the Norwich Union Workhouse, he was the last of seven children born to John and Mary Darby. John Darby was a butler, of African or West Indian origin, who lived in St Stephen's parish. After the death of his father, William was apprenticed to William Batty's travelling show where he learned to be proficient at rope-dancing and tumbling and became a talented equestrian performer. He took the name of Pablo Fanque in 1828 when he was billed as 'Young Pablo' in a troupe at the Norwich Pantheon. By 1841 Pablo Fanque had set up his own troupe and toured the country. By the late 1850s his circus was failing and its last performance was in 1870. Pablo Fanque is known to millions thanks to the Beatles, being celebrated in their song 'Being for the Benefit of Mr Kite'. The words in the song are taken from a poster advertising Pablo's Circus Royal. Mr Kite was a friend of Pablo and also of Mr Henderson, also referenced in the song, and who was the beneficiary of that night's takings. (Williams, N., *The Blue Plaques of Norwich*, Norwich Heritage Economic & Regeneration Trust (HEART), 2010)

FEBRUARY 17TH

1909: On this day the report of a women's suffrage meeting held in the School of Music was published. Miss Grace Sewell opened the meeting and firstly declared that the subject should not be treated as a party question, 'but as a measure of simple justice.' Taxation was a hot topic for discussion and it was generally accepted that 'representation went with taxation. But women householders had to pay taxes, and were not represented.' Miss Sewell pointed out that women had done much for the social and moral welfare of the nation but could have far more power if they were directly represented. The meeting was not asking that all women should vote, 'nor had they asked that women should go into Parliament. They only asked that those women who fulfilled the qualification which enabled men to vote should not be debarred from that privilege merely because they were women.' This somewhat tempered approach to women's suffrage prevailed in Norwich and the meeting agreed to seek 'the Imperial franchise for women in the same relations that it is now granted to men ... and pledges itself to do all in its power to obtain the same by constitutional methods.' (*Norwich Mercury*, 17 February, 1909)

FEBRUARY 18TH

1797: On this day the first advertisement for what became known as the Norwich Union Fire Office appeared in the local press:

> The Public are hereby informed the POLICIES OF INSURANCE against Loss or DAMAGE by Fire, are granted at the COMPANY's OFFICE, at T. BIGNOLD'S, on the Gentleman's Walk, Market-place, on the most reasonable terms. Some of the Proprietors having withdrawn, others are come forward, and have advanced a considerable Sum of Money, which is now ready for any emergency. Those who choose to transfer their Insurances to this Office will have their Policies gratis.

The Norwich Union Fire Society was in fact Thomas Bignold's second general insurance business. In 1792 he had set up the Norwich General Assurance Company, with which he parted company after five years; he was to repeat this behaviour with the new fire venture. However, the initial advertisement was successful in persuading policyholders with the alternative Norwich General Insurance Company to transfer their allegiance to the new Fire Office. Gentleman's Walk became known as the new insurance company centre of Norwich and the birthplace of the Norwich Union Group. (Mantle, J., *Norwich Union The First 200 Years*, James & James Ltd, 1997)

February 19th

1803: On this day the Norwich Society of Artists – which became known as the 'Norwich School' – was founded. Its purpose was: 'An Enquiry into the Rise, Progress and present state of Painting, Architecture and Sculpture, with a view to point out the Best Methods of study to attain to Great Perfection in these Arts'. The society held fortnightly meetings at the Hole in the Wall tavern on Exchange Street. Meetings entailed supper and the reading of papers; there was a yearly subscription of 4 guineas. From 1805 until 1825 exhibitions were held annually in Norwich, the first instance of a provincial institution holding regular exhibitions. A founder member and first president, was Norwich artist, John Crome (born 1768). Members consisted almost entirely of landscape painters in oil and watercolour, working chiefly under Crome's influence, with a bias in favour of Norfolk scenery. Crome was known as 'Old Crome' to distinguish him from his son who painted in his manner but with inferior talent. When Crome died in 1821, John Sell Cotman (born 1782) became president and the activities of the society continued until his departure for London in 1834. (Chilvers, Ian (ed), *The Concise Oxford Dictionary of Art and Artists*, Oxford University Press, 1990)

FEBRUARY 20TH

1467: On this day the City Assembly met to discuss the state of the river, 'Because the King's River, a thing very useful to this City, is so greatly filled with dirt, so that at certain times of the year dry ground is observed in places and the flow of the water is prevented.' In addition to this, 'great and more harm occurs daily' with the dumping of waste into the river from nearby houses. It was incumbent on the assembly, therefore, that suitable remedies should be found to:

> ... remove those things which are injurious to the said river ... that every one dwelling in this City ... shall apply his helping hand towards the following works in labour or money. That is to say that every one whether he be occupier (possessor), owner (appropriator) or farmer shall heap up over against his dwelling ... all the filth in the streets opposite his dwelling to the middle [of the street] and then the owners of that dwelling shall be bound to cause to be carried away and removed all the dirt and filth out of the King's Street.

(Cottingham Tingey, J., *The Records of the City of Norwich, Vol. II*, 1910)

FEBRUARY 21ST

1951: On this day the men at the goods and cartage depot of British Railways at Thorpe Station, nearly 200 in all, unanimously decided at a lunchtime meeting to 'work to rule' over a pay dispute. That meant, among other things, no overtime working and, if it continued for some days, a considerable piling up of goods traffic at Norwich resulting in delays both inward and outward. Mr Fred Goodings, who had been employed in the Thorpe goods depot for thirty years, was an official of the men's local departmental committee and told a reporter that the case for working normally had been put to the meeting but the men had rejected it and decided to take unofficial action by 'working to rule'. It was thought this could be achieved without breaking 'a single British Railways rule.' Under the new and complicated rule book 'working to rule' tactics included things like the use of the small twin-wheeled barrows instead of the big passenger barrows for moving parcels, and 'loaders may strictly obey rules and not ride from place to place on the mechanical trolleys, but walk leisurely.' However, after five days the disagreement was resolved both locally and nationally. (*Eastern Evening News*, 21 February, 1951)

February 22nd

1875: On this day a high school for girls was opened following a conference on the Better Education of Women, held in Norwich largely at the instigation of Mrs William Grey who was the chief speaker. It was thought desirable to do more in the city for the education of girls and Jeremiah James Colman seconded the resolution. A subsequent meeting was held, at which further information was given about the Girls' Public Day School Company. A committee was formed, shares were raised, and the London Company was asked to establish the school. Jeremiah Colman believed that it met a real need and that it, 'was not necessarily antagonistic to private schools ... if there are any bad schools they are best done away with, but there is no reason why really good private schools for girls should not flourish side by side with the High School.' He believed in giving women every facility for better education. Norwich High School for Girls is now one of twenty-six schools in the Girls' Day School Trust. It is set in 13 acres of grounds, 1½ miles from the city centre and provides education for girls aged from three to eighteen years. (Colman, H.C., *Jeremiah James Colman: A Memoir*, 1905)

February 23rd

1953: On this day Edgar Blower, Chairman of the Norwich and District Food Production Council (NDFPC), published a letter in *The Times* replying to Winston Churchill's speech in which he said it was just as important then as it was during the dark days of the war, to 'wring the last ounce of food from our land.' Mr Blower, supported by Noel Armstrong, Secretary of Castle Chambers in Norwich, was pleased to inform Mr Churchill of the work done by the NDFPC since its formation in 1947. It endeavoured 'to educate its citizens to the use that can be made of garden and allotment' and cited instances of how Norwich gardeners were doing their bit along the lines of the wartime Dig for Victory campaign. 'A lorry driver in a small council garden grows one hundredweight of tomatoes, his wife keeps poultry, his boy keeps rabbits and they grow vegetables and flowers. They yet have time for Norwich City football and the speedway!' Mr Blower suggested that government 'might consider a new domestic food movement to run side by side with the Savings Movement, for if it is important to save money how much more important is it to grow food.' (*The Times*, 23 February, 1953)

FEBRUARY 24TH

1966: On this day the Town Planning Committee announced that it had agreed the best thing to do with Mousehold House was to pull it down and to turn it over to new housing. It was envisaged that this would 'add fifty houses or flats to the estate now surrounding it.' A recommendation along these lines would now go to the city council. Demolition had been 'on the cards' for months but had been staved off while various alternative uses were examined. A firm of seedsmen had asked to use the land for growing plants, while a developer wanted to purchase the property and convert the house into flats. The East Anglian Bookmakers' Association put forward a proposal to use it as a members' club house, but the new Norwich Preservation Trust decided not to take on the house as 'its fundraising efforts would not be well directed on a Mousehold House project. Restoration of a building in the centre of the city would make more public impact.' In the event, Mousehold House survived and was 'remodelled' in 1969. It is now residential and sits amid a twentieth-century development of maisonettes built in the grounds. (*Eastern Evening News*, 24 February, 1966; English Heritage 229383)

FEBRUARY 25TH

1643: On this day the Conesford gate was blocked, as were the St Giles, Pockthorpe and St Augustine's gates. The city's role during the Civil War was principally to supply troops and money to the Parliamentary forces operating elsewhere in the region. However, discussions were held about constructing several bastions against the river. The intention was probably to create a star-shaped defence on the contemporary Dutch model. There was no direct threat to the city but 150 dragoons (mounted musketeers) were raised to Oliver Cromwell at Cambridge. The horses were at least partly seized from the property of Royalist sympathisers in the city. During March more volunteers were raised for Parliament and the young men and girls of Norwich raised £240 to equip the 'Maiden Troop' of Cromwell's cavalry under Captain Robert Swallow, who became the eleventh troop of the Ironsides. By July all threats seemed to be lessening and the gates were reopened. Norwich was by no means united in its opposition to Charles I and at the end of 1643 a list was made of 432 Royalist suspects among the principal citizens because the city feared a subsequent attack by loyal Royalist gentry. (Atkin, M., *Norwich: History and Guide*, Alan Sutton, 1993)

FEBRUARY 26TH

1797: On this day Admiral Lord Nelson wrote to the mayor of Norwich to donate the sword of the Spanish Rear Admiral Don Xavier Francisco Winthuysen to the city. The sword was taken in battle and Nelson received it on-board the San Jose on 14 February 1797 together with other sword of the Spanish officers which were handed one by one to his barge crew. The San Jose formed part of the Spanish fleet at the Battle of Cape St Vincent and was in the thick of the fighting, sustaining heavy British broadsides. Mindful of his Norfolk origins and in acknowledgement of the intention to confer on him the Freedom of the City, Nelson felt it appropriate that Norwich should have a souvenir of the victory in which he played a leading role. The ship was commandeered by the Royal Navy and enjoyed active service for many years as HMS *San Josef*. Following the Battle of Cape St Vincent, the Spanish fleet took refuge in Cadiz which was blockaded by the British with a special inshore squadron of battleships placed under the command of Nelson, now promoted to rear admiral. (White, C., *The Nelson Encyclopaedia*, Chatham Publishing, 2002)

FEBRUARY 27TH

1799: On this day, an eight-year-old orphan boy, Simon Wilkin:

> ... came to live at Mrs David's house hard by the churchyard of
> St George's Colegate. Deep snow lay over the countryside and
> had been delaying the London coaches but there in the city it
> was trodden hard so that the going was more comfortable than
> it would be when the thaw came. In the characteristic jumble
> of Norwich streets the parish of St George's Colegate can
> neither be said to have been fashionable or otherwise. In 1799
> the mayor, John Herring, and some twenty other 'gentlemen',
> manufacturers and merchants, were resident there besides a
> similar number of operative weavers.

Simon Wilkin was being placed in the care of one of Mrs
David's lodgers, the Revd Joseph Kinghorn, minister at the
Baptist Church in St Mary's. Simon was to thrive, after some
misadventures, and played a significant part in Norwich life,
particularly in the realms of natural history and literature,
earning a reference in the *Dictionary of National Biography*.
He worked closely with his guardian at St Mary's Church
and together they laid the foundation stone of a new Meeting
House in 1811. (Jewson, C.B., *Simon Wilkin of Norwich*,
Centre of East Anglian Studies (UEA), 1979)

FEBRUARY 28TH

2005: On this day Norwich City FC were playing Manchester City at Carrow Road. The Canaries were fighting a battle against relegation from the Premier League and the match was not going their way. At half-time Norwich director Delia Smith tried to rally the crowd. She grabbed the microphone from the club announcer on the pitch and yelled, 'A message for the best football supporters in the world ... we need a 12th man here. Where are you? Where are you? Let's be 'avin' you! Come on!' Although Norwich lost the match 3–2, but it looked as though they would secure their position in the Premier League. But their hopes were subsequently swept away when they lost to Fulham 6–0. The on-pitch incident went almost unreported until a few days later when the media became aware. Sports writers took up the story and mobile phone images of Delia, the microphone and her green and yellow scarf appeared on numerous websites and Internet blogs across the globe. Green T-shirts were produced with 'Let's be 'havin' you!' emblazoned on the back. Delia's support for the Canaries is legendary and she has been a director since 1996. (*Eastern Daily Press*, 1 & 2 March, 2005; BBC Home, 1 March, 2005)

FEBRUARY 29TH

2008: On this Leap Year day the Norwich Union released data that showed it to be the safest day of the year in the home. Ten years of claims analysis revealed that the extra day sees 20 per cent fewer claims for theft, fire, water leaks and accidental damage compared to an average day. Leap year days also see 20 per cent less car accidents than normal, making it the third safest day of the year:

> There's no apparent scientific reason for the figures ... perhaps the extra day means that people subconsciously change their routines or habits ... perhaps the odd male is in hiding in case he is put on the spot by his partner and so isn't behind the wheel of his car!

On this day in 1996 the *Eastern Daily Press* reported that Beattie Runnacles had lived through two world wars, seen four kings and two queens on the throne and remembered the Titanic sinking, but was celebrating only her twenty-fourth birthday, despite being born in 1896. There being no Leap day in 1900, an end of century year, she had to wait until 1904 to celebrate her first official birthday. (Aviva Archive, February, 2008; *Eastern Daily Press*, 1 March, 1996)

MARCH 1ST

1797: On this day the Norwich Union insurance company was founded by Thomas Bignold. The company had 27 backers and offered its earliest existing policy to one Seth Wallace, a blacksmith, on Christmas Day that year. For years only the city of London benefited from the early insurance companies, but this monopoly ended when many parts of Britain were offered their first access to an organised fire brigade. Within 20 years and mostly with Bignold at the helm as Secretary, the company expanded to running no less than 25 fire brigades across Britain. Its home town brigade was religiously wheeled out every month, the operator required to get the engine up to a head of steam and, in the event of finding no fire to extinguish, were set to clean the front of the office building, the old Bignold House. Between 1900 and 1904 a new headquarters was built in Surrey Street, architect George Skipper conceiving the fabulous Marble Hall: 15 varieties of marble sculpted into 40 columns and multitudinous pavements. In retirement, Thomas Bignold became increasingly eccentric, forming a business to make shoes with revolving heels. This, unfortunately, led him into bankruptcy and then prison. (Shores, S., *The Brief History of Norwich Union*, Fine City Magazine, 2011)

MARCH 2ND

1727: On this day the Norwich Comedians announced their new programme which would be played at the White Swan. It is not known when the White Swan first became associated with drama, but the inn was flourishing before 1648 and its Yards were probably even then an established venue for playgoers. A contemporary description of the interior of a theatre in the mid-eighteenth century serves to represent the White Swan Playhouse at its height: 'The Pit is an amphitheatre, fill'd with benches without backboards, and adorn'd and cover'd with green cloth. Men of quality, particularly the younger sort, some ladies of reputation and virtue, and abundance of damsels that hunt for prey, sit all together in this place, higgledy-piggledy, chatter, toy, play, hear, hear not. Farther up, against the wall under the first gallery, and just opposite the stage, rises another amphitheatre, which is taken up by persons of the best quality, among whom are generally very few men. The galleries, whereof there are only two rows, are filled with none but ordinary people, particularly the upper one'. The Playhouse began its decline when Thomas Ivory opened his New Theatre in 1758. (Thompson, L.P, *Norwich Inns*, W.E. Harrison & Sons, 1947)

MARCH 3RD

1988: On this day a number 26 Eastern Counties double-decker bus fell into a 26ft-deep hole in Earlham Road when a large section of the tarmac collapsed beneath the weight of the vehicle. The bus driver, Jim Pightling from Sprowston, had attempted to pull away from Paragon Place when the road surface gave way under the weight of the back wheels. Passengers just had time to scramble off the bus only a few minutes before it slipped further into the hole. The following day readers of the *Eastern Daily Press* were confronted by the headline 'Passengers flee as bus sinks into pit'. By the evening a large crowd had gathered behind police barriers to see the latest subsidence in Norwich. Only weeks before old chalk workings under the city were blamed for the collapse which wrecked a home in the Ketts Hill area of the city. The tunnels under Earlham Road are the most investigated and were discovered in 1823 when colourful lighting was put in place and they became a popular tourist attraction. Some of the passageways were even had names, such as Beehive Lane, Bacchus Street and Royal Arch. (*Eastern Daily Press*, 4 March 1988; BBC Homepage)

MARCH 4TH

1736: On this day the city ladies read with mounting excitement of 'A Fresh and Neat Parcel of the Royal Beautifying Fluid' which had arrived in Norwich. Praise for its efficacy were not modest: 'So exceedingly valued by the Ladies of Quality, and all who have used it for its transcendent Excellency in beautifying the Face, Neck, and Hands, to the most exquisite Perfection possible. It gives an inexpressible fine Air to the Features of the Face, and a surprising Handsomeness to the Neck and Hands, which it immediately makes excellent Smooth, Fine and delicately White'. As if that was not enough, 'It takes away all disagreeable Redness, Spots, Pimples, Heats, Roughness, Morphews [blemish or birth mark], Worms in the Face, Sun-burnt, Freckles, or any other Discolouring in the Skin'. It needed only a few wipes with a little of the royal fluid, dropped onto a clean napkin, to make a lady's face 'fine, clear, soft and fair, as to cause Admiration in the Beholders'. The same retailer, William Chase, a Norwich bookseller, also stocked 'the incomparable powder for the teeth, which has given such great satisfaction to most of the Nobility and Gentry in England, for these Twenty Years.' (*Norwich Mercury*, 4/5 March 1736)

MARCH 5TH

1831: On this day the *Norwich Mercury* reported that 'Her Most Gracious Majesty the Queen and HRH the Duke of Sussex having condescended to patronise the manufacturer of Norwich shawls, Edward Blakely begs most respectfully to inform the Nobility and ladies that he will have ready for inspection on Tuesday 15th inst, a splendid assortment of the same description of shawls which Her Majesty has been pleased to select'. Between 1785 and 1885, Norwich was a major textile centre and led the way in the manufacture of shawls based on traditional Indian styles and designs. Edward Blakely was one of many who specialised in the Norwich Shawl, fashionable for nearly a century. In 1848 an employee of Blakely, William Piper, went to London and 'obtained an introduction from the Countess Spencer to the Queen and was able to effect sales of Norwich shawls with Her Majesty, the Queen Dowager, the Duchess of Kent and many members of the aristocracy'. In 1851, Edward Blakely went to the Great Exhibition and showed Anglo-Indian scarves, shawls, dresses and brocades. He was rewarded by two orders for shawls made 'in the pure Indian style' from Her Majesty. (*Norwich Mercury*; Clabburn, P., *The Norwich Shawl*, Norfolk Museum Service, 1995)

MARCH 6TH

1783: On this day the citizens of Norwich were able to read in *The Norwich Directory* of the Council's proposals for improvements to the city streets. As the road through the city was 'both difficult, dark and dangerous', it was proposed opening and widening such parts as might render the whole airy and easy of access:

> To this end, the great entrance to the Market Place, through Brig's Lane, should be opened; at least the turn from the Rampant Horse Street, or Horse Market, should be rounded, by taking away the corners. From the Market Place to the Red Well, the Cockey Lane and London Lane is so narrow and irregular, that frequent interruptions, and sometimes accidents, happen by carriages meeting. Persons on foot must squeeze themselves into a dark alley, or burst into a shop to avoid being run over or crushed against the walls, while in wet weather, they are drenched by torrents of water from the houses, or plunged into a gutter, knee deep. If the Back of the Inns would admit of carriages, from the Hog-hill to London Lane, it would be a safer thorough-fare.

(*The Norwich Directory*, Norwich City Council, 1783; The Wensum Wordsmiths, *Mischief and Mayhem*, 1998)

MARCH 7TH

1883: On this day Major Blandy, officer-in-charge of the newly formed Salvation Army, invited all the cabmen of the city to a free tea. This was done 'because of the trouble being made for the various drivers on account of the noise and rows in the streets frightening the horses.' It had been intended to set the 304th Corps up in the Old Skating Rink but it had got into a bad state of repair 'and it was no uncommon thing when it rained for someone to open an umbrella to keep the rain off.' A new search was made and the Army bought Mack's Yard, from where the stage coaches had once departed to London. A cycle factory had been on the ground before the Army bought the land and, in the manufacture of the cycles, the smoke and fumes from the furnaces caused such a nuisance to the inhabitants of St Giles that a petition was got up and signed by those living in the neighbourhood. A law suit followed and in the end the cycle-maker was compelled to move from St Giles and so the land put up for sale and purchased by the Army. (Norwich Citadel Centenary 1882-1982, Souvenir Brochure)

MARCH 8TH

1600: On this day Will Kemp, Elizabethan actor and clown, jumped over the wall opposite the Maddermarket Theatre to complete his Nine Daies Wonder, a Morris dance from London to Norwich. Kemp was already famous in Norwich and London as a performer of jigs. He was a member of Shakespeare's players and there at the building of the new Globe Theatre in 1599. Soon afterwards, on 11 February 1600, be began his nine days dance. He afterwards wrote a pamphlet of his experiences and dedicated it to Mistress Anne Fitton, a maid of honour to the Queen. Approaching Norwich he agreed with mayor Roger Wiler that he should rest prior to his entry into the city to give time for the Aldermen and other notaries to gather. He recorded that he was advised 'to stay my Morrice a little above Saint Giles his gate, where I took my gelding and so rid into the City'. On 8 March, Kemp resumed his dance at St Giles Gate and jigged to St Stephen's Gate and on to the marketplace where he unfortunately trod on a young lady's dress 'off fell her petticoats from her waste ... her cheeks all coloured with scarlet'. (Kemp, W., *Nine Daies Wonder*, 1600)

MARCH 9TH

1852: On this day Thorpe Hamlet, a suburb on the east of Norwich, was constituted a separate ecclesiastical parish, from the civil parish of Old Thorpe (or Thorpe St Andrew). The need arose as the city expanded and swathes of terraced housing were built to accommodate the increasing population, in particular the workers from the newly built railway at Thorpe Station. Close by was the Nest, Norwich City's football ground until the 1930s. The Church of St Matthew was erected in 1851 on land given by the Dean and Chapter of Norwich, set into the slope of a hill close by the river Wensum. Originally a Chapel of Ease to the nearby parish church of Thorpe St Andrew, it was built in a neo-Norman style but made extensive use of the modern brick. Thorpe St Andrew was once known as Thorpe-next-Norwich or Thorpe Episcopi, the latter because a manor house in the old village of Thorpe was formerly a country seat of the Bishops of Norwich. Thorpe, spelled *Torp* in the Domesday Book, is an Old Norse word meaning hamlet or small village and serves as a reminder of the 9th- and 10th-century Danish invasions of Norwich. (*Kelly's Norfolk Directory*, 1900)

MARCH 10TH

1971: On this day around 300 students were occupying the Arts Building at the University of East Anglia in support of an American student who had been sent down after being convicted of a drugs offence. If expelled, the student would be drafted to fight in Vietnam. The sit-in began after a march to Earlham Hall and a petition of a thousand signatures, which had been raised two days earlier. The National Union of Students and nine other Student Unions sent messages of support. The sitters-in were 'people who are talking together and looking happy and listening to good sounds ... and besides the fun scene there are rooms for academic study if that is what you really want to do.' The main problem was not the conviction but that he was further punished by being sent down. This amounted to double jeopardy and punished twice for the same offence. The Vice-Chancellor refused to readmit the student or discuss the matter while the Arts Building was occupied. The sit-in was called off on 17 March leaving behind £2,013 worth of damage. The Code of Discipline was to be reviewed 'as a routine matter'. (Sanderson, M., *The History of the University of East Anglia Norwich*, Hambledon & London, 2002)

MARCH 11TH

1839: On this day, at a meeting of the Town Council, the mayor struggled to allay fears about the violent activities of the city Chartists. A few days earlier an alarming report was circulating about the arming of the Chartists with pikes and other weapons. 'Some are formed like a common halberd, others have a crescent at the bottom and the blade pointed forward, with a sharp edge, supposed to be designed for cutting the girths or reins of horses. It is said that about 60 will leave Norwich armed with these weapons, some of them with pistols'. The mayor confirmed that pikes had been manufactured, but there were 'not a great number of them'. In August pikes and guns were taken by the police from various persons and John Dover, keeper of a beer shop in St Paul's, was apprehended on the charge of giving an order to a smith to make pikes for unlawful purposes. Police were called to contain a demonstration on Mousehold Heath and special constables sworn in, while the West Norfolk Militia was held in readiness for immediate action. In spite of appeals from the Bishop they continued their demonstrations, though eventually some order prevailed. (Mackie, C., *Norfolk Annals, Vol. I*, 1801–1850, 1901)

MARCH 12TH

1915: On this day Harry Daniels was at the Battle of Neuve Chapelle, serving with the 2nd Battalion the Rifle Brigade (the Prince Consort's Own). The company commander ordered Daniels to make up a party to destroy the German barbed wire ahead of them. He turned to his friend Tom Noble and said, 'Come on, Tom, get some nippers'. The two men jumped from their trench and began to cut the wire. Both were hit by gunfire. Noble died and Daniels lay in a shell hole in No Man's Land for 4 hours before he managed to crawl back to his trench. Both men were awarded the Victoria Cross. Daniels spent several weeks in hospital but eventually returned to Norwich, where he had been brought up at the Norwich Boys' Home. He was greeted as a local hero, and many functions were held in his honour. On the last day of his visit, the sheriff presented him with a 'purse' containing £20. Cheering crowds lined the streets as he went to the station to catch a train back to London and from there to rejoin his battalion. (Meeres, F., *Norfolk in the First World War*, Phillimore & Co. Ltd, 2004)

MARCH 13TH

1851: On this day Lucy (Cecilia) Brightwell, the Norwich authoress and etcher, wrote in her diary that George Borrow had visited her after he had been 'to see the Bosjemans (or Bushmen) exhibiting at the Assembly Rooms, men about 4½ft high, strange and disgusting creatures, with a strange inarticulate language full of clicks.' Miss Brightwell was a close friend of the Borrows and on the same day Borrow accompanied her to the Norwich Museum, where they 'looked at the casts and were much struck with one which he said appeared alive. It proved to be Pitt. Next it [was] that of Oliver Cromwell, a wonderful huge unhewn, rugged, astounding visage. He declared it reminded him of Stonehenge.' Borrow then remarked, 'The nose is a wonderful thing, and after all strength is always shewn in the nose. They talk of forehead and all that, but the nose is the thing.' Miss Brightwell began her diary, 'Read, Seen and Done', in 1843 and in the back kept a 'List of Books published by me' including Doings of Great Lawyers published in 1866. She also recorded snippets of sermons, random thoughts and knitting patterns. (NRO MS 69)

MARCH 14TH

1878: On this day the first item on the Guildhall meeting was 'The Reckless Driving of the Railway Men'. The mayor said he wished to mention a 'matter of very great importance – the reckless driving of the railway men with their wagons, especially through the smaller streets'. He had witnessed a scene recently which was 'somewhat alarming'. A railway wagon was driven through London Street at the rate of at least 8 miles an hour, which was much faster than he (his Worship) should think of driving with his chaise. It was almost impossible to get out of the way and people were pressing themselves against the walls, owing to the wheels reaching over the paths. He frequently noticed these railway men driving too fast and thought it would be as well if Mr Kennet wrote to the superintendent of the Goods Department asking him to caution the men and advise them to drive more slowly. Mr Kennet suggested it might be better to bring the matter before the Watch Committee so that the Chief Constable might take steps in regard to the matter since he was sure 'it was a matter that ought to be attended to.' (*Eastern Daily Press,* 14 March 1878)

MARCH 15TH

1794: On this day, clock and watchmakers, Amyot and Bennett of Brigg's Lane, placed an advertisement in the *Norwich Mercury* to announce that they wished to:

> … respectfully inform their Friends and the Public that they have received … an assortment of PATENT HORIZONTAL LEVER WATCHES, the superiority of which is said, by the Patentees, to consist in simplicity of mechanism and exactness of time-keeping, and which, from having established a correspondence with the Patentees, they are enabled to sell on the same terms as the Manufactory.

James Bennett was apprenticed to Peter Amyot and gained the Freedom of Norwich as a watchmaker in 1781. Amyot and Bennett became partners in 1790 and their business was among the most respected in the city. James Bennett was elected Common Councilman for St Peter Mancroft ward in 1800 and High Sheriff in 1826. In addition to timepieces he specialised in optical instruments and established a correspondence with Mr Dolland, one of the first opticians in London. Many clocks and watches are attributed to him including a white dial long-case clock, a mahogany sedan timepiece and a Regency ebonised musical bracket clock, which plays seven tunes. (Bird, C. & Y., eds., *Norwich & Norfolk Clocks & Clockmakers*, Phillimore, 1996)

MARCH 16TH

1820: On this day *The Times* reported a theatrical riot which took place at the Norwich theatre. On the Monday Miss Brunton had appeared in the character of Rosalind without incident. On the Tuesday she appeared as Maria Dorillon in Elizabeth Inchbald's controversial play *Wives as they Were, and Maids as they Are*, which had been attacked as subversive for its portrayal of women. Notwithstanding the excellence of her performance, the house was very thinly attended. As if this was not enough for poor Miss Brunton, on her final performance:

> ... much confusion arose in consequence of part of the audience calling for God Save the King, which was sung, while others vociferated God Save the Queen. At length two regular battles took place ... [but] at the commencement of the farce, on Miss Brunton's appearance, loud applause superseded the tones of displeasure.

But as the battle raged among the audience Miss Brunton was led off the stage. The manager tried to reason with the audience but he and the remaining actors were driven from the stage, which was occupied by some of the rioters while 'the respectable part of the audience immediately left the house'. (*The Times*, 16 March 1820)

MARCH 17TH

1815: On this day the agricultural reformer, Thomas Coke, known as 'Coke of Norfolk', was attacked at a cattle show being held on the Castle Ditches by the Norfolk Agricultural Association. Discontent was rife after the passing of the Corn Law Bill which considerably added to the burdens of an already harassed populace. Things came to a head when Thomas Coke, Lord Albermarle and a number of other leading Norfolk agriculturists were pelted with stones by a mob alleged to be 10,000 strong. Ugly demonstrations were directed chiefly towards Coke, and somebody fixed a loaf of bread to the end of long pole and raised it above the crowd shouting, 'We'll have his heart on a gridiron'. Coke and others took refuge in the cattle pens until an enterprising butcher opened the gate which enclosed a bull and gave the animal's tail a twist, whereupon it charged at the mob enabling Coke to reach the Angel Inn. It was not until the Brunswick Hussars had been called, and the Riot Act read, that the disturbance subsided. Coke escaped through the back gate of the Angel and drove with speed to Quidenham Hall. (Thompson, L.P., *Norwich Inns*, W.E. Harrison & Sons, 1947)

MARCH 18TH

1611: On this day Robert Garsett of Norwich died, and was buried in St Andrew's Church on 23 March. He was the last entry for that date in the Burials Register under the Julian calendar before it was changed to the Gregorian calendar. Robert Garsett had held many offices in the city, being Constable of Mancroft ward in 1571, Councillor between 1590 and 1599, Surveyor 1594-5, sheriff in 1599 and Alderman of the Wymer ward 1600–11. He came to Norwich in the 1550s, attracted to the city which was prosperous for his craft as a tailor. He lived on Princes Street and there he suitably entertained his many distinguished guests. In 1589 he built a new house which incorporated a frame of timber from an Armada galleon. Some of the timbers bear the date 1589 causing it to be known as Armada House for some years. It is now known as Garsett House. With the advent of the electrical tramway system in Norwich in 1899 much of the original house was demolished to enable trams to avoid an otherwise sharp right turn into Redwell Street. In 1951 the house was purchased and given to the Norfolk & Norwich Archaeological Society. (Varney, Revd W.D., *Robert Garsett: Citizen and Alderman of Norwich*, 1991)

MARCH 19TH

2000: On this day Norwich City Football Club beat Ipswich Town 2–0. New caretaker-boss Bryan Hamilton's first job when he took charge of the Canaries was this tough-looking fixture at promotion-chasing Ipswich, the club where he had made his name twenty-five years earlier. Hamilton didn't make too many changes from the last side that Bruce Rioch had fielded. He brought in Lee Marshall in place of De Blasiis and called up forwards Anselin and Coote to warm the substitute's bench. The Portman Road (Ipswich) faithful naturally found the Canaries' recent troubles vastly amusing, but they were certainly not laughing by the time the half-time whistle sounded in this typically hard-fought local derby. Hero of the house was leading scorer Iwan Roberts, well on his way to winning a second successive Player of the Year award. Rarely have travelling Norwich fans enjoyed a half-time internal more as they chomped on their snacks that Sunday afternoon. It was a truly wonderful start for the new boss Hamilton, who had given the sceptical City fans exactly what they wanted at the very first time of asking. He would be hard pushed to maintain anything like this level of performance and achievement in the coming weeks. (Hadgraft, R., *Norwich City: The Modern Era*, Desert Island Books, 2003)

MARCH 20TH

1929: On this day a meeting was held by the Norwich City Council on the London Street Improvement Scheme. Although it ultimately resulted in the defeat of the project put forward by the Executive and General Purposes Committees, it was agreed that its most useful purpose had been to direct attention to the larger traffic problems of the city. London Street congestion was by no means singular although it was 'the most important shopping centre in the city.' Even if the widening scheme had been accepted, the result would have been to transfer the problem to some other street in the vicinity and the process would have had to be repeated somewhere else. An amendment was carried, drawing the attention of the various committees to the difficulties of the city as a whole.

> What those difficulties are is obvious to everyone who has business to transact in the city. Narrow thoroughfares in which potentially speedy traffic is held up by stationary vehicles of the shopping public, and footpaths totally inadequate in many places to the throng of pedestrian shoppers are the rule rather than the exception. And the need for radical changes in the traffic scheme becomes more acute every year.

(*Eastern Daily Press*, 20 March 1929)

March 21st

1988: On this day the new Anglia Television logo was revealed at presentations in Norwich and London. The triangle, in Wedgewood Blue, Cambridge Blue and Gold, replaced the Anglia knight which had served the company for almost thirty years. The silver figure had been discovered in the window of a London jeweller's shop when Anglia was looking for a symbol of its identity. More than 100 years old, the knight had originally been commissioned by the King of the Netherlands, who was patron of a society called the Falcon Club which met once a year to compete in falconry trials and other sports. In 1850 the king was so sure he would win the contest that he commissioned a trophy from a London silversmith. It was modelled on the statue of Richard the Lionheart but made to represent the Black Prince. To the king's dismay, the trophy was won by an Englishman who brought it home, where it remained in the possession of the victor's family until the year Anglia went on air (1959). Certain modifications were made to the pennon on the lance, and the magnificent silver trophy became the symbol of Anglia Television. (*A Knight on the Box, 40 Years of Anglia Television*, Anglia Television Ltd, 1999)

MARCH 22ND

1667: On this day the Bishop of Norwich preached at the King's Chapel (London) where he was heard by the diarist, Samuel Pepys. Pepys, however, was unimpressed: 'It being Easter Sunday, I heard the Bishop of Norwich, Dr Reynolds, the old Presbyterian, begin a very plain sermon.' Pepys did not stay long but 'quickly moved on to the Queen's Chapel where I heard Italians sing, and indeed their music did appear most admirable to me.' Having sided with the Presbyterians in 1642, at the Restoration Reynolds was appointed chaplain to Charles II. His sermons thereafter became increasingly about peace, unity and moderation, none of which held much appeal for Pepys whose living depended heavily on the activities of the navy. Back in Norwich, Dr Reynolds (1661–76) was equally derided for his work on the north transept of Norwich Cathedral. His Restoration Chapel was said to be 'destitute of all architectural interest' and, some years later, it was described as 'rambling' and 'unpleasant'. He died at the Bishop's Palace in 1676 and was buried in his newly built Bishop's Chapel. (*The Diary of Samuel Pepys* (various editions from 1660); Atherton, I. (et al.), *Norwich Cathedral: Church, City and Diocese, 1096-1996*, The Hambledon Press, 1996)

MARCH 23RD

1923: On this day the founders of the Norwich Society gathered for their first meeting at Curat House, an ancient building that was then a popular meeting place and restaurant in the city. After the First World War, Norwich was a crowded place, full of churches and narrow streets, its people trying to adjust to the losses and privations the war had brought, and hoping for better things. It is not hard to understand the growing voice, soon to make itself felt in political change, that called for a sweeping away of the old, the inadequate dwellings in the 'yards' ... spirit and vitality were there but people wanted more. 'Let's do away with all this and give the people something decent' was the feeling of the day. It took courage and tenacity to temper such a powerful sentiment, but that was the task undertaken by the founders of the Norwich Society. These citizens were not against change: indeed from its earliest days the Society proclaimed its faith both in renewal and preservation and its first task was to obtain recognition for things of value. (Anderson, A.P. & Storey, N.R., *Norwich: Eighty Years of the Norwich Society*, Sutton Publishing, 2004)

MARCH 24TH

1783: On this day Parson Woodforde left Weston Longeville for Norwich to witness a Procession that combined celebration of the conclusion of peace (in the Americas) and the patron saint of the Norwich woollen trade, Bishop Blaise. He wrote: 'after breakfast we set forth at 8 a.m., Mrs Davy and Nancy in the chaise, myself on horseback, Will, Ben and Lizzy on horseback, Jack went behind the chaise as I was willing that all should go that could.' They arrived about 10 a.m.: 'the road we went was filled with people on horseback and foot, going to see the fine sight'. He describes the order of the procession and declared:

> We were all highly delighted indeed with this day's sight – it far exceeded every idea I could have of it. Hercules, Jason and Bishop Blaise were exceedingly well kept up and very superbly dressed. All the Combers were in white ruffled shirts with cross-belts of wool of diverse colours – with mitred caps on their heads. The shepherds and shepherdesses were little boys and girls on horseback ... I never saw a Procession so grand and well conducted.

(Beresford, J. (ed.), *James Woodforde, A Country Parson 1759-1802*, Oxford University Press, 1979)

MARCH 25TH

1981: On this day the naturalist, writer and broadcaster, Ted Ellis, recorded in his diary that he found himself in Norwich with 'an hour's enforced idleness [which] allowed me to enjoy an early burst of sunshine to the full as I strolled without any set mission in mind ... not having acquired the habit of window-shopping'. He wrote, 'I found myself taking note of the colours and shapes of buildings in the mass and the textures of flint, brick and tiles, while stains of moss and algae and weeds of the crannies and neglected corners received a probing glance. Suddenly, at a crossing, I was confronted by a bed of multi-coloured polyanthus. In a flash I was taken back to my first encounter with these exotic, bright-eyed primroses as a child. Gold, scarlet, crimson and purple, rich as velvet, they seemed at that moment more glorious than all other flowers I had encountered in the wild or in gardens. The memory of that happy surprise goes back close on 70 years ... it is difficult to convey in words this joy that comes from recognising the favourites of childhood: perhaps it can be likened to hearing again some old sweet song'. (Ellis, T., *Countryside Reflections*, Wilson-Poole Publishers, 1982)

MARCH 26TH

1979: On this day the department store Bonds celebrated its centenary. A dinner was given for Bonds 400 members of staff and guests at St Andrew's Hall together with six great-great-grandchildren of the founder, Mr Robert Herne Bond. Bonds of Norwich was well-known through the county for over 100 years and, like so many aspects of Norwich trade and manufacture, had its beginnings at the end of the nineteenth century. Robert Bond bought a drapery shop in Ber Street in 1879 and the family lived above the shop. Mrs Bond looked after their six children and members of staff who 'lived in'. By 1896 the drapery and warehousing had spread to Bridge Street and his oldest son, William, joined the business. Mrs Bond added a highly successful millinery department selling over 1,000 hats each Saturday. By 1939 the store employed over 200 people. Staff worked on commission and the showroom girls wore long green dresses and black shoes. At the centenary dinner all the directors, except one, were members of the Bond family. When Bonds was purchased by the John Lewis Partnership in 1982 it retained the Bonds name for some years. (Gurney-Read, J., *Trades & Industries of Norwich*, Gliddon Books, 1988)

MARCH 27TH

1507: On this day the city was in deep chaos, reeling from the huge fire that had swept through Norwich, from Tombland in the east to St Giles in the west, destroying most of the timber and thatched houses as it went. It is thought that more than 718 houses were burned to the ground and others were still smouldering. Another fire two months later destroyed an additional 360 homes and it was to be some years before the area was rebuilt. Almost half of the city's housing was lost and led to a ruling that all new building should have tiled roofs. One of the few houses to survive the conflagration is the Britons Arms in Elm Hill, one of only two thatched buildings remaining in the city. It stood in a churchyard, apart from other buildings, and is a unique example of a 'beguinage', home to a small group of single women who devoted themselves to a life of prayer and charitable work. Such places were rare in England, and Norwich is the only English city where there is definite evidence of informal female communities following a religious vow. (William, N., *The Blue Plaques of Norwich*, Heritage Economic & Regeneration Trust, 2010)

MARCH 28TH

1936: On this day an American staying at the Annesley Hotel, Edmund G. Burbank, published a Letter to the Editor entitled 'Hidden History of Norwich'. Mr Burbank caused no small interest in his search for information relating to the Norwich weaving industry, the editor hoping that, 'Somewhere, possibly either in long unopened deep boxes or maybe in the lumber room or even the false roof of one of the Georgian houses that abound in Norwich there may be hidden the material for writing a most important chapter of Norwich history.' Mr Burbank gave a run-down of the city's weaving and spinning industry, lamenting, 'Little enough is known about the worsted industry in Norwich in the eighteenth century when it was the despair of Somerset and Devon. After Marlborough's stirring campaigns on the continent, Norwich stuffs began to encroach in markets which previously Exeter had looked upon as her own.' Each year the East Indian Company placed large Oriental orders with city manufacturers and 'Factors and correspondents in St Petersburg and Lisbon kept the Norwich merchants informed of market conditions.' Mr Burbank was interested in the seventeenth- and eighteenth-century industrial history of Norwich and hoped to reconstruct that long-neglected aspect of her past. (*Eastern Daily Press*, 28 March 1936)

MARCH 29TH

1849: On this day the trial of James Blomfield Rush began in Norwich, heard by Mr Baron Rolfe. Rush, accused of the murder of the Recorder of Norwich Isaac Jermy and his son, conducted his own defence, and in the course of the trial on two days he spoke for nearly 14 hours. Mrs Jermy, who was badly injured during the attack, was unable to make the journey but her maid, who had been shot in the thigh, was permitted by the doctor to give evidence. She was carried from Wymondham to the court in a bed constructed in a manner similar to that of a sedan chair by two men with relays at certain places. Admission to the trial was by ticket. As mayor, Samuel Bignold had six tickets allotted to him and every magistrate was given two seats. Every nook and corner of the court and public galleries was filled. On the evening of the sixth day of the trial his Lordship summed up. The jury retired for ten minutes and on their return announced their verdict, 'Guilty!' Thus ended what was probably the most memorable murder trial of the century. (Bignold, Sir R., *Five Generations of the Bignold Family*, Batsford Ltd, 1948)

MARCH 30TH

1909: On this day there were 2,511 people borrowing books from the Norwich Public Library, a statistic included in a ground-breaking book by C.B. Hawkins, *Norwich, A Social Study*. The new century bore witness to the on going Victorian concept of 'social conscience' and libraries seen as a means by which the common man could better himself. During the year, 4,400 tickets had been issued to readers, although rather more than a quarter of the borrowers were children.

In the lending department there are 24,200 volumes, nearly 8,000 of which are fiction. The total issues amounted to 86,800 ... in poetry and drama there were only 817 issues during the whole year. The reference department possesses 18,600 volumes besides a valuable collection of books and pamphlets on local history ... the reading room attached to this department is used by over 400 people every day, mainly for the purpose of reading magazines, though there are a certain number of readers who ask for works on science and natural history. An average 1,000 people make use of the news rooms every day. For a total expenditure of under £2,000 this is a very fair record of work.

(Hawkins, C.B., *Norwich A Social Study*, Philip Lee Warner, 1910)

MARCH 31ST

1851: On this day there was a general census to record the people in each house at midnight on the night of 30–31 March. The census had a unique accompaniment: an official, though voluntary, count of all attendance at places of worship on the previous day. Despite many objections and criticisms, the majority of returns were sent in, listing the number of churches in each denomination, the number of free and paid pew sittings available, and the number of those attending. The results were published in 1854 by Horace Mann, the Registrar's appointed officer. From the mass of statistics he produced an astonishing report, beginning with the religion of the Druids! Its final conclusions were that nationally 5¼ million had attended Church of England services, and 5½ million had attended those of other religious bodies. The largest part of the population had gone nowhere. In the Norwich returns, although the Church of England was far stronger than any other single denomination (15,087), the number of non-conformists was greater (16,185 discounting Roman Catholics, Latter Day Saints and Jews). These conclusions gave Nonconformity something of a new status and underlined for all churches the need for missionary endeavour. (Barringer, C. (ed.), *Norwich in the Nineteenth Century*, Gliddon Books, 1984)

APRIL 1ST

1982: On this day the audience at Norwich Folk Club, then at the York Tavern, were intrigued by the appearance of two odd-looking characters who sidled in and sat at the back during a singers' night. Journalist and broadcaster, Keith Skipper, recorded in his diary that 'one was a rather unkempt old man with a bushy grey beard, flat cap and walking stick'. The other was a menacing figure with a scarred cheek, Brylcreemed hair and an outrageous tie. After listening for a while, the old man asked if he and his boy 'Sid Kipper' could sing one of their songs. They did, and the folk music scene was never the same again. The following year, Henry (Dick Nudds) and Sid (Chris Sugden) were dubbed The Kipper Family and 'discovered' at Sidmouth Folk Festival. They appeared at clubs and festivals all over Britain and made six albums and countless radio appearances. They performed at ordinary folk clubs and it would be several songs into the act before the penny dropped – numbers such as 'Like a Rhinestone Ploughboy' and 'Arrest These Merry Gentlemen' were parodies, mostly on the traditional and entirely sensible folk singers, The Copper Family. (Skipper, K., *Keith Skipper's Norfolk Diaries*, Halsgrove, 2005)

APRIL 2ND

1904: On this day more information emerged about 'the Parish Umbrella', mention of which had been made in an earlier issue of St Peter Mancroft Parish Magazine. The umbrella had first been mentioned in the Churchwardens' Accounts for 1764 and was described as 'a very large umbrella', sometimes referred to as 'the Minister's', and at other times 'the Parish Umbrella' which was provided for the use of the Clergy when performing duties at funerals in the churchyard in wet weather. It was also used to shelter bridal parties from the outer gates to the church porch, long before the modern idea of erecting awnings on those occasions was thought of. There was also a Parish Umbrella belonging to St Giles' which was, in 1904, 'still preserved' although it was thought that the umbrella which belonged to St Peter Mancroft was 'much larger and capable of sheltering an average marriage or funeral party of a dozen persons standing close together'. The eighteenth-century accounts record £2 3s for 'New Making the Umbrella' which was not an extravagant sum when the size of it was considered, also the strong frame, which was made of rods of whalebone, was very expensive. (St Peter Mancroft Parish Magazine, April 1904)

APRIL 3RD

1854: On this day the Jenny Lind Infirmary for Sick Children admitted its first inpatients. It was named for Jenny Lind, the 'Swedish Nightingale' (born 1810), one of the best known and most popular entertainers in mid-nineteenth century Europe. Jenny began her career in Stockholm at the age of ten and in 1847 gave her first performance in Norwich, which proved so popular that a third concert had to be added to the schedule at short notice. She returned in 1848 and appeared twice at St Andrew's Hall raising £1,253 which she donated for the benefit of the poor of Norwich. At first there was little agreement as to how the money should be spent but following a public meeting it was decided that Norwich should be the first British city outside London to establish a modern institution for the care of sick children. Yet opposition came from people who saw no need for it, there being already a dispensary and district general hospital. After considerable wrangling 'The Jenny' was finally opened and in its first year admitted fifty-one children and treated 275 as outpatients. (Lindsay, B., *'The Jenny', A History of the Jenny Lind Hospital*, Norfolk & Norfolk University Hospital, 2004)

APRIL 4TH

1817: On this day, Good Friday morning, Wright's Norwich and Yarmouth steam packet had just started from the Foundry Bridge, when the engine's boiler exploded and blew the vessel to pieces. Of the twenty-two persons on board, five men, three women, and one child were killed instantly. Six women with fractured arms and legs were conveyed to the hospital, where one died. The remaining seven escaped without much injury. A subscription of £350 was raised for the injured. The packet was owned by John Wright who had bought a former captured French boat and installed a steam boiler. A competitor challenged his boat to a race and someone tied down the steam escape valve hoping to produce more power. As it was not an accident, John Wright had to pay compensation to the injured which made him destitute. Soon afterwards, a packet was introduced on the river, worked by four horses, as in a threshing machine; the animals treading an on board path 18ft in diameter. The vessel was propelled from 6-7 mph, as wind and tide favoured. This packet did not run long, before steam packets were again introduced. (Bayne, A.D., *A Comprehensive History of Norwich*, Jarrold & Sons, 1869)

APRIL 5TH

1154: On this day, with much pomp and ceremony, the remains of St William of Norwich were removed to the cathedral chapel, formerly the Chapel of the Holy Martyrs. The cultus of the boy saint had spread so rapidly that Prior Richard determined the body should be moved from the Chapter House to the cathedral. From the outset 'miracles and visions began to occur from week to week, until the crowds that came to make their offerings were found to be a serious inconvenience'. Norwich was keen to have its own saint and enjoy such notability and income that might derive from pilgrims and donors, and the Norfolk gentry vied with one another in offering their homage. However, the choice of St William was unfortunate in that he was alleged to have been murdered by two Jews 'out of hatred of Christianity'. The case for the crime was never proven and the cult lasted fewer than 100 years: pilgrims grew steadily uneasy with a following that engendered anti-Semitism and based on tenuous credentials. (Jessopp, A. D.D., & Montague Rhodes, J., Litt.D., *The Life and Miracles of St William of Norwich by Thomas of Monmouth*, Cambridge University Press, 1896)

APRIL 6TH

1820: On this day a prize fight took place at St Faith's between Cox, the Blacksmith of Norwich, and Teasdale, the noted prize fighter from London who had been brought to Norwich and passed off as a countryman under the feigned name of Johnson. More than 5,000 persons were present. The 65-round battle lasted 1 hour, 13 minutes. Cox fought with great resolution and drove his adversary over the ropes eleven times but in the end 'superior science' prevailed. In the 65th round, Cox received several violent blows on the left eye, which had been cut on one of the stakes in a fall in the second round, and victory was declared in favour of Teasdale. After the battle the imposture was discovered and a hand bill circulated, declaring all bets void. The friends of Teasdale denied any deception and insisted his name was really Johnson. The fuss died down and some time later Cox was involved in another fight which lasted 88 rounds. Cox was brought to the ground by a tremendous blow under the jaw. His head and face 'presented a frightful spectacle and not a feature of his countenance could be distinguished.' (Mackie, C., *Norfolk Annals, Vol. I*, 1901)

April 7th

1943: On this day Bill Holman wrote in his diary:

> Terrific gale blowing today; wind north-west. Struggled down
> to Earlham. On the way saw two barrage balloons break away.
> Bet there wasn't a balloon left by nightfall. Went through
> Blackdale Plantation, counted five large pine trees down. From
> the plantation to park dare not open my eyes as the wind was
> blowing dust off the fields like huge smoke clouds, everywhere
> was obliterated. Fifteen trees down on the park, some huge elms
> among them, and boughs and branches scattered everywhere.
> Near the entrance to Earlham Park a large elm lay right across
> the road and every house which stood a bit high had tiles off.

Bill was a keen naturalist and kept a diary between 1929 and
1987. He recorded various aspects of the weather, sightings of
birds, animals and wild flowers, mainly in his walks in Earlham
Park and the fields around the city. He was employed as a
night worker in the print room of the *Eastern Daily Press* for
his entire working life, so was free to enjoy his own interests
during the daytime. (Reeve, C., *Norwich The Biography*,
Amberley Publishing, 2011; Norfolk Record Office MC535)

APRIL 8TH

1996: On this day, Easter Sunday, Bishop Peter completed his year-long diocesan pilgrimage. He went first to Weston Longville Church for the Easter Eucharist and:

> After coffee and sandwiches in the village hall, I went for a short walk and did my last sketch ... I rode into Norwich on the back of a motorbike, accompanied by ten outriders. It was an exciting, if rather chilly, journey and when we arrived at St Julian's Church we were met by a phalanx of photographers and Anglia Television. After the statutory photographs, I prayed for a while in the Cell and then with twenty or so local parishioners and clergy, walked to the cathedral close. Here I was met by the children's marching band (The Falconers) from Sprowston, the same group who had met me when I arrived at Pulls Ferry last May ... we processed into the cathedral ... and once again I knelt at the tomb of Herbert de Losinga, the first Bishop of Norwich. I prayed my Pilgrimage Prayer and then the choir sang ... I pronounced the Easter blessing, and we processed out, through the great west door.

(Nott, The Rt Revd Peter, *Bishop Peter's Pilgrimage, His Diary and Sketchbook 1995–96*, The Canterbury Press, 1996)

APRIL 9TH

1948: On this day 'Whiffler' had a talk with Alison MacLaren about the forthcoming revival at the Theatre Royal of *Tom Jones*, Edward German's opera based on Fielding's novel. As in the previous year the show was to be presented with a combination of amateur and professional talent, the principal roles being filled by well-known London artists and the Chorus to be sung by members of the Norwich Amateur Operatic Society. Although *Tom Jones* was not so well known as German's Merrie England, it was still 'the favourite of a great many people.' The opera had disappeared quite quickly from the professional repertoire but Miss MacLaren thought that the amateur input would lift the performance, 'one of the great advantages of having amateurs to rehearse was that they possessed, without exception, great enthusiasm. Each one of them was keen to sing, or they would not be there voluntarily.' 'Whiffler' asked Miss MacLaren if she supported the opinion sometimes heard in other parts of the country that Norfolk people were not good singers. She emphatically disagreed, 'Judging from the singing I have already heard, if that opinion is correct then the standard elsewhere in the country must indeed be very high.' (*Eastern Evening News*, 9 April 1948)

APRIL 10TH

1912: On this day, newlyweds Edward and Ethel Beane of Norwich boarded RMS *Titanic* travelling second class. Ethel Clarke was nineteen years old when she married 'Ted' Beane – their fathers both worked at Bullard's Brewery, and Ethel herself was a barmaid in the Lord Nelson, a public house on Dereham Road. Ted was a bricklayer but worked for half the year in America and then back in Norwich for the other half. After *Titanic* hit the iceberg on 15 April, Ted pushed Ethel into Lifeboat 13 then dived overboard and swam in the icy sea until he was clear of the vessel and could be picked up. Extraordinarily, Ethel helped to pull a swimmer from the sea into her lifeboat, only to find that she had saved her husband. On 20 April, Ethel sent a telegram to her mother, 'Both arrived safely, *Carpathia*. Will write. Ethel. New York.' The *New York Times* reported that Ted had 'stood back at the cry of "No, only women" when his bride was placed in a lifeboat … but he saw that it was only half full … he jumped into the sea … and Ethel Beane's arms pulled him in.' (Balls, J., *Titanic - The Norfolk Survivors*, Nostalgia Publications, 1999)

APRIL 11TH

1925: On this day a Norwich volunteer veteran, George Curtis of Eade Road, celebrated his ninetieth birthday. George confessed that life had become 'a little irksome' since his career as a carpenter and his membership of the 1st Volunteer Brigade Norfolk Regiment had meant an existence full of incident and change. 'I remember,' he said, 'when I was only eleven ... there was a man called William Farham, who had been convicted of murder ... when it became known the execution was to take place in Norwich there was a great deal of excitement.' People congregated in front of the castle all eager to see the sight and 'I remember the vast concourse swaying this way and that and the sun beating down on the upturned faces.' After more reminiscences, George's daughter called time, 'You've talked enough for today.' The old man smiled, 'Age,' he said, 'has its drawbacks. Time was when I could sit up the night and yarn to my pals till the early hours of the morning. Can't do it now.' George said that the secret of old age was 'an open-air life and no worry', shouting, 'No worry!' to the departing reporter. (*Eastern Evening News*, 11 April 1935)

APRIL 12TH

1746: On this day an advertisement in the *Norwich Mercury* heralded the uptake of the new sport of cricket, which was described as 'a manly diversion.' Cricketing opportunities were available at 'The Union Coffee House, at the end of the Cockey Lane, and facing the Gentleman's Walk in the Market Place ... being commodiously fitted up, is now opened for the reception of Gentlemen.' Refreshment came in the form of 'the best of coffee, tea and chocolate, also the best of all sorts wines, arrack, rum, brandy, etc.' All the London papers were provided as were bats, ball and 'a very commodious piece of ground ... to continue as long as the weather will permit every Tuesday and Friday.' There were people who disliked the game, however, and complained of 'The Practice of idle men playing at cricket in Chapelfield, and using abusive language to the annoyance of those who frequent that pleasant promenade in Norwich.' In due course all sports, including 'cricket of the impromptu variety', was prohibited in Chapelfield Gardens. In 1781 cricket, however, took place at the Back's bowling green and the first 'Cricket Week' was held during Norwich Assize Week, August 1827. (Cricketing References in Norwich Papers, 1701–1800, Millennium Heritage Libary)

APRIL 13TH

1884: On this day Madame Cave-Ashton's Opera Company arrived at the Theatre Royal for yet another successful season. The press recorded, 'So powerful a company and so fine an orchestra could not fail to win appreciation.' On the Saturday night *Maritana* was performed and drew a full house, 'The sparkling and effective melodies with which this opera abounds drew forth the enthusiastic applause of the audience.' Unfortunately Madame Cave-Ashton was suffering from a 'relaxed throat' but persevered with 'remarkable courage and success to the close of the opera.' The usual storm of approbation greeted Mr Parkinson's 'Let me like a soldier fall' and, notwithstanding the extraordinary effort which this song calls forth, the singer was obliged to repeat it. Miss Louise Lyle received a similar compliment for her rendering of 'Alas, those chimes' as did Richard Cummings 'for the effective way in which he gave "So my courage now regaining".' During Gounod's grand opera *Faust* the cathedral scene was introduced and the band of the 4th (Queen's Own) Royal Hussars played in the famous Soldiers' Scene. The Company was a firm favourite in Norwich and returned the following year with another full programme. (*Eastern Daily Press*, 21 April 1884)

APRIL 14TH

1956: On this day, 'The Boy John' wrote one of his letters to the *Eastern Daily Press.*

Well after tha spring cleanen my Aunt Agatha took Mrs W- up ter Norridge, an they went ter this posh new shop wuss just opened. Poor Mrs W- had a calamity there. That wuss on them moven stairs. They wore a gorn up ter tha' next floor. She follered Aunt Agatha, but harf way up she got tha wind up, she cum a scrappen orf down agin, a knocken people about wot wore a gorne up. She dropped har shoppen bag, har oranges an onions wore a rollen downstairs, an yit they kep a gorne up agin. At larst she got down agin. Har umberalar wot she stuck tew, had opened out. Some fellar what stood there sed, 'What'd yow cum down by parashute Missus?' Well tha' starf wore werry good ter har, an they helped har to git har goods tergarther. She got orl her onions orlrite, but she lorst three oranges. Mrs W- wuss upset, she told Aunt Agatha she thought a drop o' short would settle har narves, but Aunt Agatha took har ter heve a cup o' tea.

(Grapes, S., *The Boy John*, The Norfolk News Co., undated)

APRIL 15TH

1978: On this day a sealed black japanned metal box which had resided at the Castle Museum since November 1940 was, by the terms of Miss Fountaine's will, to be opened. The box had belonged to Norwich resident Margaret Elizabeth Fountaine, a tireless world traveller and collector of butterflies. She bequeathed some 22,000 butterflies, in ten large mahogany cabinets, to the Castle Museum together with the box which, said the will, must not be opened until 1978. When the seals on the box were broken and the lid lifted, twelve identical volumes in matching bindings were revealed, each roughly the size and thickness of a London telephone directory. They were Miss Fountaine's diaries, from 1878 until 1939, a few months before her death in Trinidad. The date for opening the box was 100 years from when she began the diaries. They ran to well over 1 million words and told the extraordinary story of her life as a clergyman's daughter, her decision to leave home, her travels, and the disastrous love for an Irish singer of alcoholic tendencies. In 1980 the first volume of her diaries was published to critical acclaim. (Fountaine, M., *Love Among the Butterflies*, Carter, W.F. ed., Collins, 1980)

APRIL 16TH

1879: On this day an unusual scene was witnessed at a meeting of the Norwich School Board. A motion to increase the staff was supported by the majority and opposed by a minority, the latter asserting that the proposal could be carried out only by rescinding a resolution passed almost unanimously at a previous meeting which gave consideration to the increased costs involved.

> Finding their last effort useless to stem the current of expenditure into which the Board had plunged, and justly indignant at the treatment they received, the minority left the room and Canon Heaviside intimated that it would be a matter for consideration whether they entered it again ... a deputation went to Canon Heaviside's residence and presented to the gentlemen constituting the minority a 'memorial', signed by the ratepayers, urging that the Board should continue to protest against reckless extravagance, and so keep the ratepayers better informed of what is going on.

Ultimately the minority agreed to resume their duties, 'in the hope that the public attention called to the proceedings which led to their withdrawal would have the effort of strengthening their hands to discharge effectively the duties that devolved upon them'. (Mackie, C., *Norfolk Annals, Vol. II*, Charles Mackie, 1901)

APRIL 17TH

1919: On this day the Tombland Fair took place. Although there was a welcome change in the weather, and the fair brought a large number of people into the city, 'the glories of the great cattle and sheep markets of a quarter of a century ago appear to have gone forever. It is true that both cattle and sheep were penned in larger numbers than last year, but compared with two years ago the figures showed a decline.' It had been expected the cattle pens would have improved but during the week several of the regular Irish dealers had been unable to get their stock over 'on account of there being no boats available.' The Pleasure Fair was larger than usual and had about the same scope and quality as in recent years. The principal 'raree-show' (or peep box) is one displaying stuffed versions of a foal without fore legs, a six-legged lamb, twin calves with one body but separate heads, and various other monstrosities of the freak order. The outside canvas announcing these wonders 'has the distinction of having been painted especially, as a friendly compliment to the proprietor, by a naturalist of national celebrity.' (*Eastern Evening News*, 17 April 1919)

APRIL 18TH

1925: On this day a small boy, aged about two and a half, 'very fat, full face, complexion fresh, hair brown (cut bobbed style)' was found wandering alone in Magdalen Street, bearing a 'bluish-grey woolly coat, blue knickers and gaiters combined, brown button boots, fawn woollen hat and woollen vest.' Passers-by noticed the child but no one was able to learn anything about him, so he was taken to the nearest police station. 'The little fellow appeared to have been well cared for, and as his clothing and face were clean the officers at the sub-station regarded the case as one of an ordinary "lost" and expected an anxious parent to come in at any moment and claim the child.' However, no one came forward and the child was taken to the Norwich Infirmary. A photograph appeared in the newspaper but it was not until a week later that the public learned that William James Larter, fish merchant, had been summoned for abandoning Cecil Gibson Larter, aged two. Larter claimed that the child had been abducted by its mother, but the court decided that he had deliberately left the child, and sent him to prison with hard labour for three months. (*Eastern Evening News*, 18 April 1925)

April 19th

1884: On this day Alfred Bartram, a Lakenham fish dealer, was before the Guildhall court on a charge of using obscene language. Two years earlier Mr Bartram had been summoned on this charge by Louisa Bartram, as the language, which was of 'a most disgusting nature' was addressed to her. The Defendant had since absconded but gave himself up to the police shortly before the hearing. Mrs Bartram then denied all remembrances of the language, even though it was read over to her from the depositions, and persistently refused to give evidence against her husband. The Bench, considering that it was impossible to 'forget the language of such a nature', and believing she was bearing false evidence, proposed adjourning the case until the following day when further evidence was to be supplied. Inspector Mason said that Detective Barlow had sought additional evidence but found none. Mrs Bartram again denied any recollection of the expressions used. The court acknowledged that the Defendant had been in prison four days and 'as he was now thoroughly repentant' it was hoped the bench would see fit to dismiss the charges against him. The bench reluctantly agreed and Mr Bartram was discharged. (*Eastern Daily Press*, 19 April 1884)

APRIL 20TH

1453: On this day Margaret Paston wrote to her husband John about the visit of Queen Margaret of Anjou to Norwich. News that the queen was pregnant, after eight years of marriage to Henry VI, made the visit all the more exciting. 'The Queen came into this town on Tuesday last past in the afternoon' she wrote, "she sent for my cousin, Elizabeth Clere, to come to her; and she durst not disobey her commandment and came to her"'. When Elizabeth arrived 'into the Queen's presence the Queen made right much of her and desired her to have a husband ... and reported of her in the best wise, and said, by her troth, she had seen no gentlewoman that she liked better than her since she came into Norfolk'. Margaret Paston, though, had cause to add, 'I pray you that you will buy me a gift for Whitsuntide that I might have something for my neck. When the Queen was here I borrowed my cousin, Elizabeth Clere's necklace, for I durst not for shame go with my beads among so many fresh [gaily attired] gentlewomen as were here at that time'. (Virgoe, R. (ed.), *Illustrated Letters of the Paston Family*, Macmillan, 1989)

APRIL 21ST

1940: On this day the Victorian lepidopterist, diarist and indefatigable traveller, Margaret Fountaine, died in the West Indies. She was born in South Acre, south of Norwich, but after her father died in 1877 the family moved into the city. Leaving South Acre was 'a very great trial to us all' and it was a large household which moved into Eaton Grange, 'a necessarily sizeable house in its own grounds with outbuildings and a tennis court'. There were eight children ... a cook, at least one maid, Lucy (the Parlour maid), and a gardener (Parfitt), later replaced by a boy, who also looked after the girls' three pet goats. There was a German governess, Fraulein Hellmuth, who had lived with the family at South Acre, she left, but later returned for a while. And above all there was Hurley, the children's nurse, with whom Margaret appears to have had a much closer and more affectionate relationship than with her mother. Margaret travelled to her new home by train and then cab, 'all feeling the usual sensation of extreme slowness of the motion of a carriage after having just left the train'. (Fountaine, M., *Love Among the Butterflies,* Cater, W.F. (ed.), Collins, 1980)

APRIL 22ND

1460: On this day, at the City Assembly held on 'the Vigil of St George', it was decided that to maintain standards on 'cloths of wool called Woollencloth Norwich Cloth' it should conform to a single standard. 'A certain signum (seal) lying in the common chest shall be newly executed so that cloths … shall be made sufficient in this form.' The standards must also be agreed to by the weavers and fullers. The weavers must take no material but 'such as he will undertake to make a cloth sufficient in length and breadth' and the fullers, too, must play their part in maintaining trade standards. If any cloth should be found faulty the perpetrator could expect to be fined. It was also noted that all spinners and carders should also look to their workmanship and not buy shoddy goods and, worse, sell them. It was ordered that every person who had cloth to sell should offer it for sale himself so that he can oversee the quality. If he was unable to sell the cloth himself it should be done by 'his wife or his children or servant'. (Cottingham Tingey, J. (ed.), *The Records of the City of Norwich, Vol. II*, 1910)

APRIL 23RD

1624: On this day John Kettle, basket maker, was elected Feast Maker for the Company of St George, and was required to 'bear the charge of the feast … or pay the fine of 40 pounds'. Mr Kettle had no wish to participate in the feast making and was unwilling to pay the fine. He was several times ordered to pay the money, which he consistently refused to do, and was twice more brought before the company.

> When asked if he would 'bear the feast … he would give no direct answer' and continued to withhold the £40. The following month the company again summoned Mr Kettle but this time sent word that he would not attend. More messengers were sent for him but he replied 'What shall I do there? I was yesterday with the mayor and Alderman, and they were worse than devils.' In answer to his fine he said 'Let them set twenty [pounds], I will pay none'.

Finding 'there was no end of his shuffling' the corporation chose another Feast Maker and Mr Kettle was sent to prison for non-payment of the fine. (Mackerell, B., *History of the City of Norwich Both Ancient and Modern*, 1737)

APRIL 24TH

1869: On this day members of the newly formed Norwich Velocipede Club were preparing for their first exhibition at the Corn Hall. Jolly & Son, city coachbuilder, advertised that they were attempting to introduce the 'latest novelty in locomotive machinery' to Norwich and had 'arranged to supply from a noted French maker the celebrated bicycle velocipede, so much in vogue in Paris.' The first velocipede journey of any distance was performed in March by Mr B.W. Jolly, who cycled from Norwich to Yarmouth in 2 hours, 30 minutes but was 'considerably retarded by the roughness of the roads and a powerful gale'. The club exhibited 'one of the old-fashioned dandy horses, the original of the velocipede tribe' but it was added, 'the new velocipede is more easily managed.' The first velocipede races took place under the auspices of the Norwich Gymnastic Society at the Newmarket Road Cricket Ground, and by the end of 1869 there was a marked increase in the number of local cyclists. Accidents to inexperienced riders were frequently recorded, and complaints were made by drivers of the alarm occasioned to horses by the appearance of these 'new-fangled machines'. (Miles, J. (ed.), *East Anglia, An Anthology*, The National Trust, 1990; *Norfolk Chronicle*, April-June, 1869)

APRIL 25TH

1801: On this day the citizens of Norwich read an advertisement in the *Norfolk Chronicle*. The Church Stile, an inn close by the north gate of St Peter Mancroft, was a favourite setting-up place for travelling showmen whose speciality was wild animals. The notice ran:

> To the Lovers of Natural Curiosities – To be seen alive in a genteel room at Mr Peck's Church Stile … the largest Rattlesnake ever seen in England, forty-five years old, near nine feet long, in full health and vigour. He is well secured, so that ladies and gentlemen may view him without the least danger. The Proprietor begs to return thanks to those who have honoured him with a visit … N.B.A quadruped to be put in the Rattlesnake's cage at 12 o'clock on Thursday night. Admittance, Ladies and Gentlemen, 1s, working people and children, *6d*.

It was customary to admit persons free of charge to travelling menageries who produced live cats and rabbits (no questions asked) at the pay-box of the show. It is to be wondered what care these animal lovers exercised over their pets during the show! (Thompson, L.P., *Norwich Inns*, W.E. Harrison & Sons, 1947)

April 26th

1779: On this day news reached Norwich that the child prodigy, William Crotch, aged four, had been taken to London in January where he played the organ at the Chapel Royal in St James's Palace in the presence of the king. It was reported that, 'as soon as he has finished a regular tune, or part of a tune, or played some little fancy note of his own, he stops, and has some of the pranks of a wanton boy ... some of the company then generally give him a cake, an apple, or an orange, to induce him to play again'. Born in Norwich to a master carpenter, William showed early musical talent. He was described as possessing 'a pleasing countenance rather handsome, having fine blue eyes and flaxen hair' and 'if any person plays a tune he never heard with his right hand on the organ will put a base to it with his left hand and will name every note that you strike on an organ or any other instrument and he always knows if any person plays out of tune'. He was known as 'The Musical Phenomenon' and by his own admission was a precocious child. (*The London Magazine*, April, 1799)

APRIL 27TH

1942: On this day a formation of twenty-five German aircraft dropped high-explosive bombs on the city in a raid lasting 2 hours. A second raid followed the pattern of the first, lasting about an hour and a quarter, but this time with a higher proportion of incendiary bombs. Norwich was resourceful: it carried on, encouraged by a visit from the king. Destroyed department stores reopened within the premises of their competitors, and small shops found other spots in the city and traded anew. Spirits were high but could not mask the great damage done to the city fabric. Not only were there great gaps in Orford Place, All Saints Green and St Stephen's Street but there was also a cost to be counted in historic buildings. In the old city the churches of St Benedict, St Julian, St Michael at Thorn and St Paul were destroyed, as were the parish churches of St Bartholomew, Heigham and St Thomas's, Earlham Road. In a shattered St Stephen's area, the bombing destroyed the thatched Boar's Head Inn that had survived earlier civic attacks. (Anderson, A.P. & Storey, N.R., *Norwich: Eighty Years of The Norwich Society*, Sutton Publishing, 2004)

APRIL 28TH

1805: On this day Dr Henry Bathurst was consecrated Bishop of Norwich. Then aged sixty-one, he was possibly the oldest a bishop had been at the start of his occupancy. He is remembered as the idlest of Norwich's bishops, his tenure having been dubbed the 'dead see'. Bishop Bathurst preferred playing cards to administration. 'I cannot see to read but I can see the dots on the cards' he explained. Historians have not treated him kindly and even in his own time, though always remarkable for 'great geniality and affability', he was considered lax in the government of his diocese. He spent considerable periods away from it, and by the time of his death at the age of ninety-three it cannot be imagined that he could have had much grasp of the affairs of the thousand and more parishes that it contained. In his early sixties he began to talk frequently about 'life's last stage'. The 'stage' lasted more than thirty years. He died in office in 1837, the only nonagenarian Bishop of Norwich to date. A brooding and bewigged statue of him stands in the north transept of Norwich Cathedral. (Linnell, C., *Some East Anglian Clergy*, The Faith Press, 1961)

APRIL 29TH

1942: On this day E.C. le Grice witnessed the height of enemy bombing, later called the Assault on Norwich:

The outstanding remembrance is of the choking dust and smell of soot and gas, for the blast certainly acted as a chimney sweeper par excellence. Our family sheltered under the stairs ... Bomb after bomb fell shaking the house to its foundation, for we counted 29 H.E. bombs within a few hundred yards of us. Windows were shattered, ceilings crashed down, the crockery on the cupboard shelves was shaken off, a sugar basin emptied itself on my daughter's head, to be followed by the milk jug, and finally when one bomb fell just opposite, the voice of a warden was heard to say, 'Don't you think you had better come out of there?' We thought we had better come out, and happily that proved to be the last one in the district that night. One bomb fell in my garden ... it hit and smashed the thick branch of an apple tree, took the whole end off my garden hut and made a crater 3 feet across.

(Le Grice, E.C., *Norwich: The Ordeal of 1942*, The Soman Wherry Press, undated)

April 30th

1823: On this day Mr Stebbings of Norwich was brought before the city mayor to answer charges that he had sold his wife for £6 10s to a Mr Turner. Mr Stebbings thought he made a good deal when he took up with his 'more favourable wife', Turner having made a down-payment of £4 on the old Mrs Stebbings. Turner took the ex-Mrs Stebbings home and immediately turned his lawful spouse out of the house. When the now-destitute Mrs Turner applied to the authorities for poor relief, they were not satisfied with her story. Both husbands were ordered to appear before the mayor, together with their rightful wives, to undergo investigations as to their legal marital position. After listening to their individual versions at length, the bewildered mayor finally ordered each husband to take only his original and legal wife back into her rightful home and support her. The unhappy four were subjected to a hustling from a jeering crowd which had gathered outside the Town Hall, and had difficulty in making their way home. Whether Stebbings ever returned the £4 down-payment to Mr Turner is not recorded. (Richings, D. & Rudderham, R., *Strange Tales of East Anglia*, S.B. Publications, 1998)

MAY 1ST

1923: On this day the first female Lord mayor was 'made' in the city tradition laid down in 1835. Ethel Colman (1863–1948) was the eldest surviving daughter of Jeremiah James Colman and she accepted office with some trepidation, her sister Helen Colman acting as Lady mayoress. During her life she saw the fruition of the struggle for suffrage, with which she was actively involved, and equality in the welfare of the employees at the Carrow works for which she campaigned. In her early days she regularly taught at the Carrow Men's first-day school. She was also joint-editor of the Carrow Works magazine. She was not latterly politically active and left municipal affairs after her year of office although she returned briefly to politics in 1927 as Deputy Lord mayor to Mr Witard and was for many years vice-chairman of the Libraries Committee. An ardent supporter of congregationalism, she was a Life Deacon of the Princes Street Church. Following the tradition of her family, she was a keen collector of art and bequeathed to the National Art Collections Fund paintings from the Norwich School and the Pre-Raphaelite period. (Palgrave-Moore, P., *The mayors and Lord mayors of Norwich 1836–1974*, Elvery Dowers Publications, 1978)

MAY 2ND

1538: On this day Henry VIII granted a charter to reform Norwich Cathedral as a secular cathedral to be served by a Dean and chapter, instead of a prior and monks. Monastic rule at Norwich Cathedral was ended after more than 400 years. The Benedictine priory, one of the greatest houses in East Anglia, was the first with a cathedral to be 'dissolved'. The last prior was William Castleton, who became the first dean. Twenty-two monks were retained and translated into six prebendaries and sixteen canons. All were dispensed from the habit and Rule of their Order and were given the duties of serving God in the church and praying for the king. The priory was transferred to the new Dean and Chapter. Although the fabric subsequently fell into disrepair services continued to be held there. In the nave is a monument to the most expert of the cathedral's singing men, Osbert Parsley. For fifty years (1535-85), he sang the daily services and his career encompasses the momentous changes in religious observance that occurred in the sixteenth century. (Gardiner, R., *The Story of Norwich Cathedral*, Workshop Press, 1977; Atherton, I., Fernie, E. & Harper-Bill, C., *Norwich Cathedral: Church, City and Diocese 1096–1996*, The Hambledon Press, 1996)

MAY 3RD

1800: On this day the crisis over the price of a loaf of bread threatened the peace of the city. Wheat was scarce that spring and bread was expensive. The philanthropic United Friars Society organised its annual distribution of bread and soup, giving out over 28,000 tickets for a penny loaf and a quart of broth. By March the need had become so great that the mayor raised a subscription of £1,100 and opened six soup shops where families could buy soup at a half-penny a pint, one pint per family. In April it was reported that 16,000 indigent poor were receiving two meals a week from the Soup Institution. The permitted price of bread had risen steadily for twelve months. At the end of April 1799 a standard penny loaf had to weigh 9oz; a year later it reached its lowest weight of below 4oz. To avoid further unrest the mayor, sheriffs and aldermen, attended by the peace officers, visited the marketplace on Saturday 3 May and reasoned with the discontented crowds. May saw a slight improvement in the price of bread and the crisis passed. (Jewson, C.B., *Jacobin City, A Portrait of Norwich 1788–1802*, Blackie & Son, 1975)

MAY 4TH

1991: On this day Chris Sutton made his debut as a substitute for Norwich City. He came on as substitute at home to Queens Park Rangers and went on to score 43 goals in 121 league and cup games, before joining Blackburn Rovers for £5 million. Chris was the son of Mike Sutton, who wore seven different numbered shirts during the club's struggles in the Second Division and they were one of a number of father and son City players. Terry Ryder senior appeared in three 1st team games for Norwich, his first at Swansea Town in March 1925, but all the games were lost. His son Terry junior made his debut at Notts County in 1946 and went on to appear in 51 league and cup games. Frank Cassidy was a regular member of the club's Reserves side but only played in one 1st team game. His son Nigel Cassidy was a prolific goalscorer in junior football and made 3 appearances for the Canaries' 1st team. Kevin Bond made 161 appearances for the club between 1976 and 1981. His father John Bond was City manager from 1973–1980. (Hayes, D., *Norwich City FC, An A-Z*, S.B. Publications, 1998)

MAY 5TH

1811: On this day a bell ringer in the St Peter Mancroft belfry had a 'singularly narrow escape'. At the close of the first day's poll in the mayoral election, the bells were raised preparatory to the ringing of a few peals and it was necessary for someone to go up amongst them in order to turn the clappers of the three largest before the company 'pull off'. This was undertaken by seventy-eight-year-old James Vines, a ringer of over fifty-two years. After having deliberately placed the clapper of the tenor in its right position, he turned to stand on the frame to continue positioning the clapper. As he did so his weight caused the tenor to start moving until 'she at length came down with a tremendous hum'. Realising the danger, he threw himself onto the neighbouring bell, catching his leg as he went. Had he stood 2in nearer, 'either his legs must have been severed from his body, or himself been precipitated into the berth of the bell, in which latter case he would have been crushed to a mummy without the least vestige of human form remaining.' Mr Vines descended to the ringing chamber pale and joined in the peal. (*Norfolk Chronicle*, 11 May 1811)

MAY 6TH

1914: On this day the *Eastern Daily Press* carried the obituary of John Godfery Howlett, a partner in the footwear firm of Tillyard & Howlett, later Howlett & White which in turn was the parent company of Norvic Shoes. John Godfery (never Godfrey) had a nervous apprehension of cities and commerce, not uncommon among those who had been brought up in the country amid agricultural pursuits. As a boy he described himself as 'a clod-hopping farmer's son, working on the land'. He was a shy man but having taken time off to visit Alabama he returned from America with enough confidence to enter his father's shoe business in 1857. He later said, 'the firm's employees then consisted of George Hicklington, an admirable workman, one clicker blessed with the name of Hercules Samson, and one packer, John Williment'. John Godfery was:

> ... one of those rare men whose enthusiasms survive the deadening influence of the years; men who carry into old age the spirit of a youthful and alert outlook on the world ... and, what is still rarer, he kept to the last a living and open mind for new ideas.

(Wheldon, F.W., *A Norvic Century and the Men who Made It 1846–1946*, Jarrold & Sons, 1946)

MAY 7TH

1814: On this day the *Norfolk Chronicle* announced that Jeremiah Colman had taken over the stock and trade of the mustard and flour mills at Stoke near Norwich 'lately carried on by Mr Edward Ames'. Mr Colman 'respectfully informs his customers and the public in general that he will continue the manufacturing of mustard, and he takes leave to assure those who may be pleased to favour him with their orders that they shall be supplied in such a manner as cannot fail to secure their approbation'. One of Jeremiah's accounts books for 1814 records that £51 2s was paid to Mr Ames for mustard. Following speculation as to why Mr Colman had taken over the Stoke Mills, it transpired that the two families knew each other well. One of the Colmans had been engaged to Sarah Ames, daughter of Edward, and although she had died before the marriage could take place the closeness between the families continued. Jeremiah Colman continued to visit Edward Ames and his remaining two daughters, Ann and Maria, in Yarmouth. Jeremiah's daughter recalled, 'their names always bring before my eyes a childish recollection of alarming looking personages and rich plum cake.' (Colman, H.C., *Jeremiah James Colman: A Memoir*, 1905; *Norfolk Chronicle*)

MAY 8TH

1373: On this day the anchoress, Dame Julian of Norwich, had a vision that inspired her to write *Revelations of Divine Love*, believed to be the first book written in the English language by a woman. Very little is known of her early life, though some believe she was a nun from Carrow Abbey. After a serious illness she wrote that she had received 'Divine Revelations' and decided to enter an anchorage. Her cell had a window through which she could see part of the inside of the church of St Julian. She kept the 'Ancren Riwle' of conduct for recluses, which allowed her to have a servant, or possibly two, who would buy food and look after her. She was permitted to have two meals a day, avoiding flesh and lard. She could keep a cat. Her 'Revelations' dealt with the likeness of God, God's love of mankind, the nature of man, and how one may come to God. St Julian's Church was badly damaged during a bombing raid in 1942, but has been well restored and Dame Julian's cell reconstructed. It is now visited by pilgrims from all over the world. (Solomons, G., *Stories Behind the Plaques of Norwich*, Capricorn Books, 1981)

MAY 9TH

1945: On this day Agnes Podd recorded in her diary that on Tuesday, 8 May 'the war is over in Europe. No more fighting for all the brave men and women who have saved us from untold horror. No more sirens, no more fear and already no more bombing.' For seven years Agnes recorded the impact of war on the city and reflected the daily difficulties of an elderly lady, coping with a chronically ill husband (who died in 1944) and an unmarried son needing regular hospitalisation. On 15 August she heard the king's speech, and then went out to see the fires and fireworks, 'Went through the city and onto Mousehold where we could see the whole city. Mary and Janet enjoyed it very much, they had never been out so late at night, nor seen such a sight, or streets lighted up. It was like fairyland to them and a sight they will never forget.' In November her son returned home after eight months in hospital, 'he has had 23 gold injections and is better but still not able to walk properly, but he is glad to be home again.'(Diary of Agnes Podd of Norwich, Norwich Record Office, MC2299/1)

MAY 10TH

1660: On this day Charles II was solemnly proclaimed king, signalling the end of the Civil War. The city authorities only called a halt to festivities after they had lasted for a week, including several days of bonfires, feasting and an official thanksgiving on 24 May. The bells of St Peter Mancroft, which had merrily welcomed the rise of Protector Cromwell, rang with equal cheerfulness to welcome the return of the monarchy. As observed by James Wentworth Day, church bells know no politics. One month later, Norwich Assembly voted to restore to the crown its fee farm rent and donated £1,000 to Charles II. In August the aldermen and common councillors agreed to take the oath of allegiance and supremacy, reflecting their desire to remain in power. On 20 September, the soldiery in Norwich was at last disbanded. However, not everyone in Norwich welcomed the Restoration. Independents and Presbyterians were gradually purged from office and Norfolk's regicide, Miles Corbet, was captured in the Dutch Republic and brought back to face trial. Charles II visited the city in 1671 when he was entertained by Lord Henry Howard at the Howards' ducal palace in the Maddermarket. (Rawcliffe, C. & Wilson, R., eds, *Norwich Since 1550*, Hambledon & London, 2004)

MAY 11TH

1941: On this day a county rally was held in Norwich by about 100 volunteers of the Women's Land Army (WLA), some of them having travelled over 50 miles. A parade was held outside the City Hall, where quite a crowd of spectators had assembled, and after inspection by the Honorary Director, Lady Denman, 'the procession moved off to music provided by the Norwich Lads Club Band on a march through the city. Volunteers Garner and Durrant were standard bearers, and we hope they felt their aching arms were worth the many compliments we have heard. The excellent marching and smart appearance of the girls were remarked by all who saw the procession.' The march was followed by a meeting, which was addressed by Lady Denman and 'volunteers were delighted to have the chance of making the personal acquaintance of our Director, and we hope the cheers that took the place at her farewell showed our appreciation of her visit'. WLA members made several appearances during the month in connection with the War Weapons Week held in various parts of the county, and two groups attended church parades. By 1941, over 270 WLA volunteers were given agricultural employment in Norfolk. (*The Land Girl*, June 1941)

MAY 12TH

1926: On this day Richard Twinch wrote in his memoir:

When I was seven, my father was appointed Livestock Officer for Norfolk based at the Ministry of Agriculture in Norwich ... I used to go to school by electric tram. Trams ran along the main roads to the outer suburbs. They were open in the top and it was fun in wet weather to sit in a shiny black mackintosh, wellies, and souwester to face the elements. The driver was well wrapped up with overcoat and oilskins, but not otherwise protected from the weather. One day the trams stopped running. It was the General Strike of 1926. Everything in Norwich was at a standstill. We were taken to school by parents with cars. There were no newspapers, only a privately printed sheet occasionally available. For the first time I saw my parents worried – the middle classes all feared revolution. But it all collapsed as quickly as it began. If there was violence in Norwich I never saw it. The only aftermath was an argument a week or two later between a tram conductor and a lady passenger.

(Twinch, R., *Memoirs of a Middleman*, (unpublished), 1980)

MAY 13TH

1875: On this day the centenary of the banking house Gurneys & Co. was celebrated by a dinner at Stoke Holy Cross, the seat of Henry Birkbeck. The *Norfolk Chronicle* recorded:

The original founders of the Bank were John and Henry Gurney, who, in addition to their ordinary trade of merchants, carried on a banking business, first in Pitt Street, and afterwards in Magdalen Street. They were the sons of John Gurney, who earned the title of the 'Weavers' Friend' by reason of his advocacy of their cause. The Gurneys devoted themselves exclusively to banking in 1779 and the business was removed to premises on Bank Plain. Changes occurred from time to time and Henry Birkbeck (father of the present head of the firm) became a partner. The panics of the years 1792 and 1825, which caused the failure of many banking houses, only resulted in establishing the Gurneys on a more prosperous basis. They not only survived these financial disasters, but assisted others to tide over their difficulties.

The years 1866–67 tested the stability of the house when the run on the bank was as remarkable for its intensity as it was lasting. In 1896 Gurneys merged with Barclays Bank. (Mackie, C., *Norfolk Annals*, 1901)

MAY 14TH

1705: On this day the *London Post* remarked of Norwich politics: 'Never was a city in the miserable kingdom so wretchedly divided as this ... never were such divisions carried on with such feud, such malice, such magisterial tyranny and such defiance of laws of government'. In 1681 Dean Humphrey Prideaux described the city as riven 'into two factions, Whigs and Torys ... and both contend for their way with the utmost violence'. The party 'to which every man in Norwich belongs, from the highest to the lowest, is as well known as if he daily wore clothes of the colour by which it is designated'. The city had a longstanding appetite for participatory politics, said to be 'vibrant, exuberant, partisan and sometimes violent'. In 1727 a riot followed the general election:

> After the mixed multitude had commenced the fray by throwing dirt, oyster shells, stones or whatever else their fury could lay hold on, a warm engagement ensued amongst the staffmen, who laid on all that stood in the way with passion and violence ... some of the mob cried out 'kill the sheriffs, D-n 'em, kill 'em and then we shall get the election.

(Rawcliffe, C. & Wilson, R. (eds), *Norwich Since 1550*, Hambledon & London, 2004)

MAY 15TH

1922: On this day the Bishop of Norwich dedicated the memorials erected in St Stephen's Church to the memory of the forty men of the parish who fell in the First World War. After expressing sympathy with the relatives of those who fell in the war, the Bishop went on to say that he thought it, 'well that we should from time to time be reminded of some of the sentiments which filled our hearts in the days of the war, for he feared that in many respects we had now fallen below that which we then achieved. Many had forgotten the first scene of relief that came to us on Armistice Day. We forget many of the afflicted who were afflicted still.' Sympathy, he said, ought to be 'wise, tender and understanding.' There was an old proverb which said that if you want to please people you must please them in their ways, and not in your own way. The memorials consisted of a wall tablet, a cross – designed by Hubert A. Miller of Norwich – and a communion table. The latter was richly carved, the laurel being used for decoration on the supports. The oak of the table was grown in Norfolk. (*Eastern Evening News*, 15 May 1922)

MAY 16TH

1782: On this day the Norwich watercolourist, John Sell Cotman, the eldest son of a prosperous silk and lace merchant, was born in the parish of St Mary Coslany. From an early age he showed a prodigious talent for art. His early career developed rapidly: he moved to London to join Dr Munro's teaching academy, in the footsteps of the young J.M.W. Turner and Thomas Girtin. In 1805 he returned to Norwich and, during this period, executed a fine array of watercolours, now in the city collections. During 1823 Cotman received a mixture of critical acclaim and some confusion over his experiments with technical and visual innovation, which were not always appreciated. The *Norwich Mercury* wrote of him as 'a man of unquestionable superior genius', but in 1829 the *Norfolk Chronicle* described his work as 'too gaudy, and we regret in them the absence of that sweet grey tone which is so charming in nature'. A distinctive feature of Cotman's watercolours is the heightened sense of colour, which is almost flamboyant, matched by a new technique in which he added flour or rice paste to his watercolour to form a semi-opaque medium which intensified pigments. (Moore, A., *The Norwich School of Artists*, Norwich Museums Service, 1985)

MAY 17TH

1919: On this day a War Exhibition was opened in Norwich and included a display showing the work of the Women's Land Army. The Norfolk Agricultural Committee (Women's Branch), and the little band of workers at No.33 Prince of Wales Road, put their heads together and 'did our best to coax and persuade people into lending us all that we wanted in the way of implements, such as a chaff-cutter, spade, hoe and rake, milking pail and stool, sheep hurdles, hay and straw.' The background was festooned with banners, 'England must be fed', 'We all feel fit in the Land Army', etc. and it struck the Welfare Officer as:

> … rather funny that next door to us was a hospital display … we, in the Land Army, don't need any hospital treatment … there was a little trouble to make tailors' dummies look like the girls … the cheeks were a wee bit too pink, not quite enough of the 'nut brown maid' look about them for healthy Land Army girls [but] there were many prominent citizens and agriculturists present, who inspected the exhibits in turn. Our little show proved quite a source of attraction, and was visited by some hundreds during the exhibition.

(*The Landswoman*, July 1919)

MAY 18TH

1698: On this day the traveller, Celia Fiennes, visited Norwich where she stayed for several days. She entered the city by the West Gate, passing over a high bridge that led across a causeway which looked 'somewhat dangerous, being fenced with trenches from its banks pretty deep to secure it from the water'. She liked the city:

> ... which is walled round full of towers, except on the river side which serves for the wall: they seem the best in repair of any walled city I know, tho' in some places there are little breaches ... there are twelve gates in all and thirty-six churches which are to be seen on a clear day altogether, on the Castle walls ... they are built all of flints well headed or cut which makes them look blackish and shining. The streets are all well pitched with small stones and very clean ... one that I entered in first was very broad for two coaches or carts to pass on either side and in the middle was a great well house with a wheel to wind up the water for the good of the public.

(Morris, C. (ed.) *The Illustrated Journeys of Celia Fiennes 1685-c.1712*, Alan Sutton Publishing, 1995)

MAY 19TH

1919: On this day the war heroine, Nurse Edith Cavell, was reburied on Life's Green, at the east end of Norwich Cathedral. She had been court martialled and then executed by the Germans in October 1915. After the First World War ended Nurse Cavell's body was exhumed and returned to England. King George V lead a very well-attended memorial service at Westminster Abbey before Edith's body was taken by special train to Thorpe Station, Norwich. The Bishop of London described Edith Cavell as, 'that brave woman who deserves a great deal from the British Empire.' The coffin was draped in the Union Jack. The 23rd Psalm was sung, together with the Litany, the Lord's Prayer, the hymn 'Abide with Me', and the sounding of the Last Post and Reveille. The family had asked that she be buried in Norwich Cathedral, not Westminster Abbey. From Norwich Station to the cathedral there was another procession ... Bishop Pollock described her as 'an innocent, unselfish, devout and pretty girl ... in the very hour of her death she has re-beckoned us to eternal things'. The Cavell family asked for a plain tomb with a cross, such as was used for fallen soldiers. (Souhami, D., *Edith Cavell*, Quercus, 2010)

MAY 20TH

1961: On this day Benjamin Britten and Peter Pears gave a recital at the Norfolk & Norwich Music Club, presenting a programme of Purcell, Schubert, Debussy and Britten. It was the third that Britten and Pears had given for the club. The concert took place on the tenth anniversary of the founding of the NNMC which had its inaugural meeting in April 1951, the first concert being held in the Music Room of the Assembly House on 26 May 1951. Britten had agreed to become president, saying, 'I am pleased to be connected in this way with a club with such sensible aims, especially based in such a fine place as The Assembly House. I send you all my best wishes for the great success of the club'. He remained president until shortly before his death in 1976. Britten had many associations with Norwich: he first came to the city to take viola lessons from Audrey Alston and through her met his influential teacher, Frank Bridge. Many of his compositions received world premieres in the city including *Our Hunting Fathers* (Triennial Festival, 1936), *A Ceremony of Carols* (Norwich Castle, 1942) and *Hymn to St Peter* (St Peter Mancroft, 1955). (Norfolk & Norwich Music Club programme notes, April, 1961)

May 21st

1737: On this day the citizens of Norwich were treated to an exhibition by a travelling woman glass-blower, 'the only artist of her sex'. The lady was not named, but she was proclaimed famous and 'maketh all sorts of fine images in glass, as of birds, beasts, men, women, children, swords and scabbards, ships with men and guns aboard, with many other curiosities too much to be mentioned, all being small and curious, intermixed with blue and other colours, as natural as Indian painting.' For the 'diversion of all gentlemen, ladies and others' she set up her stall at the Lower Half Moon Inn in the Market Place where her works were displayed for sale and she gave demonstrations of the art of glass-blowing, making objects such as 'pens to write with, and Grenades, which being put to the snuff of a candle, gave a report like a gun'. Spectators were invited to inspect a wheel 'turned by human power, that spins ten thousand yards of glass in half an hour' and the performance was free although a small cost of *6d* was mentioned if anyone showed interest in parting with such a sum. (*Norwich Mercury*, 21 May 1737)

MAY 22ND

1738: On this day, the three-day Norwich Races began on Mousehold Heath. The first race was open to any horse, mare or gelding that had never won above the value of £50 at one time, a handicap fixed by age. For the duration: 'No person will be allowed to keep a Booth, except he subscribes One Guinea. A Commodious Stand will be made for the Judges.' On the Tuesday the race was for a purse of £20 and ran 'according to the Rules of Horsemanship ... the best of three Heats, four Miles each Heat.' The final day's race was for horses that had never won the value of £100 at one time, each 'to carry ten Stone each, to run the best of three Heats.' Horses must have been stabled locally by the contestant for at least ten days before the meeting. No horse could win more than one plate. No less than three horses were required for each race and any differences that arose were to be finally determined by the judges. Notice of entry and horses' measurements were to have been lodged in advance, and the entrance fee paid well before the start of the race. (*Norwich Mercury*, 22 May 1738)

MAY 23RD

1890: On this day *The Times* reported on Mr Gladstone's Norwich visit 'when he took every opportunity to deliver one of those attacks against the Government which are characterised by an almost complete absence of that factor which is apparently considered quite unnecessary to the present politics of himself and his followers, viz. accuracy'. Mr Gladstone was, however, given a jubilant reception by his supporters. At precisely the announced time of its arrival, the special train bringing him from London was seen running up to No.2 platform, to which admission only had been obtained by ticket. On arrival at Thorpe Station he remarked, 'I have not been in Norwich for fifty-three years, and I need not say I did not arrive at it by this station.' From the station gates along Prince of Wales Road to the post office was one great mass of people, who cheered most enthusiastically as the carriage conveying Mr Gladstone passed along. A detachment of mounted police accompanied the carriages and the *Norwich Mercury* reported that the behaviour of the crowd 'was most commendable, and only a solitary howl of an opposing partisan was occasionally heard amidst the general cheering.' (*The Times*, 23 May 1890; *Norwich Mercury*, 21 May 1890)

MAY 24TH

1899: On this day city dignitaries celebrated the opening of its new, prestigious purpose-built shopping arcade – the Royal Arcade – designed by the leading city architect, George John Skipper (1856–1948). Skipper planned a layout which included twenty-four shops and the premises of the Conservative Club on the southern arm. It is 247ft long, 15ft broad and 29ft long. There is a slight change of alignment immediately behind the entrance from the Walk, brilliantly disguised by angle-and-bowed shop windows. The original design of the arcade, and its decorative features in particular, show that Skipper was experimenting with ideas drawn from Art Nouveau. He was clearly aware of the work of the leading architects of the day, Baron Victor Horta in Belgium and Hector Guimard in Paris. The arcade was built partially on the site of the fifteenth-century Angel Inn. Its place was taken by the Royal Hotel, so named in 1840 as a compliment to Queen Victoria on the occasion of her wedding to Prince Albert. The new hotel was fitted 'with every convenience for the reception of families and commercial gentlemen', who could promenade along new Royal Arcade. (The Royal Arcade information boards; Thompson, L.P., *Norwich Inns*, W.E. Harrison & Sons, 1947)

MAY 25TH

1925: On this day the *Eastern Evening News* reported at length the celebrations, led by the mayor and sheriff of Norwich, in support of Empire Day. Although not officially recognised as an annual event until 1916, it quickly became a tradition in the city's schools. The sheriff gave an address in which he extolled the virtues of the Empire, 'In these days of wireless, telegraphy and aeroplanes, boundaries between different countries and long distances are beginning to vanish. In this way people of the world are getting nearer to each other and gradually learning to know each other better.' All the city's schools celebrated Empire Day and at Heigham Street School one pupil remembered:

> The Lord mayor used to come and he always gave us a half day off. If we could wear a white blouse or skirt we were encouraged to do so. Everything was decorated up in red, white and blue, with red, white and blue flowers. Usually we had a Maypole ... it was a change from learning ... That was a day we sat outside to see the Big Union Jack – all very patriotic.

(Heigham Street, Women's Oral History Project, 1995; *Eastern Evening News*, 25 May 1925)

MAY 26TH

1804: On this day the daughter of a Norwich watchmaker, Alicia Meynell (born 1782), became the first woman in the Jockey Club Records to have raced and won against a man, a record unequalled until 1943. She styled herself 'Meynell', perhaps at the request of her Massingham family, as she led a colourful life and was nicknamed 'Norfolk Nymph'. Alicia met and fell madly in love with Colonel Thomas Thornton who encouraged her to become an expert horsewoman, so much so that a bet was placed that she could make good her boast of riding in a real race. At York races in May 1804 Alicia's notoriety drew huge crowds. She raced well but her horse tired and she failed to win. A year later she was styling herself 'Mrs T', although she was only Colonel Thornton's mistress, and demanded a rematch. She arrived in an extravagant outfit consisting of a purple cap and waistcoat, yellow shirt and purple shoes with embroidered stockings. This time she rode against Frank Buckle, one of the premier jockeys of the day. She romped home in style and Buckle was never allowed to forget the day he was beaten by a woman riding side-saddle. (Robson, P., *Wild Women*, Pier 9, 2011)

MAY 27TH

1922: On this day the author Dorothy L. Sayers accepted a position as copywriter with advertising agency S.H. Benson's. One of her most successful projects was a large campaign commissioned by Colman's of Norwich. 'The difficulty in all our campaigns', admitted Colman's, "is to get our advertisements read. Mustard to the man in the street is, by its nature, a dull subject"'. Dorothy got to work and the 'Mustard Club', became the focus of the agency's efforts. Large posters appeared on the buses and hoardings saying 'Join the Mustard Club' and Dorothy wrote *The Recipe Book of the Mustard Club: A Treasury of Delectable Dishes* to great success. There was, of course, no Mustard Club in reality but once the fictional characters were established, their 'adventures' appeared in newspapers. The 'President' of the club was Baron de Beef, and the 'Secretary', Miss Di Gester. Letters and cartoons appeared in the national press, and stage stars, such as Delysia and Phyllis Titmuss, lent their names to the advertisements, as did the restaurants Simpsons and the Café Royal. The great joke of the day was 'What is a canary?' Answer: 'A sparrow who has joined the Mustard Club!' (Hitchman, J., *Such a Strange Lady*, New English Library, 1975)

MAY 28TH

1809: On this day the inhabitants of Norwich were much alarmed by an incident when the 3rd Western Regiment of Local Militia, commanded by Colonel Chadd, assembled for parade on the Castle Ditches. As the muster-roll was called, one of the privates answered as usual 'Here', but added 'with an empty belly!' This insubordination resulted from 'some irregularity respecting their pay' and the private was ordered to the guardhouse. The whole company to which he belonged immediately left the ranks, rescued him, and disarmed the guard. Others followed their example, paying no regard to their officers by marching on the colonel's lodgings and disarming the guard there. They returned to the parade ground and surrounded the Castle Inn where officers were at breakfast, threatening any man who dared to obey their officers. After some hours the militia were given an undertaking that they would in future be paid regularly but, on demanding their 'marching guinea', were told that the cost of their uniform was to be taken from it, which caused further dissent. The colonel then offered advance payment, plus their arrears, upon which assurance 'they became very peaceable and in the afternoon appeared on parade in a perfectly orderly manner'. (*The Times*, 1 June 1809)

May 29th

1907: On this day a meeting was held of the newly formed Norfolk and Norwich Model Yacht Club at Whitlingham Reach. The club was started in Norwich by sailing enthusiast George Colman Green, and had its headquarters at the Bell Hotel. The British Model Yacht Racing Association had been started in Norwich about three years earlier but it was felt that a separate club was needed for the local area. A proposal was made for a dedicated model yachting tank for Norwich as members found the river 'dangerous and dirty' and did not feel justified in encouraging boys to the river banks at Whitlingham. The tank should be '100 or 120 yards square with cement bottom and sides and a broad sunk path round its entire margin so that no bending or stooping will be required.' Reaching poles, buoys and lifebelts were necessary as a guard against accident. Colman Green thought that 'as a municipal asset the value of this work cannot be doubted, and we hope to secure as central a site as possible.' The club held its first Annual Regatta in September with 600 enthusiasts present. (Colman Green, G., *Norfolk and Norwich Model Yacht Club*, Millennium Heritage C623.8201)

MAY 30TH

1973: On this day the controversial alterations to Hay Hill were completed. Geoffrey Goreham reported:

> The greenery has gone from Hay Hill and a new concept of open space has replaced the simplicity and formality of the past. It has been rather an expensive metamorphosis and yet, after much delay and criticism there is, in Hay Hill a measure of informality and excitement which has not altogether erased the old image.

The ring of cars around the green oval was replaced by 'a passing panorama of true pedestrian activity. People can meet here, argue here, dance, play music and hold public meetings here if they wish.' The new appearance of Hay Hill 'could be said to have been in the mind of time since dealers sold hay on the slope and carrier carts rumbled over the cobbles to the White Horse Inn that stood there.' The most argued-over aspect was the C & A building which 'climaxed' the hill. Its proximity to the 'magnificent Gothic dignity of St Peter Mancroft' was considered a problem in that 'no ultra-modern building deserves such unfair competition. Small wonder the C & A building attracts criticism like barnacles on a ship.' (*Eastern Evening News*, 30 May 1973)

May 31st

1641: On this day mayor Thomas Carver died, having held the office for only a month. That same day Adrian Parmenter, a leading Parliamentarian and Alderman, was hurriedly elected to serve until the following May. Parmenter was responsible for collecting excise tax and seizing estates of Royalist sympathisers during the turbulent years of the 1600s. In 1648 his house on Hog Hill (now Timberhill) was attacked by a violent mob. The efforts of his wife Hannah to placate the rioters by offering them food were to no avail. They broke in and ransacked the house, causing considerable damage and stealing property. Excise duty was a value added tax on essentials and therefore widely resented by the poor, especially when it was extended to meat and beer. There was violent opposition to it in Norwich and at one point Parmenter declared that his officers were too frightened to collect the tax, one being threatened by a butcher's wife wielding a cleaver. Following his initial stint as mayor, Parmenter was again forced to stand the following year when the elected Thomas Gostlin, a staunch Royalist, was arrested and imprisoned. (Williams, N., *The Blue Plaques of Norwich*, Heritage Economic & Regeneration Trust (HEART), 2010)

JUNE 1ST

1913: On this day 'The man who made diamonds', the 11th Baron Stafford, died at Costessey. Lord Stafford, otherwise Sir Fitzherbert Edward Stafford Jerningham, owned Costessey Hall having inherited his title and estates from his brother. He was profoundly interested in chemical research and during the twenty years he lived at Costessey was said seldom to have left the grounds. He was decidedly eccentric. When workmen came to the hall he would point out what needed doing then leave them to get on with the work, turning the key in the lock as he went out. Food and drink were brought in by the butler but they were thus kept in confinement until the work was completed. He once accompanied his gamekeepers on their nightly manoeuvres to catch poachers, but they were assailed with stones whereupon Lord Stafford returned home and never went again. Unmarried, he lived the life of a recluse, devoting long hours to his researches in chemistry. He was credited with two main aims, only one of which he achieved. He succeeded in making artificial diamonds but died before achieving his second objective, to make them economically. Natural stones, despite their cost, remained cheaper than Lord Stafford's artificial diamonds. (*Bawburgh News*, July 2008)

JUNE 2ND

1927: On this day pioneering travel writer, H.V. Morton, published his observations on driving around England during 1926 in a 'bull-nosed Morris'. He wrote:

In moonlight Norwich from the castle walls lies with shining roofs, the green light rippling the length of the thin spire of the cathedral and falling into the dark, narrow streets. A drover behind his sheep crosses the empty market square in a pool of lamplight; and it seems that centuries have slipped back; that the Norwich looms are clacking once again, that along the deserted riverside are the ghosts of Flemish masts ... Norwich has been called the 'city of churches'. It struck me also as a city of public houses and canaries. In hundreds of little homes the shoemakers of Norwich breed prize canaries ... If you wanted to stop the traffic, the quickest way would be to walk through the city with a first-class Norwich Plain Head on your finger ... I came here knowing nothing about the city except that it ... once was the third city in England, that when its weaving trade went north after the coalfields, Norwich just put on a flinty face and learned how to make women's shoes. Trust Norwich to survive!

(Morton, H.V., *In Search of England*, Methuen, 2000)

JUNE 3RD

1728: On this day Norfolk landowner, John Buxton wrote to his son, Robert:

> Your mother did not go to Laxfield until yesterday in the afternoon; I was obliged to take the chariot to Norwich on Saturday: it was expected then we should know who were to be our candidates for the ensuing election but they came to no determination. I believe there is a general approbation of Sir Edmund Bacon but the difficulty is to find him a proper partner, and till such a one is found he does not care to declare himself ... I do not much trouble myself about it though should like to see ourselves represented by gentlemen of worth.

However, John attended numerous public meetings in Norwich: 'there was one last Saturday, of the principal gentlemen of the Harbord [family] and I believe there will be no opposition', and indeed, there was not. On election day, John met Sir Edmund Bacon at Harford Bridges 'where gentlemen and freeholders' congregated 'to wait on him into the town, and he entered with upwards of 1,200 men'. (Mackley, A. (ed.), *John Buxton: Norfolk Gentleman and Architect*, Norfolk Record Society Volume LXIX, 2005)

JUNE 4TH

1939: On this day the chairman of Norfolk County Council (Mr Colman) and Mrs Colman were 'at home' at Crown Point to members and senior officials of the Council and their wives, in order to celebrate the council's jubilee. The guests, after being received by Mr and Mrs Colman on the Saturday, enjoyed the grounds in the glory of a June afternoon. An opportunity was afforded them of inspecting the paintings of the Norfolk School and later they took tea. At 4.45 p.m. an adjournment was made to the Billiard Room where there was speech making. Afterwards Mr and Miss Tree gave a demonstration of 'thought transmission' and Mr Tree, with Major E.W. Denny as his assistant, performed some clever card tricks which 'baffled both his audience and his assistant'. After Mr Colman had given the assembled company a run down of council matters since its inception in 1889, he called on Sir Thomas Hare to address the gathering. Sir Thomas said he was the world's worst speaker. He did not quite know what the meeting was all about but expected others present did. If anyone wished to ask a question, he was sure the chairman would be pleased to answer it. (*Eastern Daily Press*, 5 June 1939)

JUNE 5TH

1850: On this day Miss Margaret Creake of St Andrew's, Norwich, died. She was the last of three very eccentric and parsimonious sisters. In her will she directed that relatives who chose to prove their identity should receive 1s each; a legacy of £20 was left to one neighbour and one of £10 to another. Each homeless person above sixty-eight years of age in London, Ireland and Scotland was to receive £50, and all her real estate was to be employed in building and equipping a hospital for aged persons. The property was valued at only £20,000, and insufficient to meet the wishes of the testatrix. Over 1,000 persons visited the deceased's house, 'the filthiness of which was beyond description'. Shortly after Miss Creake's death a chemist named Woolner, with whom she had been intimate, committed suicide by poisoning. It was immediately rumoured that Miss Creake had met with her death by foul means by the hand of Mr Woolner. The coroner ordered the exhumation of the body from St Clement's churchyard but, after an examination of the remains, Miss Creake's death was attributed to natural causes. No explanation was given for the demise of Mr Woolner. (Mackie, C., *Norfolk Annals, Vol. 1*, 1901)

JUNE 6TH

1944: On this day, in the early hours of the morning, large formations of Liberator aircraft from the American 458th Bombardment Group at Horsham St Faiths were seen passing over the city, the whole sky vibrating with activity. The hopes of months had become reality – D-Day had arrived. The group helped prepare for the Normandy Invasion by striking gun batteries and French airfields in support of the assault. Additional B-24 Liberators went from 467th Bombardment Group at Rackheath, whose airmen were known as the 'Rackheath Aggies'. Their aircraft bore such names as Blond Bomber, Belle of the East and Perils of Pauline. The celebrated Witchcraft flew 130 missions without an abort. Horsham St Faiths had been made available to the American Eighth Air Force in 1942 and designated Station 1232 (HF). Servicemen from both groups socialised in Norwich at the Bishop's Palace which became the American Red Cross club, with the bishop retaining an office in the buildings. A Memorial Library of the 2nd Air Division of the US 8th Air Force is housed in the Norwich Forum, a 'living memorial' to nearly 7,000 young Americans who lost their lives during the Second World War. (Memorial Library; Banger, J., *Norwich at War*, Wensum Books, 1974)

JUNE 7TH

1806: On this day the *Norwich Mercury* advertised a farm for sale which stood in the parish of Eaton but is now the Eaton Golf Club. The club, which stands beside Newmarket Road, was founded in 1910 and is one of the oldest golf courses in Norfolk, is constructed on the site of ancient barrows that at the start of the nineteenth century was:

> ... a farm at Eaton, chiefly in the occupation if Mr Rice Wicks, comprising an excellent dwelling house, a lime kiln in full trade, with cottages, 330 acres of arable and 60 acres of meadow, leasehold of the Dean and Chapter of Norwich. Also a very good dwelling-house in the occupation of the Revd Michael Brown and about 60 acres of arable land lying between the road leading from St Giles Gates and the turnpike road to Eaton. Also 60 acres of very good arable land lying to the left side of the turnpike road, adjoining Mile End Lane.

The four barrows, or tumuli, once formed part of Eaton Heath but even by the early ninettenth century 'two of them have been nearly levelled by the plough.' (Rye, W., *History of the Parish of Eaton in the City of Norwich*, Roberts & Co., 1915)

JUNE 8TH

1793: On this day the prosperous linen-draper, James Oakes of Bury, recorded the dwindling demand in Norwich for his goods. He had travelled up two days before and dined at the Maid's Head before visiting friends and business associates in Cawston and Colney, taking in a tour of the Pockthorpe Brewery in the afternoon. He wrote:

> I never met with a more depressed Markett, never Sold one Bundle of Yarn not withstanding every possible Endeavor. This is the 4th Month of attending at Norwich without being able to make any Sales. The manufacturers can get no Remittances owing to the Difference of Exchange & have nothing to do except a few East India orders which came in yesterday.

In July he tried his luck again but wrote, 'this is the 4th or 5th month [I] have been at Norwich and returned without selling a Bundle of Yarn'. It was not to get any better: the following year he again recorded that 'the Trade of the City [is] in the most desponding State imaginable – did scarcely any Business.' He again took refreshment at the Maid's Head and completed 'the little Business I could do in Norwich before 12 O'clock.' (Fiske, J. (ed.), *The Oakes Diaries* 1778–1800, The Boydell Press, 1990)

JUNE 9TH

1959: On this day auditions were held at the Royal Hotel in Norwich for prospective announcers and newscasters for the new Anglia Television station which opened that year. More than 780 applications were received from hopeful candidates, who had to read news items, make announcements about forthcoming programmes and conduct an off-the-cuff interview with a member of Anglia's staff, Philip Bray. Philip posed as an American film actor, an Irish playwright, an Australian sheep farmer and a guardsman who had refused to go on guard. Anglia's first newsreaders were 'Sandy' Newman Sanders, Drew Russell and Colin Bower. Across the road, work was forging ahead on conversion of the Agricultural Hall into studios and signal-reception areas. It was hoped that 200,000 of the 350,000 homes with television in the area would view the new channel. There was opposition, however, from Labour MPs, led by Christopher Mayhew, who were reportedly 'working furiously' to prevent the interruption of serious programmes by advertisements. They attacked the Independent Television Authority for abuse of the term 'natural break' used to describe 'advertising breaks'. Anglia TV went on the air in 1959 complete with advertising. (*A Knight on the Box, 40 Years of Anglia Television*, Anglia Television Limited, 1999)

June 10th

1965: On this day Allan Smethurst's 'The Singing Postman' entered the Record Retailer EP (extended play) charts at No.20. The record had been released on 19 December the previous year and caused such a stir that both BBC's *Look East* and commercial rivals Anglia Television put him on their screens – and by March the record was outselling the Beatles and the Rolling Stones in several East Anglian towns. Allan was an exponent of the Norfolk accent, his self-penned lyrics catching the mood of the county. His signature number was 'Hev Yew Gotta Loight, Boy?', in which a Norfolk courtship proceeds at a pace regulated by the lady's reiterated demands for a light for her cigarette, which earned him the Ivor Novello Award for the best novelty song of the year. In Norwich his most popular song was 'Norwich is a Fine City' which ended with a rousing 'Up the Canaries!' Allan quit the music business in 1970, later admitting he had an alcohol problem and that he had spent all his money and was penniless. In 1994 the Norwich-reared writer D.J. Taylor said that 'the Postman' reminded him of 'a mostly roseate universe ... watching the crab boats set out [and] taking rattletrap trains into Norwich for the winter sales.' (Skipper, K., *Hev Yew Gotta Loight, Boy? The Life and Lyrics of Allan Smethurst 'The Singing Postman'*, Countryside Books, 2001)

June 11th

1804: On this day the Royal Artillery, two troops of the 1st Dragoons, 24th Regiment of Foot, Colonel Patterson's Battalion, the City of Norwich, Regiment of Volunteers (on permanent duty) and the Rifle Corps, had a sham fight at Bramerton; one party (as English) marched by Trowse, and the other (as French) by Thorpe to Postwick grove, and crossed the Yare on floating bridges, formed by wherries placed alongside each other and planked over. The troops were in motion at 6 a.m. The representation of an action was on a very extensive scale. The English of course were victorious, and were regaled with several barrels of porter, and marched back to Norwich. The vanquished returned to Postwick grove, where their spirits were 'recruited' with brown stout. They then returned to the city, about 4.30 p.m. The concourse of spectators in carriages, on horseback and on foot, was immense. The Volunteer Infantry and Rifle Corps had been formed two years earlier at a public meeting held in the Guildhall, for the purpose of conforming to the regulations of the Acts for the Defence of the Realm. (*The Norfolk and Norwich Remembrancer*, Matchett and Stevenson, 1822)

JUNE 12TH

1802: On this day was born the writer and first woman sociologist, Harriet Martineau, fifth child of Thomas Martineau, a Norwich bombazine manufacturer. Harriet was educated at home before attending Revd Perry's school, but when Thomas died in 1826 his business failed, forcing the family to earn their own livings. The Martineaus were committed Unitarians but Harriet recorded her lack of religious concentration:

> The Octagon Chapel at Norwich has some curious windows in the roof – not skylights, but letting in light directly. I used to sit staring up at those windows and looking for angels to come for me, and take me to heaven, in sight of all the congregation – the end of the world being sure to happen while we were at chapel. I was thinking of this, and of the hymns, the whole of the time, it now seems to me. It was very shocking to me that I could not pray at chapel. I believe that I never did in my life. I prayed abundantly when I was alone; but it was impossible for me to do it in any other way; and the hypocrisy of appearing to do so was a long and sore trouble to me.

(*Harriet Martineau Autobiography*, Vol. I, Smith, Elder & Co., 1877)

JUNE 13TH

2001: On this day Christie's of London offered for sale a rare William III silver tankard bearing the mark of Elizabeth Haselwood of Norwich, the city's only woman silversmith. The price realised was £17,625. Elizabeth was the widow of Arthur Haselwood II, the most prolific maker of plate after the Restoration until his death in 1684. He was the son of Arthur Haselwood I, the first of an unusual continuing family of gold and silversmiths of three generations and each named Arthur Haselwood. Elizabeth was unique in carrying on her husband's business in her own right, employing her own mark 'EH' under an open-headed Crown. As early as 1685, one year after her husband's death, she regilded the Mace for Norwich Corporation at the cost of 42s 6d. The Haselwood shop was in London Street on the south side, next to 'the Cockey', by Little London Street. Elizabeth died in 1715, aged seventy-one, leaving her shop to her son, Arthur Haselwood III, and is buried with her husband in the south aisle of the Church of St Andrew. Of her work, fifteen church and twenty-nine secular pieces survive, including a beaker in the Royal Collection. (G.N. Barrett, *Norwich Silver and its marks 1565-1792*, The Wensum Press, 1981/Christie's Bid Department)

JUNE 14TH

1821: On this day the Rosary Cemetery opened, the first-ever private, non-denominational cemetery of its kind in England, established 'on the broad principles of Christian equality'. It was the brainchild of Presbyterian minister Thomas Drummond, who bought the land, once a market garden, with his own money in 1819. He fundamentally objected to the law that citizens had to be buried according to the rites of the Church of England in parish churchyards. It took two years to lay it out; the chapel is the work of Edward Boardman. Drummond had intended it for all denominations but the Church of England ignored it until Bishop Bathurst gave it his blessing in 1821. The founder was himself buried there in 1852, and just over 100 years and nearly 18,000 internments later, it came under the care of the Norwich Corporation. Much of the Rosary is delightfully untidy, weathered stone and green-stained angels stand in natural growth: it remains essentially a Victorian cemetery, 'an inspiration of Christian principle created on the hills of Thorpe Hamlet'. There are memorials to many eminent city Victorians who were the powerful hierarchy of the nineteenth century – the non-conformists merchants, manufacturers, radicals, painters and reformers. (Goreham, G., *Norwich Heritage*, F. Crane, 1977)

JUNE 15TH

1819: On this day Mary Wright, aged twenty-two, married Isaac Sewell, aged twenty-five. The wedding was held in the tiny Quaker Meeting House at Lammas and the newlyweds set off in a chaise for a week's honeymoon at Cromer. Daughter Anna (future author of *Black Beauty*) and son Philip were born into increasingly reduced circumstances as Isaac's business failed. Determined to educate her children at home, Mary turned to writing to earn enough money for books. In 1824 her first book, *Walks with Mamma, or Stories in Words of One Syllable* was published anonymously. It was one of the first children's books ever bound in cloth and earned her the 'little fortune' of £3, enough to buy books for her children's lessons. Her most famous work, *Mother's Last Words*, was published in 1860 and became an instant success, selling over 1 million copies within Mary's lifetime. She wrote a steady stream of verse, often in ballad form, intending to 'instruct and improve children and members of the working classes'. Her temperance ballad, 'The Rose of Cheriton' (1867) describes a household ruined by alcohol. Her poetry combined simplicity of language with clear moral and religious instruction. (Gavin, A.E., *Dark Horse, A Life of Anna Sewell*, Sutton Publishing, 2004)

JUNE 16TH

1835: On this day the *Norfolk Chronicle* reported that 'Guild Day was celebrated in Norwich for the last time. The Civic Procession to the cathedral was headed by the regalia borne by the respective officers on horseback. Snap, too, made his final appearance'. Guild Day might have gone, but Snap, the Norwich Dragon, was by no means bowing out of public life, having appeared as a succession of effigies for over 400 years. Such was, and is, the affection of the city for its traditional dragons that during May and June 1976 a Snap Festival of Norwich was held. Two dragons, like grotesque puppets from an oriental theatre, still hang from the roof of Norwich Castle Keep. Their mouths open as if each were roaring a challenge at the other and if a slight draught catches one, he seems alive and about to circle his opponent. Snap became a legend in Norwich and for centuries was the central feature of a procession which evolved from a religious pageant in honour of St George to a grand civic occasion on Guild Day during which the new mayor was sworn into Office. (Lane, R., *Snap: The Norwich Dragon*, Trend Litho Ltd, 1976)

JUNE 17TH

1902: On this day a gathering took place at the Criterion Cafe in White Lion Street, organised by schoolmasters Robert Webster and Joseph Nutchey. This energetic, moustachioed duo were the leading lights at a local football team known as Norwich Church of England Young Men's Society. They recruited another local sportsman, Arthur Turner, and unfolded plans to create the biggest football club for miles around. The new Norwich City FC subsequently made its home on Newmarket Road and gained admission to the Norfolk and Suffolk League. The first match was a 1–1 friendly with Harwich. City wore blue and white in those days and were known as The Citizens ... these were exciting times and enthusiastic fans adopted the anthem 'On the Ball City', apparently pinching it from another Norwich team. The local pastime of breeding canaries also became associated with the club and provided a new nickname, with club colours changing to yellow and green. Bigger crowds necessitated a new ground ... the Canaries took flight and landed at The Nest. This was part of a disused chalk-pit in Rosary Road and required the grandstands from Newmarket Road to be transported there by horse and cart. (Hadgraft, R., *Norwich City, The Modern Era*, Desert Island Books, 2003)

JUNE 18TH

1951: On this day the Festival of Britain got underway in Norwich, with a special service in the cathedral on the Sunday. Princess Elizabeth performed the opening ceremony from the City Hall balcony. Three grand street processions took as their theme 'Norwich Through the Ages'. 'Queen Elizabeth I' and her train of courtiers rode through bomb-scarred streets where patches of wasteland were still being reclaimed. Horned Viking warriors sat in their longship borne along on a sturdy lorry. The Triennial Musical Festival was held concurrently, which brought great names to the city – Sir Malcolm Sargent, pianists Clifford Curzon and Eileen Joyce, and the violinist Max Rostal. Popular events were interspersed among the classical concerts. The ventriloquist Peter Brough and his 'doll' Archie Andrews entertained audiences at the Odeon, followed by Tom Jenkins and his Palm Court Orchestra. At St Andrew's and Blackfriars Halls was an Industrial Exhibition that commemorated Norwich's past and looked hopefully towards the post-war future. Festival visitors were taken on guided tours of the silk factories in St Mary's and Mile Cross while Boulton and Paul proudly showed its contribution to the armed forces and civil defence during the Second World War. (McCutcheon, E., *Norwich Through the Ages*, The Alastair Press, 1989)

JUNE 19TH

1947: On this day Sir Alfred Munnings was received as an Honorary Freeman of the City of Norwich. He was undoubtedly the most celebrated pupil of the Norwich School of Science and Arts and was a brilliant advertising artist for Caleys (chocolate factory), celebrated painter of rural and equine life, and irascible president of the Royal Academy. Freedom of the city was an honour rarely bestowed, even on its own citizens. The ceremony took place in St Andrew's Hall where, years before, he had watched Henry Wood conduct and listened to the music of Sir Edward Elgar. He spoke movingly about his youthful days in Norwich, and Tom Copeman, editor of the *Eastern Daily Press*, wrote: 'Munnings, who for one dreadful moment lost his notes, gave a wonderful impression of his love for Norwich and of the happy freedom of his early painting days – gorse, commons [and] village inns'. Unfortunately, a reception given that afternoon by the Norwich Art Circle was far from wonderful. Munnings caused confusion by avoiding the official welcoming party and complained about the gallery layout, in particular the use of palm trees 'when you've got a gallery full of Norwich School paintings'. (Goodman, J., *The Life of Alfred Munnings 1878–1959*, Erskine Press, 2000)

JUNE 20TH

1977: On this day Anglia Television was responsible for a spoof drama production that has since achieved worldwide cult status. 'Alternative 3' was intended as a successor to the famous Orsen Welles 'War of the Worlds' hoax of the 1930s and purported to be a science fiction documentary centring on the supposed discovery that top British scientists were vanishing as part of a secret American-Russian conspiracy. They were said to be colonising Mars because the earth was dying from pollution and global warming. Actual news footage of natural disasters and droughts was used and former ITN newsreader Tim Brinton was the presenter. Director Christopher Miles (brother of the actress, Sarah Miles) said, 'if the programme has done nothing else it has made people more aware of the threat to the ecology of the world.' The programme was the final episode in a weekly series, 'Science Report'. The series was not due to be recommissioned and the spoof programme was originally meant for April Fools' Day 1977 but was delayed by industrial action although the on-screen credits dated the film to 1 April. Within minutes of the programme finishing the Anglia switchboard was flooded with calls. (*Daily Express*; *Daily Telegraph*; *The Times*, 21 June 1977)

JUNE 21ST

1933: On this day HRH the Prince of Wales opened the first Norwich Municipal Airport at the old 350-acre Mousehold aerodrome. He flew in and was met by the mayor of Norwich and the Bishop of Norwich and his wife. The prince addressed the crowds in front of the new Norfolk and Norwich Aero Club and afterwards inspected men of the Royal Air Force. The club had been launched six years earlier and during the 1930s offered summer and winter holidays which involved flying, either as the main or subsidiary feature. The club owned aircraft of the two-seater Hornet Moth and Gypsy Moth types. Visitors lived on the aerodrome 'with all the facilities of a good residential club at your disposal for £2 10s per week'. The clubhouse boasted a 'large lounge, Mess, Billiard Room, Photographic Dark Room, Table Tennis Room, Bar, Bathroom, a number of bedrooms, a covered Lawn Tennis Court ... and ample garage space.' The club had drawn such distinguished aviators as Amy Johnson, Bert Hinkler and Alan Cobham with his flying circus, but its success was soon overshadowed by the gathering clouds of war. (*Eastern Daily Press*, 22 June, 1933; Heaton, T., *Norfolk Century*, Eastern Counties Newspapers, 1999)

JUNE 22ND

1785: On this day the surveyor, Isaac Lenny, wrote in his Commonplace Book: 'Went to Norwich & saw the Balloon & bough't a Bath Stove at Mr Browns in the upper Market.' The balloon he saw was piloted by the ingenious mechanic, James Deeker, who took off from Quantrell's Gardens in a high wind and, after hitting some trees, made a flight of 45 minutes, landing at Topcroft, some 13 miles south of the city. This was Mr Decker's second attempt, the first having been three weeks earlier, on a very wet and windy day. Parson Woodforde had been on hand to witness the event:

> About 3 o'clock this Afternoon a violent Tempest arose at Norwich ... very loud thunder with strong white lightening with heavy rain ... immediately after which Mr Deeker's Balloon, with Deeker himself him in a boat annexed to it, ascended from Quantrells Gardens ... it was out of Sight in about ten minutes.

The balloon only travelled as far as Sisland when the storm forced it back down to earth. A 'vast concourse of people' assembled and it was unfortunate about the weather, although many thought Deeker most courageous to attempt the ascent so soon after the tempest. (Lowestoft Local Studies Library 168A5/1)

JUNE 23RD

1846: On this day PC William Callow of the Norwich Police died, the first Norfolk police constable to die from injuries sustained in the course of his duty since the formation of the 'new police' in the county in 1836. Constable Callow's duty, together with a number of fellow officers, was to escort a large number of refractory paupers from the workhouse at St Andrew's Hill to the city goal at St Giles Street. A jeering crowd of some 2,000 persons had assembled along the route, throwing large stones, bottles and sticks. number of police officers were injured but the mob did not disperse. As the policemen left the prison they were met by the mob hurling volleys of stones, and a full-scale riot ensued. Under considerable pressure Inspector Peck gave the order 'right about face – quick march – go in for them!' Innocent people became embroiled in the riot, people trampled and shrieks of 'murder' were heard and more stones were thrown. Several people sustained severe injuries, including Constables Barnard (spinal injuries), Day and Harman (head wounds) and the aforementioned Constable Callow, who died seven days later from his head wounds. (Storey, N.R., *A Grim Almanac of Norfolk*, The History Press, 2010)

JUNE 24TH

1547: On this day Matthew Parker (1504-75), cleric and eldest son of William Parker of St Saviour's parish, married Margaret Harlestone, daughter of a Norfolk squire, before clerical marriages had been legalised by parliament and convocation. He was to tread the dangerous path between the old Roman Catholicism and new Protestantism as Henry VIII's three sovereign children played politics with religious adherence. He was consecrated Archbishop of Canterbury in 1559 and worked courageously to formulate the tenets on which the Anglican Church still stands. He might, though, wish to be remembered as something other than a busybody. As a reforming cleric he was noted for sending out detailed enquiries and instructions and is credited with the term Nosey Parker. During Kett's Rebellion he happened to be in Norwich and went out to preach to the rabble congregating at the city gates. The rebels demanded he give them his horses but he quickly sent a message to his servant to treat their hooves with green oil to make them appear lame. It worked and the following morning he pretended to go for a walk to Cringleford Bridge where his servant was waiting with his horses, 'cured' of their lameness. (Solomons, G., *Stories Behind the Plaques of Norwich*, Capricorn Books, 1981)

JUNE 25TH

1960: On this day the last cattle market was held near the castle and the sales were moved to the new purpose-built livestock market at Harford Bridges on the southern outskirts of the city. For generations the Norwich Cattle Market was an integral part of life in the city. It once formed a section of the old castle bailey. In the mid-1930s a total of 212,000 head of stock were sold here annually at a value of over £1,250,000. Fairs were held on the cattle market at Easter and Christmas, which meant boxing booths, tented shows of freaks, strong men and wild animals, helter-skelters, toffee apples and 'kiddies' roundabouts were just some of the fun to be had. In the austere post-war years the travelling fairs brought welcome colour and entertainment to the city. As the fairs became larger and larger, steam-powered rides gave way to those driven by electrical generators and decked out with electric light bulbs. The Castle Mall, completed in 1993, is situated on 7 acres of the old cattle market site and the Easter and Christmas fairs are held elsewhere. (Anderson, A.P. & Storey, N.R., *Norwich: Eighty Years of the Norwich Society*, Sutton Publishing, 2004)

JUNE 26TH

1830: On this day King George IV died, but the news did not arrive in Norwich until the following day, sent by an express despatched from the *Sun* newspaper office in London to the proprietors of the *Norfolk Chronicle*. The great bell of St Peter Mancroft Church was tolled. On the 29th the High sheriff proceeded on horseback from the Norfolk Hotel, accompanied by a marshal and javelin-men, and other officials, to Shire Hill, where the accession of King William IV to the crown of these realms was proclaimed, and three cheers given. A procession round the city was headed by the band and kettledrums of the 1st Royal Dragoons, and five troops of the regiment.

> The Colonel politely declined the mayor's invitation to himself and his officers to take refreshments at the Guildhall ... and the offer on the part of the corporation to present the non-commissioned officers and men of the Royals with 10 guineas with which to drink his Majesty's health was also declined, on the ground that the troops, in attending the civil authorities, had only performed a duty.

The funeral of the late king was observed 'with the complete features of the Sabbath' and the great bell of St Peter Mancroft tolled from 8 p.m. until midnight. (Mackie, C., *Norfolk Annals, Vol. I*, 1901)

JUNE 27TH

1923: On this day the Carrow Bridge was opened with considerable pomp by the Prince of Wales, the future Edward VIII. Designed by City Engineer A.E. Collins, it is a single-leaf bascule lifting bridge. There had been an earlier bridge downstream, built in 1810, and another in 1833, but in the 1920s the City Council began negotiations with Colman's. By the end of the nineteenth century a new crossing was needed, but plans were delayed by difficulties over the site and the First World War. After pressure from Colman's, who did not want their factory divided by a public road, the new bridge was moved upstream. Colman's contributed £10,000 and Boulton and Paul £5,000 towards the total cost of £42,000. During construction a Bronze Age copper alloy spearhead was found, as well as remnants of the city's mediaeval defences against attack from the river. The bridge mechanism was much affected by the temperature: during the winter of 1962–63 it took 12 minutes 20 seconds to lift, rather than the normal 3 minutes, and on one occasion in the very hot summer of 1976 it refused to lift until 8 p.m., despite repeated hosings. (Cocke, S. & Hall, L., *Norwich Bridges Past & Present*, The Norwich Society, 1994)

JUNE 28TH

1864: On this day public outrage at the activities of Father Ignatius and his Third Order on Elm Hill spilled over into violence. The previous day a pilgrimage of 'over four hundred enthusiasts' had taken place to St Walstan's Well at nearby Bawburgh as a challenge to the Bishop's authority. The crowd had 'moved as one long flexible column through the town' and services were held at the well, vials and vessels being filled with the holy well water. On their return to Norwich cries of 'No Popery!' were heard and Ignatius received an anonymous letter telling him that his priory would be set on fire, together with anyone who happened to be within its precincts. A mob of many thousands gathered and detachments of police began to arrive. The brothers barricaded themselves in and some of the sisters arrived to lend support. Their armoury was mixed: Sister Faith brought her rosary, Sister Hope carried a magnificent rolling pin; but Sister Charity was made of sterner stuff – she brought a kettle filled with vitriol (sulphuric acid). In the event, the monastery survived to fight another day but eventually, in 1866, Ignatius left Norwich. (de Bertouch, The Baroness, *The Life of Father Ignatius, O.S.B.*, Methuen, 1904)

JUNE 29TH

1935: On this day Mona Barrie's *Mystery Woman* was showing at the Haymarket, the new Will Hay film *Dandy Dick* was eagerly awaited at the Regent, and *The Night is Young*, with Evelyn Laye and Ramon Novarro, was on at the Carlton. Evelyn Laye was very popular and the new film was described as 'a drama in which music, while predominant, is never obtrusive'. An additional attraction at matinees only was *It Happened in Spain*. On the Hippodrome programme was *The Age of Innocence* starring John Boles and Julie Haydon with Irene Dunne as the 'other woman'. The Theatre De Luxe was showing Miles Mander in *The Case for the Crown*. By the 1930s the 'silver screen' had taken hold in Norwich, there being nearly twenty establishments to visit. When the 'talkies' arrived in Norwich they caused something of a sensation, the first starring Al Jolson in *The Singing Fool*. The city's love affair with the cinema had begun as early as 1901. The cameras were at Queen Victoria's funeral and that very night Norwich was one of just three cities in England to screen the event. (*Eastern Daily Press*, 29 June 1935; Heaton, T. (ed.), *Norfolk Century*, Eastern Counties Newspapers Group, 1999)

JUNE 30TH

1911: On this day the Royal Agricultural Show was held at Crown Point where the Lady mayoress, Mrs Agatha Gurney, Mr H. Rumsey Wells and Mr Walter Rudd made a determined effort to boost the faltering weaving trade in the city by promoting Norwich-made textiles. A portable building was constructed by Bolton & Paul and the name Norwich Master Weavers displayed above the entrance. It was agreed that the aim was to 'revive the old Norwich industry' and that the exhibit should be 'suggestive and historical' rather than a mere shop display. A jacquard loom was on show with a weaver 'weaving a good fabric of distinctive old Norwich patterns', and a painting representing Bishop Blaize, the patron saint of woolcombers was displayed. Samples of dressing gowns, blouses, tennis shirts, etc., made from cloth woven in Norwich were obtained from T. Wells & Son of St Andrew's Street. Thomas Wells was a well-known hatter and cap maker and his son, Herbert Rumsey, became famous throughout the world for his 'Doggie' caps. The business finally closed in 1974 and the premises on St Andrew's Street are now occupied bytThe Rumsey Wells public house. (Morris, T., *Made in Norwich, 700 Years of Textile Heritage*, Nick Williams, 2008)

JULY 1ST

1702: On this day Robert Harsonge was appointed the new Assay Master for Norwich following vociferous protests against the 1697 Britannia Silver Act which proposed to stop all hallmarking outside London. The Norwich Assay Office had opened in 1595, and stood where Jarrolds stands today, to test the purity of finished silver and confer its own standard mark, a castle over a lion, on approved items. In 1581 the castle and lion were joined by a crowned rose, a rose sprig being recorded in 1643. An earlier office for goldsmiths had been established in 1423, the first recorded goldsmith in Norwich being Salomon 'the goldsmythe' who was granted a lease of land by the Abbot St Benet's in 1141. Norwich was only the second provincial town after York where goldsmiths were allowed to use a town mark. Although Norwich was re-confirmed as an Assay Office in 1702 only three pieces of Norwich silver bearing the Britannia mark are known. The city's silversmiths and goldsmiths were few in number and soon afterwards the production of articles assayed at Norwich ceased. The most important collection of Norwich silver is at Castle Museum and contains 100 pieces. (*History and Guide*, Norwich Castle Museum & Art Gallery)

July 2nd

1927: On this day 'a delicate operation' was taking place at the cathedral when, 'for nearly 3 hours a little group of men occupied the organ loft of Norwich Cathedral.' The assistant organist, R.J. Maddern Williams, was involved in 'the exacting task of recording for His Master's Voice Gramophone Company', a pioneer undertaking. To record successfully 'is a test both of nerve control and endless patience ... a footfall, a slight cough, or an untimely voice interposition is sufficient to spoil a record. And recording is an expensive process.' The recording van was parked outside the great west door and between the organ loft and the van 'the only connecting links were microphones hung in the nave and choir, and lengths of electric land lines.' Endless tests were carried out in preparation for the real thing. 'Are you ready?' called the recording manager to the operators before each test. Then to Mr Williams, 'Are you quite happy?' Mr Williams nodded and a 'Silence, please' order given to the 'group of interested persons', before he 'raised his hand at the sound of the buzzer, then lowered it, and at this signal the organist immediately started to play.' (*Eastern Evening News*, 2 July 1927)

July 3rd

1400: On this day a City Court Roll referred to a tenement abutting 'Super le Tombelond', one of the many spellings of the modern Tombland. Towards the end of the nineteenth century the area known as Tomland was 'a large piece of waste ground extending in length from north to south, broadest at the south end, narrower at the north end, and narrowest in the midst by reason of the houses which are built on the east side under the Precinct Wall of the Cathedral Church'. The modern Tombland derives from at least ten derivations 'which name some affirm is had from tombs or sepulchres as having been a great burying place in old time'. Kirkpatrick did not, though, think this the origin of the name:

> It is true that a Church of St Michael DID stand anciently on part of this ground, and that many people were buried in and near it, but I don't think that that was the reason of the name …
> I should say the meaning of Tomlond is Townland, as having been common ground in old time, belonging to the citizens.

(Kirkpatrick, J., *The Streets and Lanes of the City of Norwich*, 1889)

JULY 4TH

1860: On this day Shephard Taylor recorded two incidents at the Norwich Hospital. One concerned a case of opium poisoning. An old woman in reduced circumstances had taken 2oz of laudanum to be 'quit' of her troubles. 'Mr Williams used the stomach pump, at first apparently with good success. The old lady was then consigned to the porter who was instructed to give her a brisk aiding in the field, during which, however, she unfortunately died.' Secondly, a man was admitted and diagnosed as having 'paraplegia' caused by 'an entire horse or stallion seizing hold of the young man by the back of his neck as he was stopping down in front of him, the result of which was serious injury to one of the cervical vertebrae.' The accident had occurred more than thirteen weeks previously, thus Shephard found it 'unusual for a man to live so long after a fracture of the spine, but he is able to eat and drink, and to see him lying comfortably in bed one might think he had nothing whatever the matter with him, and yet he is inevitably doomed to die very shortly'. (Taylor, S.T., *The Diary of a Norwich Hospital Medical Student 1858–1860*, 1930)

JULY 5TH

1803: On this day writer and traveller, George Borrow, was born. He spent his formative years in Norwich, where he attended King Edward VI Grammar School. In his semi-autobiographical work *Lavengro* (1851) he called Norwich 'a fine old city', a phrase that was later fine-tuned to 'a fine city' and inscribed on the city entry signs. Borrow wrote:

> View it from whatever side you will; but it shows best from the east, where the ground, bold and elevated, overlooks the fair and fertile valley in which it stands. Gazing from those heights, the eye beholds a scene which cannot fail to awaken, even in the least sensitive bosom, feelings of pleasure and admiration. At the foot of the heights flows a narrow and deep river, with an antique bridge communicating with a long and narrow suburb, flanked on either side by rich meadows of the brightest green, beyond which spreads the city; the fine old city, perhaps the most curious specimen at present extant of the genuine old English town ... Ah! There is good blood in that old city, and in the whole circumjacent region of which it is the capital.

(Borrow, G., *Lavengro*, Everyman's Library, 1970)

July 6th

1954: On this day the Community of the Little Sisters of the Assumption began celebrating their Golden Jubilee. A Thanksgiving Mass was said at the Catholic Church of St John the Baptist offered by Bishop Parker, Bishop of Northampton. The sisters had been invited to Norwich by Canon Richard Ducket, the Foundation made possible through the benefactions of Henry, 15th Duke of Norfolk. In the Jubilee programme is written:

> On 5 November [1904], exactly one month after their arrival, the small but delicately arranged little Sanctuary in No.7, Chapel Field Road had the exalted privilege of enthroning Our Divine Lord. That grey November morning did not in the least diminish the radiant joy of Canon Ducket as he celebrated the First Mass in that little chapel. Mother Mary Castule was present, and some friends of the Little Sisters, among them Mr and Mrs Bower of No.9 (whose house some thirty years later was to belong to the Little Sisters.)

It was said of Mother Mary Petronillo, 'Norwich is her work … she made Norwich what it is and her devotedness made the Congregation loved.' The convent closed in 1987. (Little Sisters of the Assumption, Millennium Heritage Library, N271.9)

July 7th

1822: On this day there was a meeting of around 150 weavers in Friary Yard close to St James's Church in Cowgate to discuss the wage cuts announced by the city manufacturers. Two weavers were appointed from each parish to summon those neighbours who were both weavers and householders to another meeting the following day, to which about 1,100 attended. They drew up a petition and marched to the home of Alderman J.W. Robberds, Deputy Chairman of the Manufacturers' Committee, who lived in Grout's Court off Magdalen Street and had a camlet factory in St Saviour's Lane. He was no friend of the weavers, but on this occasion he agreed that the manufacturers should meet again to reconsider their decision. However, at a mass rally on Mousehold Heath the weavers decided they ought to have representatives present and, on the day of the meeting, huge crowds gathered in the marketplace. As the day progressed the crowd grew restless and violence broke out. The Dragoon Guards were put on alert but the news came that the manufactures had agreed not to cut wages and they were stood down. For once, the weavers had prevailed. (McCutcheon, E., *Norwich Through the Ages*, The Alastair Press, 1989)

JULY 8TH

1931: On this day approval was given to the proposals of the Trustees and Committee of Management of the Orphans' Home in Chapel Field, that all their assets and liabilities should be transferred to Anguish's School of Housecraft. The following year the Orphans' Home was sold for £1,300. The Orphans' Home was founded in 1844 by a group of women Quakers, including the author Amelia Opie. It was originally in Pottergate but in 1870 moved to premises which had previously been The Bowling Green Hotel. The object was 'to provide a home for girls, destitute children of married parents, who are both dead, and to educate and train them for domestic service, or some other means of supporting themselves respectably and becoming useful members of society'. The Anguish charities – the Boys' Foundation and Girls' Hospital – were set up with a bequest by Thomas Anguish, mayor of Norwich in 1611, who died in 1617 and left money in his will to set up schools for the education of the city's poor boys and girls. There is a monument to him in St George's Tombland where five of his children are seen to have predeceased their parents. (Norfolk Record Office Information Leaflet 39)

JULY 9TH

1940: On this day Norwich suffered its first aid raids of the Second World War, before London or any other provincial city. Almost since the outbreak of the war the city's sirens had sounded almost daily and nightly. One local resident recalled: 'I remember Londoners staying here, who said that they were glad to go home at weekends to get some sleep!' But on the 9th at 5 p.m. no sirens sounded and the attack on the Boulton and Paul factory came without warning. In this first raid, twenty-six people were killed and many more injured. This was just the beginning of an air onslaught which by the end of 1940 had resulted in over 260 separate raids. The city suffered its last air raid on 6 November 1943; during the raids a total of 1,400 civilians had been killed or seriously injured with some 4,700 houses destroyed or fatally damaged. Miraculously, the cathedral with its splendid spire managed somehow to survive, even during the raid in June 1942 when incendiaries struck the roof. Overnight destruction of familiar streets and buildings had far more impact on people than the greater damage over a wider area. (Smith, G., *Norfolk Airfields in the Second World War*, Countryside Books, 1994)

July 10th

1797: On this day the young Elizabeth Gurney wrote in her journal, 'Some poor people were here, I do not think I gave them what I did with a good heart.' Her father was John Gurney, a Norwich banker and woollen manufacturer, and a member of the Society of Friends. As Elizabeth Fry she was to find fame as a prison reformer but in her youth was shy and reserved but sometimes frivolous, often confessing to being 'in a most idle mind', intending to have 'an indolent dissipated day'. But she counted her many blessings:

> A good father, one whom I dearly love; sisters formed after my own heart, friends who I admire and good health which gives a relish to all ... I must beware of not being a flirt; it is an abominable character; I hope I shall never be one, and yet I fear I am now one a little.

She admonished herself not to talk at random and 'beware and see how well I can get through this day without one foolish action. If I do pass this day without one foolish action it is the first ever passed so.'

(Bardens, D., *Elizabeth Fry, Britain's Second Lady on The Five-Pound Note*, Chanadon Publications, 2004)

JULY IITH

1940: On this day William Dennis wrote in his diary:

> ...had very little sleep last night as had the 'honour' of having
> four air raids. Siren first went at 1.15 a.m. and we all kept up
> until the All Clear at 2.45 a.m. Mother got up for the second
> one, but we all stopped in bed until the fourth All Clear went
> at 7.20 a.m.

William and his brother lived with their widowed mother in
Beaconsfield Road and worked for over fifty years at the Bally
& Haldenstein shoe factory in Norwich. During 1940 he
recorded his work and leisure time at the local pubs. He was a
keen darts player and, later in life, refereed darts matches at the
Norwich Federation of Industrial Clubs. He wrote:

Mother has had the wireless repaired. One valve went screwy
but still using it for a while. Bombs dropped at 9 a.m. this morning
and school children conducted to their shelters until 10.30 a.m. but
no siren sounded. Estimated that Norwich air raid victims now total
over thirty ... Some local factories having lookouts placed on roofs
of high buildings with strong field glasses to give ample warning of
approaching enemy aircraft.

(Diary of William J. Dennis, 1940–1966, Norwich Record
Office, MC2048)

JULY 12TH

1370: On this day the English nobleman Henry le Despenser was enthroned as Bishop of Norwich. He was known as the 'Fighting Bishop' for he appeared as keen on carrying a sword as a prayer book. In rumbustious mediaeval fashion he had fought for the man who was to become Pope Urban V, and was rewarded with his appointment to Norwich. During the Peasants' Revolt of 1381 the bishop led a company that helped suppress the uprising. Despite these apparently unholy activities he is also remembered for the painted reredos in the cathedral's St Luke's chapel. The five panels combine a legacy of mediaeval painting, possibly at its greatest, and the Fighting Bishop presented it to the cathedral. In 1383 le Despenser led what became known as the Norwich Crusade. He raised a large amount of gold, silver, jewels, rings, dishes, plate, spoons and ornaments, especially from ladies and 'other women' and it was said that one lady gave him £100. He journeyed to Calais with some of the army he had hired and raised the standard of the Holy Cross but after unsuccessful manoeuvres in Ypres he returned to Norwich, having failed in his objective. (Wilton, J.W., *Monastic Life in Norfolk and Suffolk*, Acorn Editions, 1980)

JULY 13TH

1758: On this day a short but severe thunderstorm wrought its fury on a house standing alone on the causeway near Sandling's Ferry in the city of Norwich. Lightning struck off the roof tiles and pierced the house where it 'tipt off the top of an old chair ... snapt the two heads of the bed posts, rent the curtains, drove against the wall ... forced out an upright of a window frame a yard long and sent it a right line into a nearby ditch'. This shaft of electricity peeled plaster off the walls and melted a row of pewter dishes. 'An ancient woman' sitting in a passageway was scorched all over, 'her skin almost universally red and inflamed ... her shift burnt brown, stockings singed ... her shoe struck off'. The lightning missed:

> ... another old woman, sitting knee to knee with her companion as it shot along the passage. Those nearby heard a violent explosion and thought the whole house would collapse. It turned red, as if on fire, but it remained standing and the whole smelled as if fumigated with brimstone matches.

(Cooper, S., *Account of a Storm of Thunder and Lightning*, Proceedings of the Royal Society of London, 1683–1775)

JULY 14TH

1931: On this day 'Whiffler' turned the attention of his 'Over the Tea Table' column towards Tombland. A reader had written:

> Passing the historic building which we now know as Samson and Hercules House I was gratified to find the decorators busily at work. The old woodwork has been renovated already, and now those two quaint figures which apparently support the portico are receiving attention. Neither Samson nor his colleague, Hercules, could be expected to be altogether immune from the ravages of time, to say nothing of the vagaries of our English climate, and most sorrowfully, had I seen that both old fellows had literally 'got it in the neck' as well as in other parts of their anatomy.

Samson appeared to have suffered more over the years than Hercules but:

> ... skilled hands have now repaired the wounds of the two old fellows who have guarded the building since our boyhoods ... when I saw him yesterday I was glad to see that Samson's extremities looked once again in a healthy condition. His friend, Hercules, looked by contrast wretched. But I anticipate that in a few days both will once again look their old dignified selves.

(*Eastern Evening News*, 14 July 1931)

July 15th

1986: On this day the medieval Guildhall, built eighty years before Christopher Columbus discovered America, opened as a Tourist Information Bureau, being moved there from Tombland. The Guildhall was the centre of city government from the early fifteenth century to its replacement by City Hall in 1938. It was constructed between 1407 and 1413 on the site of the old Toll House, a small thatched building used for collecting the market tolls and which had been pulled down at the time of the 1404 Charter. John Marowe, a Master Mason, was employed at the rate of one silver groat daily, plus one silver groat per week, as Senior Craftsman, assisted by three other craftsmen who were paid one silver groat daily. The labour force consisted of around fifty petty offenders and miscreants, who were unpaid. At the time of construction Norwich was one of the largest and wealthiest cities in England and the Guildhall is the largest surviving mediaeval civic building in the country outside London. The Tourist Office, now the Tourist Information Centre, is housed in the Forum. (*Norwich, a Fine City*, Norwich City Council, 1992)

JULY 16TH

1792: On this day the court sat before Lord Kenyon and a common jury at the Guildhall to hear Boyle vs The Norwich Stage Coach proprietors. Mr Erskine alleged that his client had suffered at the hands of a drunken coachman. Mr Boyle, who was a hairdresser, 'took a place in the Norwich stage coach [which] set out from the Swan with Two Necks ... and it would have been very convenient if the passengers also had had two necks as well as the swan, for they had a great chance of losing one of them.' When challenged, the coachman said that the bottle under his belt was 'physic for his horse' but Mr Boyle considered the horses 'went with a sufficient degree of velocity and wanted no physic ... the coachman therefore applied it to himself – it was a bottle of brandy'. He became 'mad and furious' and drove his horses in a manner certain to cause an accident. Mr Mingay for the defence said that his clients were aware of their responsibilities. Mr Bolye had been excused his fare and given compensation. Lord Kenyon concluded that as the plaintiff had received money he found in favour of the defendant. (*The Times*, 16 July 1792)

JULY 17TH

1737: On this day new rules came into force that were aimed at reducing the high levels of disorderly conduct, induced by alcohol, that occurred in the city's inns and taverns on a daily basis. All public house keepers were forbidden to permit or suffer any person or persons to play at cards, dice, tables, loggarts or ten pins (both forms of bowling) 'or any other Unlawful Games, in their respective Houses, Grounds or Yard, under the Penalty of forfeiting every Day they keep such Houses or Grounds 40s'. Anyone found playing these games was fined 6s 8d. The court of mayoralty decreed that the mayor, sheriff or other officers were empowered to enter any public house where they thought to find these unlawful games taking place and to imprison both the keepers and the players. Furthermore, any constable who failed to make a search of any suspected houses was also to be fined. Loggarts was the cause of much aggravated violence since it involved throwing small logs at a stake, thus teams had ready-made weapons in the event of drunken disputes. The mayoralty warned that 'all and every Person and Persons offending shall be prosecuted with the utmost Severity.' (*Norwich Mercury*, 16 July 1737)

JULY 18TH

2002: On this day HM the Queen opened the Forum. Neil Storey wrote:

> Like its neighbour the City Hall, its architecture had been a point of controversy, but rather like City Hall I believe the appeal of this new building will endure. It is certainly far more appealing than the building it replaced. The Forum contains the new library; Origins, a centre telling the history of the city and county in modern and interesting ways; there are also plans for BBC Television and local radio to be based here in the near future.

The old Central Library was destroyed by fire in August 1994 when most of the contents of the lending library were lost. Neil Storey was 'the first independent historian to pledge his help to rebuild the local studies collection and been involved with the reconstitution of that collection ever since.' The Forum was built on the site of the old library and before construction began, extensive archaeological investigations were carried out on what was, in the Middle Ages, known as the French Borough. The borough was established as a colony of French traders after the Norman Conquest between 1071 and 1975. (Storey, N., *Norwich, The Changing City*, Breedon Books, 2002)

July 19th

1469: On this day Queen Elizabeth Woodville was visiting Norwich, only a few weeks after her husband Edward VI, and Edward's young brother Richard Duke of Gloucester (later Richard III) had made a four-day visit to Norwich, arriving on the 18th and departing on 21 June. Queen Elizabeth, whom Edward had married in secret in 1464, was entertained at Blackfriars Hall upon her arrival. The king had visited the city mint (approximately where the hall still stands) where groats and half-groats were struck during his reign, marked Norvic or Norwic and bearing a rose – the mint mark for Norwich. There had been a Norwich mint since Saxon times and the first mention of Norwich is on coins of Athelstan (925–941) and numerous pieces of money were stamped there by the later Saxon kings. The plaque commemorating the queen's visit was unveiled by Dr Joanna Laynesmith, who first revealed the Blackfriars' connection with Elizabeth Woodville. The mint lapsed during the sixteenth century, but in 1696 it was one of the mints re-established by William III to prevent irregularities resulting from clipped coins. Between 1696 and 1698, £259,371 worth of silver coinage was struck at Norwich. (Hannah, I.C., *The Heart of East Anglia: The Story of Norwich from Earliest to Latest Times*, Heath, Cranton & Ouseley, 1914)

July 20th

1903: On this day the directors of the lately formed Norwich Mutual Telephone Company (NMT) were summoned to appear before a special meeting of the Norwich Council. They were told that as they had not provided a switchboard nor established the desired telephone system, they were no longer being considered as contractors for the new telephone system being established in the city. The Postmaster General had advised the Norwich Town Clerk in 1899 of the rival licence application for the establishment of a telephone exchange in the Norwich area. Although the NMT had been granted a licence to establish a rival exchange to that of the existing Norwich Telephone Company, they had not done so 'to the satisfaction of the Postmaster General.' Not only had the company acquired transmitter telephones that were not compatible with the switchboard, but people objected to the company 'erecting wet creosote poles in the streets of Norwich ... they should use the type of pole used by the Norwich Telephone Company.' The council were also advised that the company's wiring 'was not of the highest quality' and they were clearly not up to the task. (Clayton, E.G., *The First 100 Years of Telephones Viewed from Norwich*, British Telecom, 1980)

July 21st

1926: On this day the Norwich Pageant opened. Held at Newmarket Road Ground it was produced by Nugent Monck of the Maddermarket Theatre. Nugent wrote:

> I have taken such episodes on the City of Norwich as lend themselves to dramatic or pictorial representation. Several events of greater importance, such as the granting of the charter, do not admit of dramatic treatment, and are therefore useless in pageantry.

When it had been decided to hold a pageant representing the history of Norwich it was recognised that a gigantic task lay before those who would have to organise it, but once Nugent Monck took the helm there was little doubt of the eventual success of the venture. One of the objects of the pageant was to attract visitors to Norwich, especially Americans. It was thought that although the city was 'the first of the Old English Cities' in the affections of the American people – especially in the New England States – Norwich was rarely included in their itinerary. Over four days, locals and visitors were treated to enactments portraying the Romans, Normans, Queen Philippa, the Black Death, Queen Elizabeth I, the Pillage of the Churches and Charles II and Sir Thomas Browne. (*Norwich Pageant Programme*, Jarrold & Sons, 1926)

July 22nd

1119: On this day Herbert de Losinga, first Bishop of Norwich, died. Shortly before his death he showed, not for the first time, that he was a man to be reckoned with. He discovered that his deer park had been broken into, with 'the marauder carrying away the carcass minus the head and intestines'. The bishop declared:

> I excommunicate those who have broken into my park and killed my deer with that anathema wherewith God, in His anger, smiteth the souls of the wicked. I interdict them from entrance into the church, from partaking of the body and blood of Christ, and from fellowship in the whole circle of Christian offices. May the curse of the excommunication rest upon them in their homes, in the ways, in the fields, in the woods and in the waters, and in all the places wheresoever they shall be found. May the flesh of those who have devoured my stag rot as the flesh of Herod rotted.

During his lifetime the builders of the cathedral had often incurred his wrath at their laziness, and he declined to consecrate the churchyard of a new church at Thetford monastery unless the ancient Episcopal dues were restored to him. (Andrews, W., *Bygone Norfolk*, 1898)

JULY 23RD

1785: On this day the intrepid balloonist Major John Money of Trowse perpetuated the prevailing eighteenth-century craze of ballooning by attempting an ascent from Quantrell's Gardens. His was a charity event and the money raised from the 700 fee-paying spectators went in aid of the Norfolk and Norwich Hospital. The gathering was 'a large and brilliant assembly of the first and most distinguished personages in the city and county', including the Earl of Orford. They watched as the balloon rose and was in sight for 45 minutes before it drifted slowly to the south-east. Major Money tried to let out gas to gain height but the string which operated the valve would not open. He continued to drift for a couple of hours and eventually came down in the sea off the Suffolk coast. A Dutch boat which passed did not stop, apparently mistaking the balloon for a sea monster. After clinging to the balloon for 5 hours, chin deep in water, Money was spotted by the Harwich revenue cutter which pulled him aboard. He was put ashore at Lowestoft next morning and arrived at his home in Crown Point in a post-chaise. (Meeres, F., *A History of Norwich*, Phillimore, 1998)

July 24th

1660: On this day the wealthy city hosier, Joseph Paine of Strangers' Hall, presented the newly restored Charles II with £1,000 in gold coins which he had raised from local merchants. Paine was a staunch Royalist during the Civil War, when Norwich was Parliamentarian, and was mayor when Norwich declared its support for the restoration of the king. He set off for London with the sheriff and, it is thought, an escort of the Norwich (or City) Militia (of which he was colonel), to show loyalty to the crown. He was well rewarded as the king knighted him on the spot. The sheriff, however, was peeved as he got nothing, not even his expenses. In spite of his grand gesture, many of Paine's letters reveal his civic interests and the difficulties of war. Paine lived at Strangers' Hall between 1659 and 1667 and one wing of the building was built as his private chamber. The fire surround shows his initials and those of his wife, Emma, alongside a dragon (or Norwich 'Snap') indicating that he was a member of the Guild of St George. (Strangers' Hall Museum, Norwich)

July 25th

1904: On this day a group of boys playing on Mousehold alerted the city to a fire by means of a bugle. At 11 a.m. the youths noticed a fire had started in the furze and bracken. One of them 'had a bugle with him [and] knowing the military fire call' sounded the alarm, which was heard at Britannia Barracks. One hundred and fifty men of the 3rd and 4th Norfolks turned out, followed by numerous civilians and the city police firemen. A strong wind fanned the flames and approximately 30 acres of the heath was destroyed. The identity of the bugler was never revealed. Summoning the fire service was achieved by various means over the years. At one time it was by the firing of a rocket from a pipe set in the pavement beside the Guildhall, a practice that later received some scrutiny after a descending rocket plunged through the roof of a printing shop on Gentleman's Walk and set it alight. After that an exploding 'mortar shell' was favoured. Some of these shells were discovered in the Guildhall as late as 1930. A constable took one home and blew his November the Fifth bonfire to pieces. (Morson, M., *A Force Remembered*, Breedon Books, 2000)

JULY 26TH

1998: On this day it was confirmed that a century of Christmas-cracker production in Norwich was drawing to an end. Around 175 workers would lose their jobs when the factory closed later that year. Since 1906 Tom Smith Crackers, founded by cracker inventor Tom Smith, had supplied the Royal Family with paper hats, novelties and excruciating jokes. Only a small group of the staff who rolled up the Queen's crackers by hand knew their contents. A company spokesman said: 'We deliver the crackers to all the Royal palaces. The staff is always sworn to secrecy about the contents and I have no doubt the family will be very disappointed we are closing, it has been an important part of our company tradition.' All that was vouchsafed outside the company was that the crackers concealed 'small but valuable' gifts and 'none of the mottos or corny riddles have ever been revealed ... One of the last tasks will be for workers to hand-make a special, farewell batch.' In the 1900s Smith's crackers were produced not only at Christmas but also to celebrate every major occasion. In 1953 Tom Smith had merged with Norwich rivals, Caley Crackers. (*Sunday Telegraph*, 26 July 1998)

July 27th

1978: On this day the Norwich Lads' Club celebrated its Diamond Jubilee. On the evening of 8 March 1918, a motley group of about thirty Norwich boys had stood outside an old building in St George's Street, anxiously waiting for the doors to be opened so that they could see what the club had to offer. The boys had been drawn there by leaflets signed by Richard Jewson, Lord mayor of Norwich, and generous gifts and cash donations from city firms and individuals made it possible for this to be a 'mini paradise' for boys between the ages of fourteen and eighteen; it opened the door to a whole new world for thousands of youngsters. The founder of the club was John Henry Dam, a revolutionary Chief Constable of Norwich who promised 'healthy and instructive recreation and amusement.' In 1926 John Dam addressed the Norwich Rotary Club saying 'too many parents tie up a dog at night and turn the boy loose to run at will.' He advocated 'manly pursuits', which led to a tradition of boxing that endured for many years. However, by the 1980s lack of money became a continual problem and it was forced to close in 1996. (Pardue, B., *Norwich Streets*, Tempus, 2005)

JULY 28TH

1912: On this day Dorothy Jewson (1884–1964) helped organise a big meeting on Norwich Market Place in support of women's suffrage. Born in Norwich, her father was Alderman George Jewson, head of the well-known builder's merchants, Jewson's. Dorothy was an enthusiastic member of Mrs Pankhurst's Women's Social and Political Union (WSPU) and together with brother, Harry, helped organise fundraising events in Norwich. As a pacifist she was opposed to the war and when Harry was killed in 1917 she left the strongly pro-war WSPU. At the 1923 general election, she became Norwich's first female MP – one of four women to be elected as Labour MPs at that election. She lost her seat in the 1924 election but for the next nine years served on the city council. Dorothy was not only a suffragette but also a trade union organiser, an advocate of birth control and a sociologist in the Rowntree mould. With Harry she wrote *The Destitute of Norwich and How They Live* (1913) and later *Socialists and the Family* (1926). Her final years were spent in Lower Hellesdon in a cottage near her brother, Christopher. (Rawcliffe, C. & Wilson, R. (eds), *Norwich Since 1550*, Hambledon & London, 2004)

JULY 29TH

1844: On this day Charles Sherwood Stratton, better known as Tom Thumb, made his first appearance in Norfolk as the star turn in Barnum & Bailey's Circus. Tom Thumb was 25in tall and weighed only 15lb. Barnum schooled him in courtly manners, his name being taken from the legendary dwarf knight, Tom Thumb, in King Arthur's court. In 1862 Barnum introduced Mercy Lavinia Bump Warren to his troupe, who stood 32in tall and weighed 29lb. Tom and Lavinia married in New York and in 1863 it was publicised that they had been blessed with a daughter, Minnie. In 1866, while they were staying at the Norfolk Hotel on St Giles Street, tragedy struck – Minnie died. Her funeral at Norwich cemetery was attended by hundreds of people. The route was lined by locals who came to see the tiny coffin, heaped with 'garlands, wreaths and posies' in the glass-sided horse-drawn hearse. After Tom died Lavinia remarried but denied ever having had a child, claiming that Minnie was only part of the show and borrowed by Barnum for the duration of the tour. (Storey, N., *Norfolk Tales of Mystery & Murder*, Countryside Books, 2009)

JULY 30TH

1900: On this day the Norwich Electric Tramways Co. commenced operations with services to Dereham, Earlham, Magdalen and Thorpe Road. It was authorised by the council in 1897 and the city's narrow streets determined the choice of the 3ft 6in (1067mm) gauge. Major street widening and demolition was required, most significantly the link through to Castle Meadow, beside the Bell Hotel. The development involved tearing down buildings and the obliteration of small streets to make way for Orford Place, which was to become the hub of the tramway system. In 1932 the council sought compulsory purchase of the tramway which, by then, was running more than thirty motor buses in addition to its fourty-four trams. Ratepayers put up strenuous opposition to the cost and the matter was put to a poll. The result was 7,775 in favour and 11,033 against. Only 29 per cent of those eligible to vote had done so, and thus Norwich never had a municipally owned public transport system. In 1933 the Eastern Counties Omnibus Co. bought a controlling interest in the tramway. The last car ran into the Silver Road depot in December 1935 amid a noisy throng, but without official ceremony. (Mackley, D., *Norwich Tramways*, Middleton Press, 2000)

July 31st

1961: On this day sixteen-year-old Miss Betty Wright arrived at the Norvic Shoe premises on St George's Plain, not knowing that it would be her workplace for eleven years.

It would be the hands-on typing of accounts, minutes and accurate shorthand and typing which would stand me in good stead to eventually becoming Private Secretary of the Group Managing Director. The noisy factory was close to the offices and these had to be visited to deliver salary slips to managers in each department – daunting for a sixteen year old. The evocative smells of leather and glue and noisy machinery were sadly removed to Norvic's state of the art factory at Vulcan Road. The St George's Plain premises had begun with Howlett & White's ladies shoe production, and opposite the famous children's Kiltie brand was made, just two of the many Norwich shoe factories. Promotion meant travelling with the boss all over the country to visit Norvic's empire in London, Mansfield and Northampton, but it became too successful and asset rich and fell victim to a financial takeover in 1972, enforcing the redundancy of both Boss and Secretary, but leaving me a lifetime love of shoes!

(Memoir of Mrs Betty Martins (unpublished), 1961)

AUGUST 1ST

1914: On this day, it was learned that Russia had mobilised and Lord Kitchener was summoned to give counsel to the king. The following day as troop trains began to roll-out all over Europe, prayers for peace were said in all the Norwich churches. On the Cattle Market beneath the castle, a small band of socialists met to protest against the inexorable slide into war, raising their voices against 'the unscrupulous system of butchery and plunder engineered by the capitalists.' Two days later, the ultimatum given to the German government expired and Great Britain was at war. The following morning's *Eastern Daily Press* carried an appeal to all former soldiers, whether regular, volunteer or territorial, inviting them to join the Norfolk Regiment's 4th Battalion. All that day streams of men made their way up the hill to Britannia Barracks or to the drill hall at Chapelfield. Two train loads of the 12th lancers arrived at Thorpe Station and 200 reservists left in a special train with much cheering and waving, an observer remarking that it was 'wonderful to see how happy were both the soldiers and their relatives.' (Kent, P. in Gliddon, G. (ed.), *Norwich: 1914-18 from Norfolk & Suffolk in the Great War*, Gliddon Books, 1988)

AUGUST 2ND

1994: On this day Norwich woke to the shocking discovery of a fire-gutted Central Library. Thousands of historic documents and more than 100,000 books, together with memorabilia and photographs from the local studies library and the American Air Division Memorial Library, a unique record of the activities of US servicemen who were stationed in Norfolk during the Second World War, were also destroyed. The building itself was so badly damaged that it had to be demolished and archivists immediately set about attempting to salvage records, including the 800-year-old Norwich City Charter and manuscripts dating back as far as 1090. These items were among more than 2 million documents stored in fireproof vaults in the basement of the library, which became drenched as fire fighters attempted to extinguish the blaze. At the height of the fire, smoke could be seen 20 miles away and more than sixty-five fire officers were in attendance at the scene. The fire burned for 4 hours. Initial reports suggested the fire had been caused by a gas explosion, triggered when the caretaker switched on the lights. He was catapulted backwards by the force of the explosion but escaped unhurt. No one else was injured. (BBC Home, 'On This Day' 1950-2005)

AUGUST 3RD

1944: On this day 370 more evacuees arrived in Norwich and were welcomed at the George White School Rest Centre. The number included sixty unaccompanied children who, together with mothers with one or two children, were billeted in the city's smaller houses. There was often difficulty in finding accommodation for large families, so as to avoid splitting them up. When a further 360 evacuees, including thirty-six more unaccompanied children, arrived at Angel Road Rest Centre, the same problems arose and more than a week later some ninety evacuees remained unbilleted. They were transferred to the Dowson School Rest Centre and a special meeting of the Emergency Committee was called. It was decided that compulsory billeting was not looked on favourably by the Chief Billeting Officer and it was suggested that if essential furniture could be found, many families could be housed in requisitioned property and Nissen huts. During 1944 alone, over 3,500 adults and children were evacuated to Norwich. In September, however, the government announced that all evacuations were cancelled although on that day a further 270 evacuees turned up at Thorpe Station and were accommodated at the Colman Road School Rest Centre. (Banger, J., *Norwich at War*, Wensum Books, 1974)

AUGUST 4TH

1903: On this day the Norwich Grand Opera House and Theatre of Varieties opened with a musical play *The Country Girl*. It was built on the site of the old Norfolk Hotel in St Giles Street. Despite being noted for 'a good class of variety entertainment', its operatic pretensions were brief and in less than a year its popularity waned. Negotiations took place with the owners of the Hippodrome Theatre (in Theatre Street) and the two agreed to swap. The Opera House became the New Hippodrome, with twice-nightly variety shows, and the old Hippodrome building became the Theatre Royal. The Hippodrome was run by E.H. Bostock and F.W. Fitt, two of the leading families in the city. Frederick Fitt, who married Fannie Bostock in 1895, served as a city councillor from 1901–22 and then became an alderman. His daughter Doris also served on the city council. In its heyday some leading names performed at the 'Hippo' including Charlie Chaplin, Marie Lloyd and Gracie Fields. The Hippodrome finally closed in 1960 and the site is now a car park. (NRO MC198/16, NRO MC 198/74)

AUGUST 5TH

1894: On this day the Norwich journalist James Hooper compiled an article entitled 'Inn Signs In and About Norwich' in which he saved for posterity the list of inn signs 'which adorned this city about the year 1750' as collected by William Arderon, FRS, 'regarded by some as the pioneer of natural sciences in Norwich.' He reported that even by 1894:

> A very large proportion have disappeared, among the more curious of which were – The Three Turks, Three Washerwomen, Whittlington and His Cat, Pump, Pease and Beans, Man i' th' Moon, Flora, Black Jack, Bacchus, Abraham Offering his Son, Hog in Armour, Wax Candle, Lobster, Mad Tom of Bedlam, Two Twins, Hole in the Wall, Five Alls, Bishop Blaise, First and Last, and Labour in Vain … The Hog in Armour, which was behind the Swan in Swan Lane, was called by the wits the Pig in Misery, just as jocular persons are pleased to call the Elephant and Castle The Pig and Tinder-box.

Perhaps the most celebrated of all old signs in Norwich was The Man Loaded With Mischief, representing a man carrying a woman, a magpie, and a monkey. This house, degraded to The Mischief, and deprived of its comic painting, still survives in Peacock Street. (*Eastern Daily Press*, 10 August 1984)

AUGUST 6TH

1799: On this day Luke Hansard, born in 1752 in the parish of St Mary Coslany, was freed from apprenticeship by redemption and admitted to the livery. Aged fourteen, he had begun working for the printer Stephen White; he slept in the corner of the shop, while Mr White's pigeons occupied the opposite corner. His apprenticeship completed, Luke started for London with only a guinea in his pocket and became a compositor in the office of John Hughes, printer to the unofficial account of proceedings, the House of Commons Journal, written by the radical William Cobbett. Luke prospered and went into partnership with Hughes, becoming known as Hansard the Printer. He never lost his Norwich burr and whenever possible he would return to 'beautiful Norwich, my home'. Eventually his son, Thomas Curson Hansard, bought Cobbett's Journal and the business remained in the Hansard family until the 1880s, when it was taken over by the Stationery Office. The name Hansard was officially adopted for their reports in 1943. By coincidence, Her Majesty's Stationery Office moved from London to Norwich and its offices are only a few hundred yards from St Mary Coslany where Luke was born over two centuries before. (Solomons, G., *Stories Behind the Plaques of Norwich*, Capricorn Books, 1981)

AUGUST 7TH

1787: On this day James Bowen of London became a Freeman of the Stationers' Company. Together with his wife and young children he moved to Norwich to succeed Peter Gedge as printer and bookseller at No.10 Cockey Lane. At the time, Norwich was one of the largest provincial cities in England and its eminence was reflected in many aspects of its social and commercial life, not least an active printing and book trade. James became a Freeman of Norwich by purchase on 15 June 1789 and prospered, taking on John Parslee as an apprentice in July of the same year. However, he died suddenly in 1790. His wife and children were left destitute but as a result of a public subscription, and the sale of her husband's shop, Anne Bowen was able to set herself up as a stationer, and a music and book seller in a smaller shop at No.4 Cockey Lane. It was unusual at that time for a woman to take on any printing or bookselling role, but Anne's business was highly successful and she was recorded as still in business there in a city directory from 1810. (*Bury and Norwich Post*, 25 March 1789; *Norwich Mercury*, 20 November 1790)

AUGUST 8TH

1834: On this day a most important case was tried by a special jury in the sheriff's Court which would affect the city's stallholders. A stallage fee, or rental, was payable to the corporation for the right to erect stalls or booths on Norwich Market Place, but a butcher named John Burrows refused to pay the charge for his meat stall on the grounds that 'the patent of his freedom exempted him from such charges'. The corporation brought an action against him for charges amounting to 16s 4d, which he ignored. The special jury found for the full amount claimed by the corporation, but again the defendant resisted payment. A warrant was then issued for his arrest and Mr Burrows was taken to London and committed to the Fleet Debtors Prison by Mr Baron Alderson. Mr Burrows was particularly aggrieved as he had taken advice from the Municipal Commissioners in the matter, and he feared that the proceedings would ruin his business. William Wilde suggested to the corporation that an instruction be issued to the Market Committee not to collect stallage in future from freemen selling provisions, but the motion was defeated by nineteen votes to nine. (*Norfolk Chronicle*, 8 August 1834)

August 9th

1843: On this day Norwich experienced a massive thunderstorm, so fierce that cellars and basements became blocked with ice and hail, and thousands of glasshouses were shattered as gardens were cut to pieces. According to the *Norwich Chronicle,* 'very old men have never before witnessed so fearful a scene of elementary strife, carrying desolation to many a dwelling and heaviness to many a heart.' At 7.30 p.m. 'thunder and lightning commingled with rain and hail to a degree that produced sensations of awe and fear in the boldest spectator.' The rain fell in 'such profusion that nothing could be seen through the falling mass.' In the Red Lion district, the Coach & Horses suffered as the torrent rushed into the ground floor and loosened quicksand beneath the cellars, causing their beer barrels to sink into the abyss. At the Bell Hotel on Orford Hill, 100 squares of glass were smashed whilst a poor woman was literally carried off her feet down the hill by the torrent. The grocery stores in the Old Haymarket were inundated and, during the night, four cartloads of ice were taken out of the shop and cellars. (Ogley, B., Davison, M. & Currie, I., *The Norfolk and Suffolk Weather Book*, Froglets Publications, 1993)

AUGUST 10TH

1835: On this day the execution took place on Castle Hill of Frances Billings, aged forty-six, and Catherine 'Cat' Frary, aged forty; it was the last time a double execution of women was carried out in Norfolk. Both women had been found guilty of arsenic poisoning: Billings for the killing of Mary Taylor, wife of Peter Taylor of Burnham, and Frary for the murder of her husband. Their trial excited such a degree of interest 'that the court on Friday morning was crowded to excess.' The 'cruel and diabolical nature of their guilt' inspired such universal horror and detestation that people flocked to witness both the trial and execution. The relations of the prisoners 'stood trembling in the court in awful expectation ... the unhappy woman Billings was mother of fourteen children, nine of them now alive, most of whom were in the court in a fainting state.' Illicit liaisons were at the heart of it all, Billings having admitted to an affair with Peter Taylor who had, more than once, 'been obliged to take the hedges, leap gates and run across fields' to avoid detection. Frary's relationship with a Mr Gridley came under scrutiny, the women being accused of casting a 'love spell' on him, but she was 'caught out' by her husband. (Storey, N.R., *Norfolk Murders*, Sutton Publishing, 2006)

AUGUST 11TH

1920: On this day an experiment took place in Norwich, one of 673 simultaneous petrol consumption tests for the Overland car, a four-seater model made by Messrs Willys-Overland Ltd of Canada. It was started from Mann Egerton's garage on Prince of Wales Road, the route taken being the main road to Thetford. The object was to ascertain the mileage that could be achieved using a gallon of petrol in an Overland Four model. At 10 a.m. the car was wheeled into the road 'without being tuned up in the slightest.' A gallon of petrol was poured into the empty tank and the journey commenced. 'St Stephen's Street, which was badly congested, was cleverly negotiated ... in the open a strong slanting headwind was met with, but an average speed of 23 miles an hour was maintained.' When the car came to a dead stop it had covered 29½ miles, 'So many miles per gallon is worthy of note, especially in these days of dear "juice". The reason ascribed for the car being able to do such a good trial was the lightness of build, and its relatively new type of spring suspension.' (*Eastern Evening News*, 11 August, 1920)

August 12th

1835: On this day the Catton Estate, which had been the first commission for landscape gardener and Norwich School Old Boy Humphry Repton, was put on the market by the executors of the late Mrs Ives, widow of Jeremiah Ives, a prominent citizen and twice mayor of Norwich. The park then covered 70 acres (28 ha). In 1788 Ives built the hall and commissioned Repton to design additional planting and landscaping for the park, plantations and shrubberies. A ha-ha and new entrance were included. Catton was then a small village on the northern outskirts of Norwich, where a number of wealthy citizens had their villas and country-boxes. Repton's famous Red Books of Catton are lost, but the gardens were described in 1947:

> The elegant little park still preserves a decidedly Reptonian air. There are oaks and some beeches which must have been planted before his time; but his hand is surely visible in the subtly arranged belts of trees which ... so gently seclude its peaceful acres from the ever-encroaching city. The disposition of the trees on the higher ground eastwards across the road is also reminiscent of Repton ... and its competence fully explains the success which he was soon to meet.

(Ketton-Cremer, R.W., *A Norfolk Gallery*, Faber & Faber, 1948)

August 13th

1802: On this day a superior residence was offered for sale by Bacons the auctioneers and Messrs Foster, attorneys of Norwich. The advertisement ran:

Residence in the City of Norwich to be sold, an elegant leasehold Mansion situated near the Bishop's Palace, with stabling for five horses, double coach house, pleasure ground, green house and kitchen garden, the ground very tastefully laid out and the green house stored with choice shrubs, etc. The kitchen garden is well planted and cropped, and walled in, together with brew house, porter's lodge, and suitable offices; the whole occupying nearly five acres. The house is fitted up in the best style of elegance, and consists of spacious drawing and eating rooms, library with a select collection of books, music room, excellent kitchen, arched cellars, and every requisite for a genteel family. It contains many paintings in oil and water colours by the best artists, pier glasses of considerable magnitude, and the furniture throughout of the best quality; the chimney pieces are of statuary marble. The premises, pictures, furniture, and several very fine statues on the ground, are to be sold together, and possession may be had immediately.

No asking price was included. (*The Times*, 14 August 1802)

AUGUST 14TH

1561: On this day, and for most of the summer, the Duke of Norfolk entertained on a lavish scale in Norwich. His guests were 'a great many lords and knights with their ladies' and their amusements included a tattoo on Mousehold Heath. Some of the guests were assigned lodgings at the Crown Inn, next door to the ducal palace. This was the best hotel in Norwich and where the judges of the Assize generally stayed; the owner was the duke's tenant. There were regular feasts for the mayor and alderman, banquets for the High sheriff and the judges of assize, and an occasional dinner for the justices of the peace. Bishops, deans, canons, rectors of city parishes and, on the lowlier benches in the hall, incumbents of livings under the duke's patronage, would also expect to enjoy his hospitality. The bowling alley and the tennis court were sacrosanct, but 'quite humble folk used to be admitted to the playhouse and drink free ale in the kitchens afterwards.' There were always beggars and destitute women and children waiting outside for the almoner's daily distribution of loaves and meat. (Williams, N., *Thomas Howard: Fourth Duke of Norfolk*, Barrie and Rockliff, 1964)

AUGUST 15TH

1666: On this day a bill of mortality was published for the parishes of Norwich which showed that the overwhelming number of deaths in the city was due to bubonic plague. It was the final epidemic of plague to afflict Norwich and it raged from October 1665 to October 1666. Sufferers were herded into pest houses and left to die, but there was little else to be done. Those who could, left the city for the country, to escape the narrow, twisting, ill-drained and dark streets in which plague was endemic. Nearly every shop around the marketplace was shut, and so many aldermen left that the Town Clerk complained that it was almost impossible to govern the city. Hundreds of unemployed people crowded the street corners, dejected and on the verge of bloody revolt. Many of the weavers made extra money during the summer months by working for farmers in the hayfields and corn harvest. That year the farmers would not take them on, fearing, not unnaturally, that they might bring the plague with them. Then the weather cooled and the plague abated, as did the simmering revolution. (Day, J.W., *Norwich Through the Ages*, The East Anglian Magazine Ltd, 1976)

AUGUST 16TH

1578: On this day Queen Elizabeth I began her Royal Progress in Norwich. She stayed for five days and lodged at the bishop's palace. The mayor greeted the royal party at Harford Bridge and escorted the queen and her entourage into the city. Pageants, shows and feasts were provided for her entertainment, principally allied to the trade and manufactures of the city. The minister and congregation of the Dutch church presented her with a silver cup. On leaving the city, the queen knighted the mayor and expressed herself as being highly pleased with her reception. Preparations for the visit had started in June: St Stephen's Gate was refurbished, streets were repaired and tidied, and the wall of St John's Maddermarket churchyard was rebuilt. In the cathedral, a series of eleven large coats of arms were painted on the north wall of the cloister and a magnificent throne was prepared for her opposite the tomb of her great-grandfather, Sir William Boleyn. His tomb bears the Boleyn arms which must have been a poignant reminder to the queen, her mother Anne Boleyn having been executed on the orders of her father, Henry VIII. (Dutt, W.A., *Norfolk*, Methuen, 1902; Lane, R., *The Plains of Norwich*, Lanceni Press, 1999)

AUGUST 17TH

1930: On this day a crowd, reported to be in the region of 5,000 people, turned up to see the first speedway meeting held at the Firs Stadium, Norwich. The city was quite late in succumbing to the new craze, but succumb it did; the August meeting proved so popular that a follow-up was held less than one month later. Unfortunately, the organisers picked the wrong day as the heavens opened and it poured with rain. A contemporary report said that, 'the riders carried on pluckily under the difficult conditions and some good sport, considering the conditions, was seen.' By the 1935 season, crowds had grown to over 7,000 as Norwich fans quickly took team racing to their hearts and it became one of the best-supported clubs in the country. The final meeting took place on 31 October 1964 when Firs was sold for development. Fans remained loyal to the sport right up until the end and were heartbroken when the site was handed over and the track and stadium were demolished. In 1976 an attempt to interest Norwich Council in a new stadium was made, but although 2,000 supporters attended, planning permission was refused. (Jacobs, N. & Kemp, M., *Norwich Speedway*, Tempus Publishing, 2004)

AUGUST 18TH

1852: On this day the Revd Benjamin Armstrong requested the Norwich officials to issue a marriage licence which, to save time, he directed should be sent by post to Beeston where the ceremony was to take place. Unfortunately they sent it to Dereham. So, in order that the wedding might come off that day:

I cantered off to Beeston with the licence in my pocket. There I found that the anxious couple had gone to Dereham by train, so I galloped to Fransham station in the hope of overtaking them. Fortunately they had been just a minute too late for the train. I next advised them to go to Beeston church as quickly as possible, while I rode round to the rectory and by the time that Mr Nelson and I had got to the church it wanted ten minutes to noon and the parties had not arrived. Moreover, the clerk was absent and he had the key of the vestry containing the surplice and book. These difficulties were surmounted by my acting as clerk and the anxious bridegroom breaking open the vestry door, so that, after all, we could just manage to perform the ceremony in the canonical hours.

(*Armstrong's Norfolk Diary*, Hodder & Stoughton, 1963)

AUGUST 19TH

1800: On this day, at Goat Lane Friends Meeting House, Elizabeth Gurney married Joseph Fry. Apart from an occasional gentle rustle, a hardly perceptible sigh, or the quiet tread of a late-comer, a profound silence lay over the gathering. Each sat, if not wrapped in meditation, at least in hush, men on one side of the aisle and women on the other. Into that deeply silent gathering entered at last the wedding procession. Young Fry, sitting on the facing benches beside his parents, with folded arms and a blush that brought tears to his eyes, saw them enter the door and he got to his feet. A slight wave of movement went over the congregation, as all heads turned, but all remained seated. Elizabeth came up the aisle on her father's arm, pale and tremulous in her quaint Puritan dress, followed by her six sisters and four brothers. Joe Fry, clearing his throat uneasily, knew that everything now rested upon him. He had to break that profound stillness. Panic-stricken, he stole a glance at Elizabeth seated beside her father. He saw a tear slip over the round curve of her down-bent cheek. It braced him. He laid his hand firmly on hers. He rose and drew her gently to her feet. (Whitney, J., *Elizabeth Fry, Quaker Heroine*, George G. Harrap, 1937)

AUGUST 20TH

1815: On this day the diarist John Bilby was signed as an apprentice to Mr Mason, tailor and hairdresser, of King Street. It was his fifth job in as many years and he was not yet fourteen years old. The family lived first in Ber Street, and then in King Street before moving to St Augustine's and then to Stump Cross. John was an extrovert and soon displayed talents beyond his trade of 'hair cutter'. In time he became a member of several musical and convivial clubs, including The Musical Sons of Good Humours. He enjoyed frolics, outings to Yarmouth races and took part in parish affairs. In 1822 he was engaged by the Norwich Company of Comedians 'to take the part of a Knight of the Garter in the play of the Coronation of George IV', and appeared at the Theatre Royal for sixteen nights. Amongst the reviews was one from the *Norfolk Chronicle* that reported, 'the Royal Banquet in Westminster Hall is extremely well arranged [and] the Equestrian Champion's entry and challenge the most exciting part of the proceedings'. John died at the relatively young age of thirty-nine. (McCutcheon, E., *Norwich Through the Ages*, The Alastair Press, 1989; Norfolk Record Office MC 27/2, 501X4)

AUGUST 21ST

1783: On this day the diarist Sylas Neville had recently returned from a trip to London and was still settling back in Norwich having spent many years living abroad:

> The new Bishop [Dr Lewis Bagot] preached at the cathedral for the benefit of the hospital. It is remarkable that I heard Bishop Yonge preach the first hospital sermon in the Assize week 1772. A very fine service for a Protestant church; the music well performed by a full band; a temporary orchestra erected before the organ in the stile of church concerts abroad. A very brilliant and crowded audience which I was glad to see for the sake of charity … the wives of some of the richest people in the county shone with diamonds.

Sylas had originally intended to practise medicine, but he subsisted increasingly on charity and the proceeds of begging letters. Late in life, Sylas mutilated the diaries and letters, apparently in an attempt to remove compromising or politically embarrassing material. On his death in 1840 his papers passed to a neighbour, the Revd Francis Howes, a minor canon of Norwich Cathedral. Howes transcribed the early diaries but destroyed the originals. (Cozens-Hardy, B. (ed.), *The Diary of Sylas Neville 1767–1788*, Oxford University Press, 1950)

AUGUST 22ND

1578: On this day Queen Elizabeth I departed the city after a stay of five exhausting days being feted, entertained, and lectured. It was said that 'the Norwich orators, unquenchable to the last, sought to inflict yet another endless oration – what one commentator called "grovelling rubbish" – on the Queen', as her Norwich visit came to an end. Anxious to avoid another long speech, she instructed her Lord Chamberlain to tell the mayor, politely but firmly, that Her Majesty would prefer to have the manuscript of the speech in order that she might enjoy it at her leisure. The manuscript was handed over and it 'was no doubt put to some laudable culinary, or other, use later in the day'. Wherever she went, the streets were packed so densely that the onlookers could barely move. On one occasion a 'comely bachelor', dressed as King Gurguntius, the mythical founder of Norwich and builder of the earliest Norwich Castle, addressed her for some considerable time. Then a boy in a silk turban, standing on a platform along the route, delivered yet more orations to be followed by 'delicate music'. (Day, J.W., *Norwich Through the Ages*, The East Anglian Magazine Ltd, 1976)

AUGUST 23RD

1898: On this day the curious case of Samuel Matthews, of Raglan Street, Dereham Road, was tried at the Norwich Police Court. He had been charged on eight summonses with unlawfully using the name and title of 'doctor' and of 'surgeon', thereby implying that he was a registered medical practitioner. To all intents and purposes this was a clear-cut case of fraudulent misrepresentation. In spite of all the prosecution evidence, the bench decided that Mr Matthews, in using the word 'doctor', did not 'wilfully and falsely pretend to be registered as such.' They dismissed the case against him but considered there had been an infringement of the law in the use of the word 'surgeon', for which the defendant was fined 12s. Unhappy at the outcome, the Master of the Society of the Art and Mystery of Apothecaries of the City of London sued Mr Matthews for 'unlawfully acting as an apothecary by attending, advising, and supplying medicines to certain persons.' A special jury was empanelled to try the case, which was admitted. Extraordinarily, Mr Matthews was afterwards presented with a gift of plate weighing 300oz, subscribed for by the citizens as a mark of their esteem and sympathy. (Mackie, C., *Norfolk Annals*, 1901)

AUGUST 24TH

1578: On this day the joy and festivity of Elizabeth I's visit to the city was succeeded by a most severe affliction. Her London train of followers had brought disease with them. The *Norwich Roll* recorded: 'her majesty's carriage being many of them infected, left the plague behind them, which afterwards so increased and continued, as it raged above a year and three quarters after.' Some 2,335 natives, including ten aldermen and 2,482 'alien strangers', died of it between August and February of the following year.

> During the infection it was ordered that anyone coming from an infected house should carry in his hand a small white wand, two feet in length: no such person should appear at any court, or public place, or be present at any sermon. The following inscription should be put over the door of every infected house: 'Lord Have Mercy on Us' and there remain until the house had been clear of the infection for one month at least. No person who had been afflicted should appear abroad until it had been entirely healed for the space of twenty days.

(*The History of the City and County of Norwich from the Earliest Accounts to the Present Time*, printed by John Crouse, 1768)

AUGUST 25TH

1919: On this day the family of Miss Harriet Copeman of Rose Cottage, Surrey Grove, were busy preparing for her 100th birthday. Her niece wrote to the Palace, 'I trust I am not taking too great a liberty in asking you to be so good as to inform H.M. The King that my aunt Miss Harriet Copeman will, if spared, celebrate her 100th birthday.' On 30th August, the telegram arrived and Miss Copeman thought it incumbent on her to reply:

> I am very much obliged to His Majesty The King for his kind and gracious words ... It was quite a surprise to me as I had no idea any communication had been made to him, nor did I imagine that so humble an individual as myself could possibly receive so great an honour ... it will be suitably framed to be kept as an heirloom ... I have to thank God for all the care and blessing with which he has given me throughout my long life. With my dutiful respect to His Majesty who I pray may be spared for many years to reign over a prosperous Empire.

Harriet was the last remaining sister of the late John Copeman, JP. (Norfolk Record Office MC 81/26/396)

AUGUST 26TH

1864: On this day the Norwich authoress Lucy (Cecilia) Brightwell had begun to notice the effect of poor eyesight which would eventually lead to her blindness. She wrote of feeling the:

> ... first sensation of blindness in the right eye ... as I stood in the sunlight a ray seemed to come sideways, and occasioned a strange feeling, some[thing] like incipient blindness. I moved out of the brightness and did not think more of it at the time. A few days after, I found a wild flower which I wished to draw. I found I could not see to do it. I took a pair of magnifying spectacles and by their aid, did the drawing ... I had always been short-sighted but found that the left eye was gradually beginning to see at a great distance. My eye glass was useless. Closing the left eye I found that the right still saw near at hand and, in fact, I have no doubt, that for a considerable time it has almost done all my work ... I have used [my eyes] very much indeed. The finest drawing, and most intimate work I could do without feeling any ill effect, and I wrote for many hours by candlelight.

(NRO MS69)

AUGUST 27TH

1549: On this day Kett's Rebellion came to its terrible and bloody conclusion when upwards of 3,500 rebels were killed during the final assault on Norwich. During the hot summer, riots became commonplace as England descended into religious and economic turmoil with the people in open revolt against the government. Unemployment, land enclosure and the high cost of living resulted in Robert Kett leading an oppressed peasantry in setting forth twenty-eight grievances and demanding their redress. There were summary executions but the mood grew angrier until a huge gathering assembled on Mousehold determined to storm the city. Mercenaries had been enlisted under the command of the Earl of Warwick, and the rebel army, when it attacked, was torn to shreds. Robert Kett and his brothers were captured, taken to London for trial and condemned to death. Robert was executed and hanged in chains at Norwich, while his brother William met a similar fate on the church tower at Wymondham. In his lifetime Kett was seen as a traitor but in 1949 a plaque was fixed to the castle wall to honour 'a notable and courageous leader in the long struggle of the common people of England'. (Mee, A., *Norfolk*, Hodder & Stoughton, 1951)

AUGUST 28TH

1912: On this day yet more heavy rain fell on the city, so that the streets were flooded, the drains became blocked by debris, and the river overflowed. It was the worst flooding in Norwich since 1878 and 'the [city] has literally hundreds of little, narrow, sunless courts, resembling nothing more than rabbit runs'. In 1912 over 3,500 homes were damaged, including many in the Norwich 'yards', whose inhabitants supplemented family finances by breeding canaries, a cottage industry for which Norwich was particularly famous. Canaries were brought by the Flemish weavers in Tudor times and the Norwich Plainhead Canary was bred and sold as far away as London. Their clear orange-yellow colour is thought to have come from feeding the birds cayenne pepper during moulting. In the floods canary-breeders lost valuable stock and one species of Norwich canary was wiped out entirely. After three days the rain ceased. The water receded, and railway and other public services were resumed. It was recorded that though 'some time must elapse before the great damage done has been repaired, it is believed that the most anxious period of a very critical time has passed.' (Reeve, C., *Norwich The Biography*, Amberly Publishing, 2011; *The Times*, 28 August 1912)

AUGUST 29TH

1939: On this day, three days before the outbreak of the Second World War, the first evacuees from London arrived at Norwich station. Evacuation was to prove one of the major problems of the early years of the war. The decision to billet the children, and in some cases their mothers, in private houses became a controversial issue, especially when it was discovered that refusing to take in 'strangers' when ordered by the authorities could lead to a £50 fine. A week earlier the Emergency Powers (Defence) Bill had given draconian powers to the authorities. Homes could be searched without warning, people removed out of areas, ports and railways commandeered and bus and train services curtailed. Compulsory billeting of evacuees was an emotive issue that filled endless newspaper columns. By the end of 1939, many of the evacuees had returned to London, though in the following years with the onset of the London Blitz thousands found themselves back in Norfolk. Following the outbreak of war, full blackout restrictions were introduced and enforced, sometimes officiously, by ARP wardens. This gave rise to considerable annoyance and there was a marked increase in road accidents in the city. (Smith, G., *Norfolk Airfields in the Second World War*, Countryside Books, 1994)

AUGUST 30TH

1788: On this day the *Norwich Mercury* hailed the arrival in the city of the celebrated actress, Sarah Siddons (1755–1831), giving readers a detailed description of her person, mannerisms and actorial skills, declaring: 'She is sparing in her gestures, but they are always proper, dignified and graceful'. Sarah opened at the Theatre Royal, then under the management of John Brunton, in the title role of the tragedy *Jane Shore*, one of her early Drury Lane triumphs. Both the *Norwich Mercury* and *Norfolk Chronicle* pronounced her first night to have been 'brilliant'. In the second week she appeared in David Garrick's *Isabella* (or *The Fatal Marriage*), another of her early successes. The *Mercury* effused:

> To particularise the points of excellence which discriminate this unrivalled actress, would be only to re-echo what has been repeated a thousand times in the London papers. Suffice it to say that the faintings of some of the female part of the audience, with the many fair faces suffused in tears, added to the glistening eyes of the other sex, have borne ample testimony of her unequalled powers.

She gave her final performance in Norwich on 15 September and never acted in the city again. (*Eastern Daily Press*, 3 October 2009)

AUGUST 31ST

1826: On this day a hoax was perpetrated on the citizens of Norwich when a bill was circulated advertising the arrival in the city of Signor Carlo Gram Villecrop, 'the celebrated Swiss Mountain Flyer from Geneva and Mont Blanc', who would perform extraordinary and astonishing gymnastic flights, 'never before witnessed in England'. These extraordinary feats had been exhibited before the grandees of Europe and 'all the resident nobility in Switzerland'. Twenty thousand people attended St James's Hill at the back of the horse barracks, arriving 'on foot, on horseback, in chaises, gigs and other vehicles.' They were promised that Signor Villecrop would:

> ... run up the hill with his Tyrolese pole between his teeth ... he will next lay on his back and balance the same pole on his nose, chin and certain parts of his body ... he will then walk on his head, up and down the hill, balancing his pole on one foot.

Other feats were to be exhibited which included 'toppling', peculiar only to the Swiss peasantry, and 'repeated flights in the air' assisted only by his pole. The non-appearance of Signor Villecrop was taken in good part by those who had turned out. (*The Times*, 31 August 1826)

September 1st

2008: On this day the *Norwich Evening News* reported that a familiar figure seen on the Norwich streets since the mid-1980s had retired. The busker David Perry, known to his fans as the Puppet Man of Gentleman's Walk, had as many supporters as detractors and was always a controversial figure. His performance consisted of dancing with a range of puppets while singing along to pop songs played on a portable karaoke machine. His main characters were 'Mick the dog', named after Mick Jagger, and 'Brenda', named after his wife. Described variously as 'infamous' and a 'dullard', the Puppet Man nevertheless attracted a cult following. He admitted that 'some people don't like my singing', but in the summer of 2008 David was hired by a Norwich nightclub to perform live in front of 2,000 students. In 2007, he was named as one of the '25 Faces of Norwich', which inspired bosses at Langley's toyshop in the Royal Arcade to donate a new line-up of puppets, saying that the Puppet Man 'adds fun to the streets of Norwich [and] puts a smile on hundreds of people's faces every day.' The Puppet Man is now a global video star courtesy of the 'viral video' medium. (*Norwich Evening News*, September 2008)

SEPTEMBER 2ND

1842: On this day celebrations were underway following a grand rowing match at Norwich, after the host team pulled off a surprise victory. Cambridge, Leander, King's College (London) and Norwich Clubs were in competition. The betting at the outset was 10 to 1, and even in some cases, 15 to 1 against the Norwich men. The contest excited lively interest. When the boats went down to the starting place, Bramerton, no small anxiety was manifested by Norwich to see that the other three boats were each 2ft longer than their own. Lots were drawn for the order in which they entered the first heat and rowing got underway, King's College winning the first heat. The Norwich men won the next heat by two seconds amid the cheers of thousands of spectators. Then came the final struggle between King's College and Norwich, King's going off first with the stroke oar 'suffering greatly' from a 'wasting attack of English cholera.' The Norwich crew, after contesting it side by side for about 300 yards, passed their competitor and came in easy victors, amid the heartfelt hurrahs of their surprised friends and neighbours. (*The Times*, 7 September 1842)

SEPTEMBER 3RD

1101: On this day Henry I granted to Bishop Herbert de Losinga and the monks of the newly founded monastery jointly his valuable manor of Thorpe-next-the-city, with its appurtenant holdings at Catton, Lakenham and Arminghall, for the benefit of his soul and those of his father and mother, his brother William, and all his ancestors and successors. On the same day, Bishop Herbert's charter to the monks was witnessed and sealed, wherein he granted the priory lands and manors including those at Plumstead and Norwich. Many lands of the bishopric described in Domesday Book were in the hands of sub-tenants and included around a dozen manors and a good many smaller holdings, with an income value of around £240 per annum. It was mainly from these lands that the priory was endowed. The monks also received offerings made in the cathedral, as well as profits from fairs held in Norwich already granted to them by the king. To compensate for having to endow the priory, and mindful of future Episcopal revenues, Bishop Losinga improved Thorpe Manor and bought additional lands and property. (Atherton, I., Fernie, E., Harper-Bill, C., & Smith, H. (eds), *Norwich Cathedral: Church, City and Diocese 1096–1996*, Hambledon Press, 1996)

September 4th

1827: On this day John Wesley left Norwich after an exhilarating few days attempting to gain the attention of the Norwich sceptics. He walked the 9 miles to Hempnall having written in his journal:

> I preached at the Tabernacle in Norwich to a large, rude, noisy congregation. I took knowledge what manner of teachers they had been accustomed to, and determined to mend them or end them. Accordingly the next evening, after sermon, I reminded them of two things: the one, that it was not decent to begin talking aloud as soon as service was ended, and hurry to and fro as in a bear-garden; the other, that it was a bad custom to gather into knots just after sermon and turn a place of worship into a coffee-house. I therefore desired that none would talk under that roof, but go quietly and silently away.

He was told that the membership was about 500 'but a hundred and fifty of these do not pretend to meet at all'. The Wesley brothers made seventeen visits to Norwich over forty years, John Wesley preaching here in 1790 when he was eighty-seven years old. (Curnock, N., *The Journal of the Rev. John Wesley, A.M., Volume IV*, Epworth Press, 1938)

September 5th

1990: On this day the press reported that 'at least one Norwich City [football] player could be earning £2,000 a week for this season's campaign', as revealed by the club's chairman Robert Chase. The editorial called it 'the price of success', in that profits from transfers were crucial to City's income in Division 1. 'This is not a position which is welcome to many of its supporters' ran the comment:

> ... but it is in accord with the realities of the business, as well as the Canaries' placing in the financial pecking order. Carrow Road ... is [like] a large main line station, picking up talented players from the Grimsbys, Gillinghams, and the stage wings of major clubs, and, after a few successful seasons, shuttling them on to the big five clubs.

The policy was paying off in terms of success on the pitch, 'while at the same time developing a stadium more in tune with modern expectations.' City's annual balance sheet showed one unnamed player earning more than £1,700 per week, putting him in the £85-90,000 per year pay bracket and, said Chairman Chase, 'I am confident that next year's accounts will show that a player will be earning £100,000.' (*Eastern Daily Press*, 5 September 1990)

SEPTEMBER 6TH

1701: On this day the *Norwich Post* was first published, just six months before the first daily newspaper, the *Daily Courant*, was published in London. It was the brainchild of Francis Burges, an enterprising young London printer who decided to try his fortune by setting up a press in Norwich in 1700. The reason why Burges chose to come to Norwich is easily apparent: it was not Norwich alone but its environs. It was a promising place for an extension of the press. Yet the venture was not without its hazards, for the press was still regarded by all in authority as an exceedingly dangerous instrument, and its liberty was qualified by great latitude in the interpretation by the judicature of the laws of libel and sedition. Burges has left evidence in a pamphlet that he published on the art and mystery of printing, that Norwich was more suspicious than welcoming at the innovation. Burges died in 1706, aged only thirty, and immediately newspaper warfare broke out in Norwich. By the end of the year the city was more plentifully supplied with newspapers than any other provincial city having not only the *Post* but a *Post-Man* and a *Gazette*. (*The Norwich Post: its Contemporaries and Successors*, Norwich, 1951)

September 7th

1687: On this day the Quaker John Gurney married Elizabeth Swanton. They lived in John's house which stood in the middle of the 'great kite-shaped city', surrounded by its ancient twelve-gated wall, with a steep cobbled street running down to his quay between St Miles bridge and Duke's Palace bridge on the river Wensum. The house was large and solid, commanding an important position at Charing, or Shearing Cross, which marks the 'plain' where the main sheep-shearing had taken place for centuries. Open spaces and town squares are still known in Norwich today as 'plains'. A sketch exists of the 'sign of the three pigeons' in which the Gurneys lived, showing a large fifteenth-century mansion standing in the fork of two streets of different levels, St Benedict Street and West Wick Street. In John's day these were called Over and Nether Westwyke. Elizabeth planted fruit trees in her garden and, living in the heart of the weaving industry, bought wool and flax, and handled distaff and spindles, though she could never have dressed her household in scarlet, and herself in purple, for quiet shades and pale colours were favoured by the Friends. (Anderson, V., *Friends and Relations: Three Centuries of Quaker Families*, Hodder & Stoughton, 1980)

SEPTEMBER 8TH

1875: On this day the first report of the newly established Co-operative Society was published. After an unprecedented number of meetings among interested parties, it was finally agreed that a Co-operative Society would be to the benefit to a certain sector of the city. Mr E.S. Cannell, a very determined man, was often urged to cease all agitation, but he stoutly believed in the principle he espoused at many a meeting and was imbued with the principle, 'Society first, Collectivism next, and Individualism last'. Heavily supported by trade unionists, a public meeting was held at the French Horn Inn and the final decision to go ahead was made. A 'Coal Ring' was formed and a truck of coal was purchased, a profit of 20 per cent being made for the new society. Regular meetings were held thereafter at the Farriers Arms every alternative Saturday to discuss the rules, hold elections and, in due course, discuss the opening of the first store. Once the society was up and running it was decided that meetings on licensed premises did not 'conduce to earnest concentration' and a room was secured at No.1 British Workman in Princes Street, a rendezvous of Temperance society life. (*Norwich Co-operative Society Limited Jubilee History 1875–1925*, 1925)

September 9th

1974: On this day Jack Robert Burton, an ordained Methodist minister and a full-time bus driver, recorded in his journal:

This was an important day because I started working with a new conductor. I become mildly paranoiac whenever I am faced with a change of conductor; it is a moment of crisis for a crew driver ... My new conductor is twenty, and his three burning passions seem to be railways, beer and football. We should be able to communicate. Working with someone who has not had time to become old and staid is a powerful antidote to the inertia of middle age. If I spend long in the company of certain mature adults I die a thousand deaths; no zest, no imagination – only moans and groans.

The following day was their early week:

... we started at 5.55 a.m. As I walked to work I paused on the bridge to admire the cathedral spire, silhouetted dramatically in the sunrise. In the seclusion of my cab I sing constantly! This morning it was Stanford's Te Deum in B flat – over and over again.

'B flat? You can say that again!' – Roy, my conductor.

(Burton, J., *Transport of Delight*, SCM Press, 1976)

SEPTEMBER 10TH

1874: On this day the Thorpe Collision occurred, and was reported by the *Illustrated London News* as:

> The worst head-on collision in the history of British railways occurred on the night of 10 September 1874 between Norwich Thorpe and Brundall stations. As was generally the case human error was to blame, although the Board of Trade inspector criticised the laxity of the system that allowed such mistakes to occur. A series of misunderstandings between the stationmaster, the night inspector and the telegraph clerk, and the dispatch of a message without the required signature, resulted in two trains being dispatched from each end of the single line. These three and the ticket collector stood helplessly on the platform at Norwich Thorpe, knowing there was nothing they could do to avert the disaster.

Both drivers and firemen were killed, as were seventeen passengers; a further four died later from their injuries. Seventy-three passengers and two railway guards were seriously injured. As a result of the accident, engineer Edward Tyer developed the 'tablet' system, where a token is given to the train driver which must be slotted into an electric interlocking device at the opposite end of a single-track section before another train is allowed to pass. (*Illustrated London News*, 19 September 1874)

SEPTEMBER 11TH

1807: On this day nine-year-old Zechariah Buck enjoyed his first day as a choir boy of Norwich Cathedral, where he would one day become the organist and Master of the Choristers. In his early career, Dr Buck initiated a novel method of obtaining good voices for the choir. He was ever keenly on the look-out for boys whose voices were likely to prove, with proper care and training, to be of more than ordinary quality. Whenever he met or heard of such a lad (it mattered not how poor and ragged he was) no trouble was spared in endeavouring to secure him. These lads were musically trained at his own expense in exactly the same manner as the choristers, and were termed 'Trial boys' or 'Triers'. As soon as a vacancy arose the 'Trial boy' with the best voice was selected to fill it, so maintaining the full strength and quality of the juvenile portion of the choir. The 'Trial boys' were not remunerated, but sent to school with the choristers in order that they might be enabled to earn a trifle during the intervals when musical instruction was in abeyance. (Kitton, F.G., *Zechariah Buck, Mus.D., Cantor*, Jarrold & Sons, 1899)

SEPTEMBER 12TH

1825: On this day, a Mr Marten was visiting Norwich with his family for the first time. He kept a diary (his forename is not mentioned) and was accompanied by his wife, daughter and a servant. They travelled by the steam-packet *Hero* from London to Yarmouth, thence by a steam vessel to Norwich. They stayed at the Norfolk Hotel and explored the city in all its facets, visiting first the cathedral and a variety of different places of worship. As an evangelical, Mr Marten took a particular interest in Meeting House buildings and attended sermons by Mr Kinghorn although:

> His preaching was not to us so satisfactory ... He appeared to be more the preacher than the minister or pastor. His pronunciation is very broad ... Mr Kinghorn is a thin tall old gentleman very plain in his attire, simple in appearance, of acknowledged talents and has entered the lists in controversy with Robert Hall of Leicester on the subject of open communion which is advocated by the latter and opposed by the former.

However, the Princes Street Congregational preacher was better suited to him and he felt 'amply repaid by the instruction and pleasure which we had received.' (Norfolk Record Office MC 26/1)

SEPTEMBER 13TH

1825: Mr Marten and his family continued their tour of the city. They strolled around the streets, but found 'the small sharp stones with which the streets are paved very annoying.' They obtained permission to 'mount the top of the elevated castle in order to have a panoramic view of the City and the hills which surround it, but we were dissuaded on account of the wind blowing so strong that it would be difficult to stand against it.' However, they walked round the castle to where it was 'loft enough to afford a view over the houses to the distant hills. Here we counted twenty-three steeples of the thirty-six churches which the Map of Norwich states to be in it and prolonged our stay because of the pleasure we enjoyed.' They toured an 'important Silk Manufactory' and were shocked to see workers as young as seven years of age, 'these are on foot from seven in the morning till eight in the evening.' The stay in Norwich was a pleasant one 'and the Norfolk Hotel entitled to praise for the goodness of its provisions ... the neatness of its accommodation; & the attention of its conductors & servants.' (Norfolk Record Office MC 26/1)

September 14th

1882: On this day, there was disorder on the streets of Norwich following the visit of General William Booth, founder of the Salvation Army. General Booth, on the first of his sixteen visits to Norwich, issued a stentorian challenge to Norwich converts to 'Get a drum, and rouse Norwich'. Two days later, serious disturbance and rioting occurred when the new army band played in the city streets, causing the *Eastern Daily Press* to consider that 'Norwich was roused indeed!' In the early days, the army premises were regularly attacked with stones; an item in a cash book for a 2*d* repair of a banner pole, and another for solicitors' fees and summonses gives a clue to street clashes and more. Complaints were made to magistrates about 'disorderly behaviour' and meetings were fiercely heckled. In 1883 Miss Emma Booth, daughter of the general, visited Norwich and violence erected again: 'During the riots which followed, Miss Booth's word were a constant inspiration … Black eyes were a common occurrence, not that a black eye was very serious, it was the stones which were far more serious.' (*Eastern Daily Press*, 6 August 1982)

SEPTEMBER 15TH

1782: On this day the diarist Sylas Neville was pleased to be back in Norwich after an absence of nearly ten years. He heard service at the cathedral:

> … which is kept much cleaner than most of our churches. Tea with my friends from Norwich at Thorpe at the Rectory. I always thought there was something extremely pretty in this village. The parsonage commands the river and meadows with the road to Yarmouth, but from the grove behind, which is on a bank, there are a variety of delightful views. The river barges under sail, rich meadows and woods, country seats with mills etc. in picturesque situations.

His friend was Philip Martineau, who was married to the daughter of the Revd Richard Humphrey, rector of Thorpe-next-Norwich. Sylas stayed with the family and took jaunts out into the countryside, 'a very pleasant ride through Spixworth, Catton, Aylsham, Etc. Catton is not more than tolerably pleasant. Here are many good country houses of the citizens of Norwich.' Once back in Norwich he took the trouble to visit Catton again, 'which I cannot think at all equal to Thorpe.' (Cozens-Hardy, B. (ed.), *The Diary of Sylas Neville 1767–1788*, Oxford University Press, 1950)

SEPTEMBER 16TH

1845: On this day the principal landed proprietors and agriculturists of the eastern and western divisions of the county met in Norwich for the fourth annual exhibition of the East Norfolk Agricultural Association. Many of the association's patrons attended, including the Earl of Oxford, Lord Ranelagh, the Bishop of Norwich, two local MPs and a representative of the Royal Agricultural Society of England (RASE). *The Times* reported:

> The quantity and quality of stock far exceeded those of former years ... the exhibition of horses, although not numerous, indicated a considerable improvement ... East Norfolk has not as yet been able to compete with the West Norfolk farmers, doubtless in a great measure, to the example of the late Earl of Leicester among the West Norfolk farmers. Above 200 farmers from the two divisions of the county sat down to dinner at the Assembly Rooms, the Earl of Oxford presiding. After a toast was raised to 'The Queen', and a few short speeches delivered, 'a conversation ensued as to the propriety of soliciting the Royal Agricultural Society of England to hold one of its meetings in Norwich, which was warmly advocated by the company.

RASE held its annual show at Norwich in 1849. (*The Times*, 19 September 1845)

September 17th

1853: On this day an extraordinary accident occurred at the residence of Mr Bunting, on St Giles Road. It appears that some years previously, the spot on which this house was situated was occupied by chalk pits and excavations. After the working had been discontinued, instead of being filled in, some portions were arched over artificially. In 1827, Mr Bunting's house was built over one of these chalk arches. No symptoms of danger ever presented themselves until about 1 p.m. on this Saturday, when, as Mrs and Miss Bunting were at dinner, part of the floor, which was made of brick, suddenly gave way, and they were precipitated, with the chairs on which they sat, into a pit 27ft deep. They were both considerably injured. On examination, it was found that a water pipe had broken, and 'the water had descended as far as to soften the chalk arch to such a degree that it gradually gave way and let the super-incumbent soil with it.' The chalk mines date back to the eleventh century when they were used to burn lime for mortar, then used in the city walls, parts of which can still be seen. (*White's Norfolk Directory*, 1854)

SEPTEMBER 18TH

1940: On this day and the one following, four bombs were dropped on the city, two incendiary oil bombs and two delayed-action high-explosive bombs. One of the delayed-action bombs fell on heathland at Long Valley, Mousehold, and exploded 12 hours later, while the two incendiaries which also fell in Long Valley caused only minor fires to heathland. The second delayed-action bomb, a 1,000-pound monster, made a crater in the pavement of Theatre Street, near Church Street, damaging a gas main and thus adding to the hazard facing the bomb-disposal squad. It certainly created great disruption in the city as it was not removed until 24 September, with the whole area evacuated and notices posted restricting entrance. The unexploded bomb was a most unwelcome neighbour for the Arts Ballet Company, which was performing at the Theatre Royal, having removed from London earlier than intended when the air raids there interrupted their work. During the month of September, the air-raid siren was sounded some 129 times, with not a single day clear. All householders were advised to have sandbags and water buckets available and for emergencies the corporation built several 5,000-gallon water tanks. (Banger, J., *Norwich at War*, Wensum Books, 1974)

SEPTEMBER 19TH

1876: On this day an ice-skating rink, the brainchild of local solicitor Mr Warner Wright, was opened on St Giles Street. It was built 'at a cost of £9,000, including fittings ... was 103ft in length, 55ft wide, with promenade gallery, smoking rooms, etc.' An outer rink, abutting Bethel Street, covered an additional area of 80ft x 40ft. For some months previously, roller skating had proved a very popular amusement and weekly returns were published of the number of people visiting the establishment. But the popularity of roller skating hadnot lasted long for in May 1876 the *Norfolk Chronicle* had announced: 'The passion for rinking having fallen to zero, the managers have introduced additional attractions in the shape of a couple of clever bicyclists and a troupe of performing dogs.' The introduction of ice skating was similarly short-lived and a theatrical licence was subsequently obtained. The rink was reopened as The Vaudeville Theatre of Varieties, under the management of Mr Hugh J. Didcott with Mr B. Isaacson as musical director. When the theatre closed in 1882 its decline was mourned by many. Since October 1993 the building has been occupied by furnishings importers, Country & Eastern. (Country & Eastern Archive; Mackie, C., *Norfolk Annals*, 1901)

SEPTEMBER 20TH

1915: On this day, a lighting order was issued for the city, following air raids on Sheringham, Yarmouth and King's Lynn. This imposed a complete blackout but exempted churches and railway stations. Trams rattled the streets with a single guttering candle lighting their interiors; the kerbs sprayed white for direction. It was an offence to light a match in the open and many people wore luminous discs as they stumbled and bumped about the pitch-black streets. There were no air-raid wardens, as in the Second World War, so patrols were carried out by special constables, due to the regular police force having been greatly depleted by the return to the colours of its many reservists. Around 700 'specials' were recruited – men who felt that even amateur soldiering was beyond them, but still wished to serve in an official capacity. They policed the city for illegal gleams and 4,042 people were fined, usually 5s, for lighting offences. But the inconvenience proved worthwhile for, apart from one nerve-racking flight by a Zeppelin that missed the city, scattering bombs at random in the surrounding countryside, Norwich remained unscathed. (Kent, P., & Gliddon, G. (ed.), *Norwich: 1914–18 from Norfolk & Suffolk in the Great War*, Gliddon Books, 1988)

September 21st

1960: On this day the Bishop of Norwich, Dr Launcelot Fleming, went to the Dolphin Inn where one of his predecessors took refuge in 1647, to reopen it as a public house. The bishop, before he toasted the success of the inn in champagne, said he hoped the inn would prove to be a place of pleasure and enjoyment to the community. Formerly known as Bishop Hall's Palace, the inn was originally the residence of Richard Browne, a sheriff of Norwich, in 1587. The 45th Bishop of Norwich, Joseph Hall (1574–1656), was turned out of his palace by the Puritans and took refuge at the Dolphin, where he lived until his death. In *Hard Measure*, Bishop Hall wrote of the pillaging of the cathedral, 'Lord, what work was here! What clattering of glasses and beating down of walls! What tearing up of monuments! What pulling down of seats! What wrestling down of irons and brass from the windows and the walls.' He lived at the inn for ten years. The inn was damaged by enemy action in 1941 and restored in 1960 at a cost of over £20,000. It is no longer an inn, having closed in 2006. (*The Times*, 21 September 1960)

September 22ND

1803: On this day dinner was taken at the King's Head by the newly formed Norwich Volunteers, following a presentation of their colours by the mayor. The King's Head was one of the principal inns of Norwich and it was fitting that it was here that the Norwich Volunteers should hold their celebrations. It was a period of intense military excitement in the city, which had been steadily mounting since March, and reached its zenith on 26 August, when the Norwich Regiment of Volunteer Infantry was formed. They held their first parade on 1 September and 'from five barrels of British brown stout they drank the King's health, and prosperity to their country and city, and success to the corps.' A week later, the assorted bits of ordnance which had been in the possession of the city for varying periods were assembled, and their possibilities as defensive weapons against a French invasion assessed. The resulting experiments were interesting but discouraging, since four of the brass guns burst. Even the gun which Kett had used in 1549 came under consideration, but was rightly judged to be of more value as a relic. (Thompson, L.P., *Norwich Inns*, W.E. Harrison & Sons, 1947)

September 23rd

1970: On this day the Norwich Terrier Club celebrated the 75th anniversary of Kennel Club recognition of prick and drop-eared Norwich Terriers as a breed. From the beginning, the Norwich Terrier encompassed what turned out to be two distinct types of dog, though early breeders thought they were of one breed with two ear types. In time it became increasingly evident that the characteristic ears were accompanied by other differences. During the 1870s a Cambridge dog dealer named Charles Lawrence, known as 'Doggy' Lawrence, introduced the Cantab Terriers which were said to have been developed from the small Irish Terrier bred from small red terriers which annually visited the Norwich area accompanying a band of gypsies on their travels from Ireland. The breed gradually evolved until Frank Jones, First Whip to the Norwich Staghounds, bred small red terriers that he called Norwich Terriers. The foundations of the 'Norwich' with breed 'standards' (with uniform ears) took several years to establish: there were so many other breeds and cross-breeds featuring in the background that a specific type of dog was elusive with breeders unable to breed 'true'. Finally, in 1932, a standard was approved and the breed had come of age. (Monckton, S., *The Norwich Terrier*, 1960)

SEPTEMBER 24TH

1836: On this day *The Times* carried a very positive report from the Norwich Festival where a concert of Mozart's *Jupiter Sinfonia* 'went off with great spirit and great éclat ... no less than seven pieces were encored during the concert'. The morning had been devoted to Haydn's *Creation* and Bishop's cantata *The Seventh Day*, and

> ... to the Norwich Festival belongs the credit of renewing the excellent custom of performing the former entire; for at the one in 1838 it was thus given for the first time after an interval of 16 years. It has been too much the practice to allow two or three popular singers to select a certain number of favourite songs, the interstices being filled up with the first choruses that came to hand, and to name the medley A Grand Selection of Sacred Music.

Here composers Mozart, Haydn and Handel are treated with the reverence they deserve, and the aid of vocal artists is employed do to them honour, not to make a merely individual display. There were progressively larger audiences throughout the Festival, 'and the success of the Festival is now regarded as certain.' (*The Times*, 24 September 1836)

SEPTEMBER 25TH

1884: On this day the Matthews Minstrels were enjoying a successful run at the Agricultural Hall. This 'well-known and old established troupe' was giving 'highly entertaining performances to large and appreciative audiences throughout the week ... The rendering of some of the most popular songs is in every way efficient, while the usual jeu d'esprite and sallies are well to the front.' A crowd-gathering parade often preceded the performance, and the show itself was divided into three. During the first part the entire troupe danced onto stage singing popular songs and exchanging wisecracks. The second part featured a variety of entertainments and the final act consisted of a skit or send-up of a popular play. This part was in the hands of the Brothers Matthews, who were thoroughly at home in the impersonations of Bones & Tambo, a popular contemporary act with comic stock characters. The press reported:

> ...very clever dancing and acrobatic absurdities' and the audience treated to 'several droll and farcical pieces ... Altogether the troupe takes a good position among those of a like nature, and lovers of this kind of entertainments should take an early opportunity of visiting the Hall before their engagement terminates.

(*Eastern Evening News*, 25 September 1884)

September 26th

1921: On this day the Maddermarket Theatre opened under the direction of Nugent Monck. The first production was Shakespeare's *As you Like It*. 'It was probably not a good performance, everybody was too tired,' Monck said afterwards. The theatre, first built in 1794 as a Roman Catholic chapel, was home to the Norwich Players, a guild of amateur actors founded in 1911 by Monck. It stands on the site of an old market where madder was sold, the chief dye of the Middle Ages. There are references to the Maddermarket as a place name as early as 1232, but although Norwich possesses a rich collection of civic records, there is no account of it as a market. Monck had a remarkable gift for getting people to work for him, craftsmen, businessmen, undergraduates on holiday, and ladies who in the twenties and thirties would give up their morning to running the office and wardrobe. In 1911 W.B. Yeats and the *Morning Post* critic called in to see him and in no time they found themselves tying the ticket numbers on the seats. Yeats admired a man who could persuade an Irish poet to undertake such a task. (Stephenson, A., *The Maddermarket Theatre*, Soman-Wherry Press, undated)

September 27th

1925: On this day the City of Norwich Education Week opened with a special cathedral service presided over by the Lord Bishop of Norwich. Similar services were held at churches across the city and the Sunday School Authorities suggested that Education Sunday should be observed as an open day. Throughout the week exhibitions were mounted at most of the schools and speakers were arranged at Norwich High School for Girls, Lakenham Council School, and at a public meeting in St Andrew's Hall. A costume entertainment was given at the Maddermarket Theatre, under the direction of Nugent Monck, with mediaeval and Elizabethan songs, scenes and revels. All manner of singing, games and dancing displays were put on throughout the week, and at St Luke's Parish Hall the Norwich Red Cross Military Band was on hand to entertain parents and visitors. The Education Act of 1918 had imposed on the Education Authority practical responsibility for the physical, mental and moral training of the children of the citizens, 'the growth of education in our city furnishes a record of which Norwich may well be proud.' (*The Handbook of the Education Week* held in Norwich from 27 September to 3 October 1925, The Education Offices, Norwich)

September 28th

1725: On this day a petition was presented to the mayor and corporation, signed by the principal traders in Norwich, requesting the use of the New Hall in St Andrew's for an Exchange, which was immediately granted. On 4 October of the same year the court, attended by nearly 200 gentlemen and principal tradesmen, came to the New Hall which was then opened and solemnly proclaimed to be an Exchange on which occasion the Recorder delivered the following address:

> This place is now opened with an intent to promote traffic and commerce. Here, formerly, God was worshipped, though in a corrupt manner; and may the consideration of the sacred use this building has been put to so far influence all that shall resort hither, that nothing in the course of business may be here transacted but with great justice and honestly. I wish success to this undertaking, and the prosperity of the city in every respect.

The hall continued operating as an Exchange for only one year, but it was open every day except Saturday and Sunday 'which proves that a considerable mercantile trade must have been carried on in the city at that time.' (Bayne, A.D., *A Comprehensive History of Norwich*, Jarrold & Son, 1869)

SEPTEMBER 29TH

1671: On this day Charles II knighted the Norwich physician, philosopher, botanist and writer, Thomas Browne, at a banquet arranged in the king's honour in St Andrew's Hall. Obliged to honour a notable local, the name of the mayor of Norwich was proposed to the king for knighthood. The mayor, however, declined the honour and proposed the name of Browne instead. The king had previously visited Thomas and his wife Dame Dorothy at their home in Orford Place to find that this pioneer of botany and zoology was dissecting a dolphin taken from the coast. Dame Dorothy prepared steaks of it for the king's table. Meetings with the restored monarch were sometimes difficult in the first few years of the new king's reign, but Thomas was respected in the city by Royalists and Puritans alike for his qualities of character and his tolerance. He wrote, 'I could never divide myself from any man upon the difference of an opinion ... persecution is a bad and indirect way to plant religion.' A conservationist, he catalogued the monuments in the Cathedral and other casualties of destruction wrought during the Civil War. (Sharp, Revd David M., *The Church of St Peter Mancroft*, Norwich, Jarrolds, 1978)

September 30th

1935: On this day, the grand opening of the new Theatre Royal took place with the musical comedy *White Horse Inn*. A disastrous fire had occurred in the summer of 1934 during an exceptionally hot June. Alfredo and his famous Gipsy Orchestra were heading a bill of variety acts for the week. In the afternoon an assistant cashier noticed flames coming from underneath the safety curtain. She rushed into Theatre Street and the fire brigade were called. But their gallant efforts were in vain. In just over 2 hours, one of the fiercest fires ever known in the city left the theatre in ruins and many valuable old playbills, precious framed pictures, costumes and musical instruments were reduced to ashes. Owner Jack Gladwin said:

> On receipt of a telegram I travelled down immediately from Brighton and determined in the train that I would build a new up-to-date theatre on the same site and none other. Nothing but my deepest sentiment for the great traditions of the theatre in Norwich would have induced me to make such a decision.

The new theatre, architecturally ultra-modern for its time, was ready in exceptionally fast time, only fifteen months after the fire. (Howard, V., *The Show Must Go On*, Wensum Books, 1977)

OCTOBER 1ST

1753: On this day, Jehosaphat Postle, of the parish of St Paul's, rose with the sun and went for his usual walk. In fact so regular was he in this practice that in his diary he often wrote 'ditto yesterday'. Jehosaphat was a brewer and he appears to have been well connected within Norwich society. He had a property at Thorpe-next-Norwich which he visited frequently and where he meticulously recorded measurements of the malthouse floor. On 15 September he wrote that 'the mayor [John Press] came in Mr Harveys Chaise with my Horses and we set out for Yarmouth.' Although the purpose of the visits is not clear, he more than once records walking 'out of the South Gate to see the Dutchmen.' Besides reading and walking, his two favourite occupations, he also gardened. In the autumn he spent many happy hours putting out some 'stock-gilliflower plants' and over a period of three days set out huge numbers of plants. Jehosaphat found time to visit the city's taverns and inns, presumably checking on the beer, but evened things up by attending church twice on a Sunday, usually St Paul's and the cathedral. (*Diary of Jehosaphat Postle of St Paul's Parish*, Norwich Record Office, MC2375)

OCTOBER 2ND

1798: On this day news reached Norwich of Horatio Nelson's triumph at the Battle of the Nile. The bells of St Peter Mancroft were rung all day in celebration. Nelson's name was famous across the country and a flood of Nelson memorabilia was soon on sale to meet popular demand. Mr and Mrs John Berry gave a grand ball in honour of Nelson at the Assembly House. Their brother, Edward Berry, had been educated in Norwich by his uncle, the Revd Titus Berry, and was one of Nelson's 'Band of Brothers' (his captains at the Nile). Guests included the mayor and mayoress, Lord and Lady Walpole, and Captain Berry's wife. The centrepiece of the decorations was a painting of a naval column ornamented with trophies and inscribed: 'Nelson – Berry - Victory' and 'Health and long life to the Norfolk Hero'. The toasts included one to 'Mrs Edward Berry, and may our gallant admiral long retain his right hand.' Later, when official news of the victory reached Norwich, the St Peter Mancroft bells were rung again and the Union flag was hung above the French tricolour from the church tower. (Lewis, C., *Nelson 'I am myself a Norfolk Man'*, Poppyland Publishing, 2005)

OCTOBER 3RD

1984: On this day citizens of Norwich were enjoying listening to the new commercial radio station, Radio Broadland, which had opened two days previously in the former Norvic shoe factory in Norwich's Colegate. Listeners became familiar with a new breed of presenters, such as Rob Chandler and Chrissie Jackson. The formula included extensive pop music and a local news service. For ten years Broadland's listening figures put it consistently in the top five of the national table of independent stations and confirmed the county's love affair with local radio. The BBC had arrived on the local broadcasting scene in 1980, setting up on Surrey Street opposite the BBC television studios on All Saints Green. As the echo of the bandsmen's trumpets died away and a cluster of balloons took to the air, producer John Mountford welcomed the county to BBC Radio Norfolk. The overriding challenge for the new station was to get 'Norfolkness' and mainstream local radio in the right proportions helped by familiar names like Keith Skipper, Rob Bonnet, David Clayton, Wally Webb and Roy Waller. In the space of ten years, Norwich became a significant broadcasting centre for radio and television. (Heaton, T. (ed), *Norfolk Century*, Eastern Counties Newspapers Group, 1999)

OCTOBER 4TH

1899: On this day the popular concert singer, Miss Clara Butt (1872–1936), sang at the 26th Norwich Festival. She gave a performance of Dvorak's 'Biblical Songs' which were sung with 'care and appropriate fervour ... but so laboured are they, and so lacking in musical idea, that the applause which followed was undoubtedly a tribute to the popularity of the singer rather than to the music.' The programme of the evening concert the following day, however, drew an audience of 1,320 and contained the remaining novelties of the festival. On the evening of the 5th, however, the reception was very much warmer when she gave the premiere rendition of Edward Elgar's *Sea Pictures*, a setting for contralto and orchestra of five poems with a maritime theme, dressed as a mermaid. Elgar (later Sir Edward) himself conducted. *The Times* critic recorded 'the exceedingly favourable reception of both works and the enthusiasm aroused by Miss Clara Butt's effective singing of Mr Elgar's cycle of *Sea Pictures*. Both singer and composer were recalled over and over again, and the songs have undoubtedly been launched on a prosperous career.' Two days after the Norwich performance, *Sea Pictures* was given its London premiere. (*The Times*, 6 October 1899)

OCTOBER 5TH

2011: On this day the comedian Steve Coogan appeared in character as 'Alan Gordon Partridge' at Waterstones in Castle Street to sign copies of his autobiography. The spoof Radio Norwich DJ and TV presenter made his debut in 1991 on the Radio 4 show *On The Hour* as a sports reporter. Later, after accidentally killing one of his guests, he hosted the 'graveyard shift' on Radio Norwich. In the 1997 BBC television series *I'm Alan Partridge*, 'Alan' returned to Radio Norwich with his devoted PA, Lynne. But his feckless character has been blamed by some for portraying the county as 'a backwater populated by yokels'. The 'socially awkward talk show host of the fictional Radio Norwich' has also been blamed for costing the city a place on the shortlist of British towns vying to become European City of Culture. The Alan Partridge character is a parody of both sports commentators and chat-show presenters and has appeared in two radio series, three television series and several television and radio specials. In 2008 Steve Coogan included Norwich, 'the city he famously ridiculed', in his UK tour entitled 'Steve Coogan is Alan Partridge and Other Less Successful Characters'. (*Norwich Evening News* 22 & 24 September, 2011)

OCTOBER 6TH

1898: On this day mineral, table water and ginger beer manufacturer, A.J. Caley & Son was incorporated as a limited company. Arthur Jarman Caley, a pharmaceutical chemist from Windsor, began manufacturing mineral water in his London Street chemist's shop. He branched out into manufacturing drinking cocoa and chocolate confectionery and in due course was joined by his son, Edward, and his nephew, Frederick Caley. New premises were found in Chapelfield and the early 1900s saw the profits and reputation of the chocolate side of A.J. Caley & Son rise considerably, with nationally known products such as Marching Chocolate being supplied to British soldiers in the trenches. Arthur died in 1894 but Caley's continued until 1939 when its assets were liquidated and amalgamated with those of Mackintosh's. John Mackintosh had bought Caley's in 1932 for the bargain price of £138,000. Although its original identity was lost it was known locally as Caley's for many years. Production continued until 1942 when the Chapelfield factory was damaged by German incendiary bombs and manufacturing ceased in Norwich for the rest of the war. In 1956 a new building was built on the old site and Norwich became Mackintosh's headquarters. (A.J. Caley & Son Archive, Norfolk Record Office, BR266)

OCTOBER 7TH

1859: On this day, as part of the great Volunteer Movement that started in Norwich in that year, the first muster of the Norwich Rifle Corps Club took place with twenty-two men present. Three companies were formed, the mayor's, the sheriff's, and Mr Gurney's. Many in the Quaker community were hesitant to join but stipulated that 'on no account could they be called from Norwich except in the actual case of invasion or rebellion.' The uniform consisted of 'a grey cloth tunic with black mohair braid and buttons down the centre, with a low, upright collar … this was surmounted by a shako of hair-cloth of the same colour, with a plume like a shaving brush, and … a black patent leather waist-belt with pouch bags.' Officers carried a sword in a steel scabbard with bronze whistle and chain. The government later provided the corps with Long Enfield rifles, with which they practised on Mousehold Heath. By then there were 1,200 volunteers who were inspected by the Lord Lieutenant of the county; standing in long lines of grey, the 'rank and file from various social grades from bank clerks down to those of weekly wage-earners.' (Mottram, R.H., *Portrait of an Unknown Victorian*, Robert Hale & Co., 1936)

OCTOBER 8TH

1971: On this day the architectural historian and diarist James Lees-Milne, watching the film *The Go-Between*, noted in his diary, 'I am constantly amazed at the historical ignorance of people who should know better. For instance ... motor cars dating from the 1930s were allowed to appear in Norwich Close in what was meant to be Edwardian times.' Joseph Losey's award-winning film was shot entirely on location in Norfolk during 1970 and brought together the playwright Harold Pinter, who adapted L.P. Hartley's novel for the screen, and a cast of international stars to huge acclaim. In Norwich the old passageway and restaurant in the Maids Head Hotel, Cathedral Close and Tombland Alley were filmed and a horse sale was recreated on Tombland. *The Go-Between* is unique in being the first film to have had its royal premiere in Norwich, at the ABC Theatre in Prince of Wales Road. It was attended by Queen Elizabeth the Queen Mother, who was greeted with a fanfare of trumpets. She wore a, 'shimmering gold dress, with gossamer thin panels with a white fur stole ... diamond necklace and tiara.' It was a sell-out performance attended by 1,300 people in evening dress. (Hartop, C., *Norfolk Summer: Making the Go-Between*, John Adamson, 2011)

OCTOBER 9TH

1600: On this day a longstanding quarrel between the families of Sir John Heydon and Sir Robert Mansfield culminated in the two men fighting a duel just outside the city boundary. They met in Ber Street, Sir Robert attended by Mr Kynvett, who happened to be his opponent's nephew. The seconds argued about the length of the rapiers, Mansfield accusing Heydon of using a longer blade, but eventually the duellists rode on alone, without attendants, to the appointed place of 'Rackey wards' (Rackheath). Sir Robert reported being wounded twice by Sir John's rapier and afterwards stabbed by his dagger; Sir John sustained several wounds and became very weak. The idea was that Sir John would be forced to sign a document, the contents of which are vague but likely to do with money owed to Sir Robert. In due course he did sign being all but 'ready to faint'. Quite how much of his condition was real was hard to say but both men lived to tell the tale. A gruesome reminder of Sir John's tendency to engage in duelling is seen in the Castle Museum where one can find his mummified hand, reputedly lost in his duel with Sir Robert. (Heydon With One Hand, *Gentleman's Magazine*, Vol. 193, 1835)

OCTOBER 10TH

1990: On this day the *Eastern Daily Press* celebrated its 120th birthday. 'We begin small ... we shall grow bigger' were the prophetic words that formed part of the first issue of what was then called the *Eastern Counties Daily Press*, when it made its debut on 10 October 1870. There were only four pages, each with five columns and a limited news scope: main stories included the latest on the Franco-Prussian war and Norwich Quarter Sessions court reports. The word 'Counties' was dropped from the title after six months. Sport was entirely racing, all quoted from the sporting press. Its front page was devoted entirely to advertisements, printed at Museum Court, Norwich, and published from Exchange Street. It cost one penny and was intended as a journal based on civil, religious and commercial freedom, although records state that 'the public were not electrified'. Circulation fell short of expectation, advertising proved elusive and expenses were crippling. That the paper survived was due to the vision of Carrow industrialist and city Liberal MP, Jeremiah Colman. Throughout the 1870s he fought efforts to shut it down and it was not until 1878 that the EDP made a profit of £73. (*Eastern Daily Press*, 10 October 1990)

OCTOBER 11TH

1859: On this day the novelist Charles Dickens gave a reading at St Andrew's Hall from *A Christmas Carol* and the trial scene from *The Pickwick Papers*. He stayed at the Maids Head Hotel and the following day read the story of Little Dombey. It was reported that:

> The reception of Mr Dickens, on his first appearance in front of a very artistically arranged screen, was cordial and enthusiastic. His voice was far from powerful, but he had remarkable expression and the power of exhibiting this in face as well as in voice. As a pecuniary speculation, it must have been highly profitable to Mr Dickens.

The describer may have been smarting from Dickens's comments on an earlier visit when, after visiting The Mall he declared that he found Norwich a disappointment 'all save its place of execution which we found fit for a gigantic scoundrels' exit'. Dickens is also reputed to have said that the Theatre Royal audiences were the least responsive he had ever met. In 1861 Dickens appeared at St Andrew's Hall and it was remarked that, 'Mr Dickens as a reader fails to do justice to himself as an author.' (Mackie, C., *The Annals of Norfolk Vol. II*, 1901)

OCTOBER 12TH

1942: On this day, teacher Rachel Dhonau wrote in her diary:

It is very hard getting up in the morning and I felt tired all day. Great excitement in Norwich because the king came to see the bomb damage. Not that I saw him, but lots of people did. There were placards all over Norwich. Great speech by Churchill – but Miss L, reading it in the train said 'Well, I can't see much in it', and listening to it, neither can I. Once I listened with bated breath to Churchill, but he now leaves me quite unmoved. Words, words, words. Some not even very sensible. We continued to freeze today in school. I shall be glad when November comes and we can have some heating.

The following day she recorded:

Colds increase. Nearly everybody has one in the staff room and they are rife amongst the children. Discussion about general industrial slackness ... We listened to the Brains Trust, which wasn't very exciting ... We were very disturbed after we got to bed by aeroplanes going out. There is a new moon and all sorts of people are saying, 'Will there be raids again?'

(Malcolmson, R. (ed), *Wartime Norfolk, The Diary of Rachel Dhonau 1941–1942*, Norwich Record Society, 2004)

OCTOBER 13TH

1843: On this day a case came before the county justices at Norwich Shirehall, in which the keeper of Hellesdon toll-bar was summoned for the unlawful demanding and taking of a toll in respect of a vehicle called a 'wheel machine'. Details of the contrivance, which belonged to a city mechanic named Matthew Fish, were given to the court. It was described as 'only a barrow worked by the feet, and not propelled by machinery.' The 'carriage' was shown outside the court and 'appeared to be a very ingenious machine, which could be worked at the rate of 10 miles an hour on a level road.' It had three wheels and was controlled by two levers. Mr Repton, the clerk to the turnpike trustees, urged that the narrow wheels cut up the road more than those of heavy carriages, and that 'such contrivances for evading toll and the keeping of horses were increasing.' These 'carriages' were considered a nuisance on the roads, no horses liked to pass them, and a highways Act 'laid a heavy toll upon the pike keepers to prevent them running on any turnpike at all.' The matter was ultimately settled without a conviction. (Mackie, C., *Norfolk Annals*, 1901)

OCTOBER 14TH

1918: On this day *The Times* reported on the third anniversary of the execution of Nurse Cavell by the German military authorities in Belgium. Edith Cavell is celebrated for saving the lives of soldiers without discrimination. The occasion was marked by the unveiling of a memorial for Nurse Cavell near the cathedral by Queen Alexandra, accompanied by Princess Victoria. Large crowds followed Her Majesty's progress through the streets, which were decked-out with flags and banners. The procession assembled on Tombland, 'it being also the site of the Cavell Memorial Home for nurses, that bears her name.' In his welcome, the Lord mayor said:

> Your Majesty will deem it fitting that in the chief city of Edith Cavell's native county ... some permanent memorial should be raised to this Norfolk heroine of whom we are so justifiably proud. This city is already famous as the birthplace of Elizabeth Fry and we desire to perpetuate the memory of this other noble woman whose fame is also worldwide ... Edith Cavell rests from her labours and her works do follow her.

Queen Alexandra also visited the Red Cross Hospital at the Bishop's Palace and the King Edward VII ward of the Norfolk and Norwich Hospital. (*The Times*, 14 October 1918)

OCTOBER 15TH

1766: On this day, at about 7 or 8 a.m., an anonymous threatening letter was found pushed under the threshold of the shop door of James Poole, a Norwich grocer. There was severe unrest in the city, 'as every necessity of life is at this time very dear' and some mills were selling flour only to other dealers, bakers and big houses. The letter informed Mr Poole that if the city bakers, butchers and market traders did not sell their commodities at reasonable rates, 'Your Tallow Chandlery and fine house will be set on fire all on one night.' The writer called Mr Poole and his fellow traders 'grand rogues' for maintaining the high price of flour, warning that 'you all know that we will raise nine hundred men and no boys, for we will clear all before us ... and we will raise twice nine hundred.' The Norwich Magistrates offered a reward of £100 for information leading to the discovery and conviction of the writers. They did the same for another anonymous letter sent the same week, but there is no record of a conviction. (Goodwyn, E.A., *Selections from Norwich Newspapers 1760-1790*, East Anglian Magazines Ltd, 1973)

OCTOBER 16TH

1928: On this day a serious fire was still burning in Norwich and but for the 'splendid work of the fire brigades one of the oldest parts of Norwich might have been swept away. Troops stationed in the city also helped in fighting the flames.' There had not been such a big fire in the city for many years and so many firms were involved that it was impossible to give any estimate of the damage, though it was believed that 'it must run into tens of thousands of pounds.' One of the largest firms of timber merchants in East Anglia, Messrs Ranson Ltd, were among the worst hit, as were the Eastern Counties Joinery Company, the furnishers Messrs A.S. Howard, Wallace Kings of Upper Goat Lane, general merchants Harrison & Son, contractors T.C.R. King & Son, motor engineers Morris & Son, and the Ordnance Survey Office. The latter's headquarters were in a fine old Georgian mansion. The United Automobile Company 'had motor-coaches and omnibuses destroyed valued at £8,000. A horse and dog were burnt to death, but there were no other casualties. The fire spread with alarming rapidity and the spectacle was a striking one.' (*The Times*, 16 October 1928)

OCTOBER 17TH

1671: On this day the diarist John Evelyn wrote:

My Lord, Henry Howard, would needes have me go along with him to Norwich, promising to convey me back againe after a day or two. This as I could not refuse, having a desire to see that famous Scholar & Physition Dr T. Browne, author of *Religio Medici*, now lately knighted. Thither then went my Lord & I alone in his flying Charriat with 6 horses ... Next morning I went to see Sir Tho. Browne whose whole house & Garden being a Paradise & Cabinet of rarities, & that of the best collection, especially Medails, books, Plants, natural things, did exceedingly refresh me. Sir Thomas had amongst other curiosities, a collection of the Eggs of all the Foule & Birds he could procure, that Country being (as he said) frequented with severall kinds, such as Cranes, Storkes, Eagles etc, & variety of Water-foule. He likewise led me to see all the remarkeable places of this antient Citty, being one of the largest, & certainely (after London) one of the noblest of England, for its venerable Cathedrall, number of Stately Churches, Cleanesse of the streetes, & buildings of flint, so exquisitely headed & Squared, as I was much astonish'd.

(De Beer, E.S. (ed), *Diary of John Evelyn*, Everyman's Library, 1959)

OCTOBER 18TH

1819: On this day a meeting was held at the Guildhall, presided over by the mayor, to again consider the matter of the best means to be adopted in order to carry out a plan for making a new street and for erecting a bridge over the river Wensum at Duke's Palace. The idea had been discussed at an earlier meeting but was adjourned when a resolution in favour of the plan was rejected by a considerable majority, in spite of the fact that £7,000 of the £9,000 proposed to be raised by shares of £25 each had already been subscribed. Not to be outdone, the bill necessary for permission to begin work was introduced into Parliament and read a second time on 17 December. Opposition to the proposal continued and the following February it was announced that the bill had not been passed, 'owing to the interference of the petitioners and that the promoters would have to commence fresh proceedings in the new Parliament.' By the following April, however, opposition had been overcome and the bill was finally passed in both houses. The foundation stone of the bridge was laid on 28 August 1821 by Mr Alderman T.S. Day. (Mackie, C., *Norfolk Annals, Vol. I*, 1901)

OCTOBER 19TH

1682: On this day the notable physician and philosopher, Sir Thomas Browne, died at his home in Orford Place on his seventy-seventh birthday. Sir Thomas was without doubt St Peter Mancroft's most famous parishioner. The worldwide authorities in the many disciplines which count this man among their original thinkers seek out the church he loved and in which he lies buried. He came to Norwich in 1637 and practised as a physician from his home in the Haymarket. To the majority of Norwich people he was their modest family physician. However, as a pioneer in many branches of learning he had to make up words where none existed, including 'electricity', 'hallucination' and 'antediluvian'. In fact, wherever the English language is spoken his reputation would survive solely on the strength of his mastery of English prose. Beneath his memorial in the sanctuary, a Latin couplet on a paving stone marks the re-interment of his skull in 1922. The skull was taken from his coffin when it was accidentally opened in 1840, and it was kept for many years in the museum of the Norfolk and Norwich Hospital until its return, when it was registered as 'aged 316 years'. (Sharp, Revd D.M., *The Church of St Peter Mancroft, Norwich*, Jarrolds, 1978)

OCTOBER 20TH

1868: On this day a Norwich soldier, George Wilde, of the 13th Light Dragoons, was admitted as a Freeman of the City of Norwich. George had been discharged from hospital the previous year, being found 'unfit for further service ... has Chronic Rheumatism ... disease did not exist before enlistment and is therefore the result of long service and exposure – has broken-down constitution which will materially affect his ability to earn his livelihood.' George had enlisted in August 1842 aged eighteen years five months, and he went on to serve for twenty-four years in Turkey and the Crimea. He accrued numerous medals for his actions during Crimean War, especially at Balaclava, Inkerman and Sebastopool; he also received the Long Service and Good Conduct medals. After a lifetime of exemplary service he returned to Norwich in 1867 and when he died, aged sixty-two, he was the last survivor in the city of the famous Charge of the Light Brigade at Balaclava. His horse was killed under him and he was wounded. A stone erected over his grave in the Rosary Cemetery noted that, 'he was one of the Six Hundred ... and went through the whole of the campaign in the Crimea.' (*Eastern Daily Press*, 26 May 1887)

October 21st

2011: On this day Norwich School held its annual Trafalgar Day service to honour the school's most famous Old Boy, Viscount Horatio Nelson (1758-1805), the hero of the Battle of Trafalgar (1805). At Trafalgar the combined fleets of France and Spain were destroyed in a manoeuvre which broke their line in two places, and finally removed the danger of an invasion of Britain. The school has celebrated Trafalgar Day since the 1940s with an assembly in the cathedral, followed by a wreath-laying ceremony at Nelson's statue in Cathedral Close. Trumpeters or buglers from the school sound 'The Last Post' and 'Reveille'. In this year the laying of wreaths was witnessed by the Head of School, Eleanor Tivey and the Head of Nelson House, Tom Gosling. During the cathedral service, Anna Herrmann read from the Book of Revelation, the choir sang Stanford's lyrical *Beati Quorum Via* and Tom Gosling gave an address. Tom reflected on the several contradictions in Nelson's character, 'He was generous and genuinely concerned for individuals yet he was also overbearingly vain', but concluded that 'his life could provide us with considerable inspiration.' (Harries, R. (ed), *A History of Norwich School, Friends of Norwich School*, 1991; Norwich School Library)

OCTOBER 22ND

1805: On this day the Norwich-born social theorist, Harriet Martineau, recorded:

My first political interest was the death of Nelson. I was then four years old. My father came in from the counting-house at an unusual hour, and told my mother, who cried heartily ... it always rent my heart-strings to see and hear my mother cry; and in this case it was clearly connected with the death of a great man. I had my own notions of Bonaparte, too. One day, when my father was talking anxiously to my mother about the expected invasion ... I saw them exchange a glance, because I was standing staring, twitching my pinafore with terror. My father called me to him, and took me on his knee, and I said, 'But, papa, what will you do if Boney comes?'

'What will I do?' said he, cheerfully. 'Why, I will ask him to take a glass of Port with me,' helping himself to a glass as he spoke. That wise reply was of immense service to me. From the moment I knew that Boney was a creature who could take a glass of wine, I dreaded him no more.

(*Harriet Martineau's Autobiography, Vol. I*, Smith, Elder & Co., 1877)

OCTOBER 23RD

1930: On this day Janacek's Glagolitic Mass – originally described as the Slavonic Festival Mass – was first performed in the UK by the Queen's Hall Orchestra, conducted by Sir Henry Wood, at a Norfolk & Norwich Triennial Festival concert at St Andrew's Hall, Norwich. The most astonishing thing about the concert is the length of the programme. The other works comprised Bruch's violin concerto, a firm favourite with Norwich audiences; the world premiere of Vaughan Williams' *Job*; Rimsky-Korsakov's *Scheherazade*; Beethoven's *Emperor* piano concerto (No.5) and Honegger's *Pacific 231*. Although Janacek's music received only a lukewarm reception at its premiere, it was due mainly to the lack of preparedness by the chorus and orchestra, together with an awkward English translation. There have been two performances since: in October 1988, conducted by Richard Armstrong, and in 2008, conducted by David Parry. On the last occasion audience appreciation was 'extravagant' in praise of the climactic and powerful finish of the chorus, which lit up the hall's decibel level monitor light. The concluding parts of the mass were just as powerful with an extended organ solo (played brilliantly by Darius Battiwalla) giving over to full orchestra until the end. (*Norwich Evening News*, 6 May 2008)

OCTOBER 24TH

1925: On this day Suckling House and the adjacent Stuart Hall were handed over to 'the mayor, Aldermen and Citizens of the City of Norwich' and declared open by the Duke and Duchess of York. The property had been purchased by Ethel and Helen Colman in 1923 with the intention of restoring it and opening it to the public. The entrance hall memorial stone reads:

> In remembrance of Laura Elizabeth Stuart of Carrow Abbey, Norwich, who greatly loving the true and the beautiful and ever seeking after them found her highest joy in service. This old and historic Suckling House and the new Stuart Hall are given by her sisters Ethel Mary and Helen Caroline Colman to the city of which she was proud to be a citizen.

Management was vested in a body of governors, the desire of the donors being that the place should be used for the advancement of education in its widest and most comprehensive sense. Suckling House had originally formed part of the Dominican monastery and was built between 1325 and 1348. Cinema City opened in Suckling House in 1978. (Colman, E.M. & Helen C., *Suckling House & Stuart Hall, Norwich*, Jarrold & Sons, 1926)

OCTOBER 25TH

1415: On this St Crispin's Day, Sir Thomas Erpingham led the English archers at the Battle of Agincourt, where 9,000 troops under Henry V defeated 60,000 French troops. Sir Thomas was lucky to survive on a day when 10,000 French lay dead in the field. The Erpingham Gate at the entrance from Tombland to the cathedral church was erected and paid for by Sir Thomas in thanksgiving for his victory. The kneeling figure in armour on the gable front represents Sir Thomas. Wentworth Day wrote:

> When you gaze on the Erpingham Gate ... think of the lumbering charge of visored knights in plate armour thundering into battle on great chargers, man and horse together weighing a ton ... the clang of swords and battle axes, the ringing thud of maces and above all, the shrill whistle of arrows from those deadly English archers, then the finest marksmen in the western world.

Thomas married Joan Clopton and when she died he married her sister, also named Joan. His daughter, by one of the Joans, was also named Joan. The turret shields show the coats of arms of Sir Thomas and his two wives. (Day, J.W., *Norwich Through the Ages*, East Anglian Magazine Ltd, 1976)

OCTOBER 26TH

1963: On this day the new University of East Anglia was receiving its first intake of students. When the early students arrived in the village they looked more like students of the 1950s than those of the mid-1960s. 'Still and television photographic evidence shows girls wearing skirts (many in the tartan and check then in fashion) and jumpers and high-heeled shoes. The young men were short-haired and wearing suits and ties.' They had the appearance of schoolteachers, secretaries and bank clerks, which must have been reassuring to those in the city, albeit a minority, who had expressed views on the negative effect that students would have on Norwich. During a reception at the City Hall someone was heard to say that 'universities are not necessary for modern youth, that all they were fit for was the army.' But UEA's students even impressed the *Daily Telegraph*, one of whose reporters gushingly found in them 'a wonderful freshness of outlook and a splendid combination of curiosity and kindness, of self-possession without aggression.' The initial attitude of Norwich to the university was, though, almost uniformly favourable. (Sanderson, M., *The History of the University of East Anglia Norwich*, Hambledon & London, 2002; *Daily Telegraph*, 29 November 1963)

OCTOBER 27TH

1792: On this day the *Norfolk Chronicle* recorded, 'On Monday last the ruthless hands of men began to execute the sentence of demolition passed upon the venerable gates of this city.' There were twelve gateways with fortified towers and between 1790 and 1810 they were demolished wholesale by the civic authorities. The walls, all built in the mid-fourteenth century, ran in a loop whose line is now followed by the inner ring road. The gates were considered an obstacle to traffic movement but their original grandeur can be seen in a set of prints etched in 1792 by John Ninham. They were published in a new edition in *Norwich* in 1861 and a further set (engraved by Ninham's son, Henry), issued by Jarrolds in 1864. One of the few surviving remnants of the walls is the Black Tower, on Carrow Hill, named after the black flints from which it is built. In 1665–6 it was used as a compulsory isolation house for victims of the plague. Just beyond Ber House and the church stood Ber Street gates, which are pictured, with formidable portcullis and towers, on the sculptured sign of the adjoining public house. (Roberts, C.V., *Norwich*, The Pevensey Press, 1989)

OCTOBER 28TH

2002: On this day, Norwich-based Anglia Television lost its on-air identity. It had been forty-three years since they had started broadcasting at 4.15 p.m. on 27 October 1959 from the Mendlesham transmitter. One of the first shows was *The Midday Show*, when the actress Susan Hampshire became one of its first on-screen celebrities. Later, special police security was laid on between Norwich railway station and Anglia House when £25,000 worth of jewellery was displayed on the show. Anglia's first major outside broadcast came in 1960 as five cameras covered the enthronement of the new bishop, Dr Lancelot Fleming, at Norwich Cathedral. *About Anglia* began in May 1960 as a twice-weekly programme and eventually extended to four nights a week. In July 1975 the popular card-game quiz *Gambit* started with Fred Dinenage as compère. In 1988 Helen McDermott joined the *About Anglia* team, sharing presentation with Christine Webber and Alastair Yates. Christine left in 1990 and John Francis joined the programme. In 2000 Granada bought the assets of Anglia's holding company (United News and Media) and when it merged with Carlton, to form ITV plc, Anglia's existence as a separate brand ended. (*A Knight on the Box, 40 Years of Anglia Television*, Anglian Television Ltd, 1999)

OCTOBER 29TH

1938: On this day His Majesty King George VI, accompanied by Her Majesty Queen Elizabeth, opened the new City Hall. Thousands of citizens thronged the streets to catch a glimpse of the Norfolk-born king and his queen. The king made a short speech, witnessed by one of the largest crowds Norwich had ever seen, which was recorded by Pathé Newsreel. He also visited Norwich City Football Club on the same day and became the first British monarch to watch a football league match. The City Hall, which overlooks the 1,000-year-old Market Place, had taken three years to complete and became the city's main centre for administration. The two heraldic lions were sculptured by Alfred J. Hardiman and the main doors have eighteen bronze plaques made by James Woodward. When the old Guildhall buildings were demolished in 1935 a great tonnage of the brick rubble was transported to the marshland of Carrow Road, to form the basis of Norwich City's new football ground. The City Hall had been officially open for eleven months when war was declared, and although there were two very near misses, the building survived the bombing. (Taylor, S.R. (ed), *Norwich: A Fine City*, Norwich City Council, 1992)

OCTOBER 30TH

1866: On this day the Prince and Princess of Wales, with her Majesty the Queen of Denmark, left Sandringham to visit Lord and Lady Stafford at Costessey Park. They were accompanied by the Duke of Edinburgh, who had accepted the invitation of the High sheriff to spend the festival week in Norwich. The royal party travelled by special train to East Dereham and thereafter by road to Costessey where they were enthusiastically greeted by a large gathering. The following morning they proceeded to Norwich and were received by the mayor and other dignitaries on the city boundary at St Giles' Gates. At the Guildhall, addresses were presented to the prince and princess by the corporation and by the bishop and clergy of the diocese. The party then went on to St Andrew's Hall to attend the musical festival. During the interval the mayor gave a luncheon and the princess was presented with an album on behalf of the ladies of Norwich containing photographic views of the city. Their Royal Highnesses then drove to Chapel Field and planted two trees in commemoration of their visit. The day ended with the opening by the Prince of Wales of the new Volunteer Drill Hall. (Mackie, C., *Norfolk Annals, Vol. II*, 1901)

OCTOBER 31ST

1745: On this day Mr Henry Baker wrote to the president of the Royal Society, Martin Folkes, concerning the Norwich Bridewell. The information came from William Arderon of Norwich who was anxious to recover lost arts, 'The wonderful art, which our ancestors knew, of cutting or rather breaking flint stones into uniform figures, of equal size, and with smooth and plain surfaces.' There were many instances of 'flint-breaking' to be seen in the city:

> ... but none is more artificially and regularly finished than the north wall of our Bridewell. It is one of the greatest curiosities of its kind, either in our city or county, and is not perhaps to be outdone in any part of the known world. It was built by William Appleyard, the first mayor of Norwich ... and, what is very strange, this flint work appears now as perfect as if it had been finished but yesterday, whereas the bricks, which were wrought in near the bottom of the wall ... are almost entirely rotted away. These beautiful flint stones are squared to such a nicety, that the thin edge of a knife cannot be insinuated between the joints without a great deal of difficulty.

(Proceedings of the Royal Society, 1744-45)

NOVEMBER 1ST

1440: On this day three Norwich Waits were required to take the city watch from the Feast of All Saints to the Feast of the Purification of the Blessed May (2 February). During the nightwatch the Waits piped certain hours which led to their forming minstrel bands, while retaining their original duties as watchmen. The Norwich Waits were important civic officials for a period of about 400 years. Their duties extended to civic church services and public festivals, celebrations, thanksgiving days, proclamations of the accession of kings and the reception of celebrities to the city. Norwich was one of the earliest cities to employ Waits, a deed of 1288, enrolled in the Court Rolls of the City, names 'William de Deveneschyre le Wayte'. The records confirm that Waits had official standing and were supported by law and even given pensions. From 1408 onwards there are numerous archival records of the Waits and their instruments. In 1426 there were three Waits, but by 1437 their number had increased by one. Another was added in 1553 and 'thereafter the company of five continued until its disbandment in 1790.' (Stephen, G.A., *The Waits of the City of Norwich through four centuries to 1790*, Goose, 1933)

NOVEMBER 2ND

1737: On this day there was to be seen, at the Lower Half Moon in the city Market Place, 'A Curious Beast taken in the deserts of Arabia, whose Name is not yet found out, and is the Admiration of all the Quality and Gentry that daily resort to see him.' A succession of such exhibitions visited the city at this time and in addition to the 'Curious Beast' there was 'a most beautiful Porcupine, taken in the East-Indies', which was said to be 'curious and surprising' in all respects. 'His Head, especially the upper Lip, resembles a Hare's in all Parts except his Ears, which in Likeness come somewhat near a Swine's.' The porcupine's quills 'succeed each other in Rows ... The whole Body concludes with a Tail, which resembleth a Duck.' Such creatures were unknown outside their native habitat and excited much interest, especially when a trumpet was sounded and the porcupine 'puts himself in a posture of Defence, by turning his Tail towards you, he shakes his Mane, shivers his Quiills, points his Darts and expands his Tail.' As if all this was not enough, there was also a tiger from Bengal and other live creatures, 'very Curious to behold.' (*Norwich Mercury*, 29 October 1737)

NOVEMBER 3RD

1987: On this day a centenary exhibition concerning the singer Jenny Lind, known as 'The Swedish Nightingale', was held in the cathedral. It was formally opened by a representative from the Swedish Embassy, and followed by a special St Luke's Day service in the cathedral. The Norfolk and Norwich Hospital's Jenny Lind Children's Department – for which Jenny had provided the initial funding – held an open day and a concert was given in St Andrew's Hall by local children in aid of the Norwich Children's Fund, compèred by Stewart White of BBC's *Look East*. Jenny had first come to Norwich at the invitation of the Bishop of Norwich, Dr Edward Stanley, whose wife had heard Jenny sing in London. At the time the stage was regarded as being 'far from respectable', although Jenny had shown that she did not live the life-style common among her theatrical contemporaries. Dr Stanley did not escape criticism for his invitation. A Dr Gifford wrote in the *Standard*, 'It is very right and proper that jackdaws should build in the church. They have vested interests there. But farewell to the primitive purity of the establishment when it affords a resting-place to nightingales.' (*Jenny Lind in Norwich, A Centenary Celebration (1820-1887)*, Gallpen Press Ltd, 1987)

NOVEMBER 4TH

1880: On this day the newly designed Chapel Field Gardens were opened to the public. mayor Harry Bullard performed the opening ceremony and afterwards the band of the 6th Inniskillin Dragoons played the national anthem. His Worship entertained a large company to lunch at the Drill Hall. The *Norfolk Chronicle* reported:

> This hitherto neglected area had been tastefully laid out as a garden, and in the centre was erected the wrought-iron pavilion manufactured by Messrs Barnards and Bishop, and exhibited by them four years previously at the Philadelphia Exhibition. It was designed by Mr. T. Jeckyll, and purchased for the city by public subscription.

The City of Norwich Water Company had built a large reservoir there in 1792 but following an outbreak of cholera in the city the reservoir was abandoned in 1849. It was filled in and the city corporation laid out the whole area as ornamental gardens. The pavilion, or pagoda, was much admired by Pevsner who called it, 'one of the most gorgeous Victorian cast-iron monstrosities of England ... not looking in the least like a pagoda, nor indeed like anything else.' It gradually became unsafe through rust and neglect and was dismantled in 1949. (Mackie, C., *Norfolk Annals*, 1901)

NOVEMBER 5TH

1788: On this day the city celebrated the centenary of the Glorious Revolution of 1688 and the accession of William III. A Norwich Revolution Society was formed and as part of the festivities a travelling menagerie was brought for display at the Boar Inn near the city centre. A large tiger, valued at 200 guineas, was exhibited to great effect since it broke loose and could not be secured again until he had devoured two monkeys and brought horror to all assembled. The tiger did not, however, live much longer because he had swallowed the monkey's brass collar and chain which 'gangrened within him and killed the beast'. The *Norfolk Chronicle* supported the current thinking and informed its readers that the centenary of the Glorious Revolution … :

> … [was] the most illustrious and happy in the British annals … Hence agriculture, manufacturers and commerce have risen to a height which has surprisingly increased the wealth of the community … science, polite literature and the arts of social life have been improved in a manner that … cannot be equalled in any part of the universal history.

(Storey, N.R., *A Grim Almanac of Norfolk,* The History Press, 2010; *Norfolk Chronicle*, 1 November 1788)

November 6th

1565: On this day Letters Patent came into effect, authorising a settlement of thirty Dutch and Walloon families in Norwich to produce textiles. The city was suffering a depression and some of the new trades introduced to compensate for the fluctuations in the fortunes of the Norwich textile industry turned out to be short-term successes. Hatters flourished for a time, but their products were not of the highest standard and the industry declined. The leather trade developed and skins were imported from Spain, but their infrequent mention in ships' cargoes suggests that it was not in any great quantity. Remarkably there is no reference to manufactured leather goods, either imported or exported from the city. However, following the introduction of the 'Strangers' (as they were called), economic revival was rapid. The industrial marriage between the English and the Strangers was not an entirely happy one, but by the 1580s the city's textile industry had been restored to its former prosperity and soon after Strangers were admitted to the freedom of the city, Norwich worsteds having been, in part, replaced by the new draperies. (Rodgers, M., *The River and Staithes of Tudor Norwich*, King Street Research Group, 1996)

NOVEMBER 7TH

1882: On this day twenty-year-old Frederick Rolfe began fourteen days' hard labour in Norwich Castle prison for poaching rabbits. He wrote:

A door swung open and a Turnkey led us inside. I shall never forget what I felt when I first saw that gloomy place, and I was fit to cry, but held back my tears somehow ... the cell was about ten feet long by six broad, and had a stone floor, and a board for a bed ... [The Turnkey] brought me a loaf of bread about the size of a good apple and a can of water, and told me that that was my tea ... I did not want a bite that night ... I kept on thinking of mother and home, and the trouble I had been and got myself into, just like some had always said I would ... they made me tread the wheel, and pick oakum, which was hard old tarry rope ... but it was then I made a vow that I would be as bad as they had painted me.

(Rider Haggard, L. (ed), *I Walked by Night: Being the Life & History of the King of the Norfolk Poachers*, Nicholson & Watson, 1935)

NOVEMBER 8TH

1817: On this day the city was bustling with news of the death of Princess Charlotte. An express had arrived in Norwich bearing the ill tidings, but there were compensations aplenty for the local cloth manufacturers.

> Three post chaises and four followed a few hours after [the express] with gentlemen from some of the first London houses, to buy up all the black bombazines that the manufacturers had on hand, some of them, however, had earlier intelligence of the melancholy event by letter brought by the express messenger, who arrived here on horseback.

It was subsequently stated:

> Notwithstanding the immediate and necessary exertions of all persons employed in the manufacture of bombazines and other articles of sable hue, they have not yet been able to satisfy the demand for goods of this description, whilst the dressmakers, &c., have found it difficult to execute all the orders they have received. During the last week all the coaches have departed heavily laden with manufactured goods.

On the day of the funeral, black was generally worn, St Peter Mancroft's bell was tolled, and the mayor and corporation attended service at the cathedral, 'The mayor substituted for the official cloak of justice one of black crape.' (Mackie, C., *Norfolk Annals*, 1901)

NOVEMBER 9TH

1862: On this day the Prince of Wales Road was opened for public traffic to create a direct and somewhat grandiose link between the city centre and Thorpe Station. It was intended as an impressive introduction to Norwich for rail travellers, a wide, sweeping curve flanked by fine buildings. Unfortunately, the scheme ran out of money, the work was curtailed and only the city end was really developed as originally envisaged. Agricultural Hall Plain is regarded as being part of Prince of Wales Road. It stands on quite a steep incline – a natural rise in the ground has been exaggerated by the remains of one of the earth embankments which formed the outer defences of Norwich Castle. The hall recalls the days when the city was an important centre for the region's farmers. Until 1960, when it was removed to Hall Road on the outskirts, the Cattle Market formed a great semicircle of livestock every Saturday around the foot of the Castle Mound from the Agricultural Hall to Farmer's Avenue. Only in recent years, with the development of Castle Mall and a general refurbishment of the entire area, has visible evidence of the old Cattle Market been swept away. (Lane, R., *The Plains of Norwich*, Lanceni Press, 1999)

NOVEMBER 10TH

1813: On this day celebrations were held in Norwich for the victories gained by Wellington over France in Spain and Germany; citizens roamed the streets shouting 'God Save the King!' In the city a bullock was roasted whole in the Market Place. The roasting had commenced at 9 p.m. the previous evening. At noon a grand procession started from the Castle Meadow, passing through all the principal streets, before entering the Market Place. 'At one o'clock Mr Lowden, the butcher, commenced to carve the bullock, but the crowd became unruly and broke over the barriers and there was a disgusting waste of good provision.' Six hundred *2d* loaves and ten barrels of stout were given away. A public dinner took place at the Angel Inn, and in the evening a huge bonfire was lit in the Market Place. Great depredations were committed in obtaining materials for the fire, and several offenders were sent to Bridewell. There was also a procession of stagecoaches through the city and an effigy of Napoleon Bonaparte was burned. A general illumination followed. Celebrations also took place in nearly every town and village in the county. (*The Bury & Norwich Post*, 10 November, 1813)

NOVEMBER 11TH

1878: On this day a trial took place to demonstrate the efficiency of the new Edison telephone transmitter and Phelps receiver. It was made over the telegraph line belonging to J. & J. Colman, between Norwich and the firm's offices in Cannon Street, London. The line ran beside the Great Eastern Railway (GER) and was 115 miles in length. The experiment began at 4 p.m. and the incessant crackling and bubbling sounds in the receivers showed that the adjoining telegraph wires were at their busiest. After a few adjustments to the Edison transmitter, a few words were recognised at each end. Remarks passed on the weather showed that a storm of sleet was going on at both ends. Later on, toward 9 p.m., when the telegraph wires had less traffic, conversations took place and the American voice of Mr Adams (Mr Edison's London representative) was easily recognised. A member of the Carrow Works Band played a cornet solo in the Norwich office and it was plainly heard in London. After the experiments, members of the GER staff who had helped with the arrangements were invited to dinner at Messrs Colmans. (*The First 100 Years of Telephones Viewed from Norwich*, British Telecom, 1980)

NOVEMBER 12TH

1886: On this day the Society for the Protection of Ancient Buildings sent its report on plans for a castle museum to the Norfolk and Norwich Museum. The idea of converting the keep and county gaol into a museum had been suggested around 1884 by architects Edward Boardman and John Gurney. Both claimed to have had the idea first, which caused friction between them throughout the project. In the October meeting of the town council, Mr Gurney had offered to pay for the estimated £5,000 of work needed to convert the keep, treadwheel house and women's prison into a museum. Almost a year later the Norwich Corporation took formal possession of Norwich Castle. A letter was sent to the Home Office to see what should be done with the treadwheel but no answer came. It was in a highly dangerous state, although an unfulfilled plan was mooted to give public demonstrations of its use, with operatives in prison garb, as a fundraiser. Work was advanced enough for interviews to be held for a museum caretaker in June 1894, and on 23 October the museum was opened by the Duke and Duchess of York. (Rodziewicz, J., *The Making of Norwich Castle Museum*, Norwich HEART, University of East Anglia, 2011)

November 13th

1785: On this day Sarah Ann Glover was born in the Close. She became a music teacher and invented the Tonic Solfa's Doh, Ray, Me, Fah, Soh, Lah, Te, Doh system. Together with her sisters, Christina and Margaret, she ran a school for young gentlewomen in a large building off Colegate. Sarah taught in a large and high schoolroom, up to eighty children at a time standing in groups, some on the groundfloor and some on a balcony. In the corner stood Sarah's 'ladder', a glass harmonicon, consisting of a row of tuned tumblers filled with water which were struck with hammers in the same way as a xylophone. Notes were struck from the tumblers to establish pitch and train the ear. John Spencer Curwen visited Sarah's singing classes to observe the use of the Tonic Solfa in the teaching of singing; it was he who popularised the system in the wider world. Sarah, however, published an instructional book, *Scheme for Rendering Psalmody Congregational*, which met with some success. Although it fell into disuse, the concept became better known after it featured in *The Sound of Music*, the 1965 film musical by Rodgers and Hammerstein. (Strangers' Hall Museum, Norwich; Solomons, G., *Plaques of Norwich*, Capricorn Books, 1981)

NOVEMBER 14TH

1997: On this day the Norwich Union Group celebrated its bicentenary in the city where the group began life. The celebrations were highlighted by a civic reception in Norwich Castle when it was announced that Norwich Union was to be granted the honorary freedom of the City of Norwich. The Lord mayor announced that it was in recognition of 'the unique part that Norwich Union had played in the business and community life of Norwich since their founding in 1797.' The freedom was conferred at a ceremony in St Andrew's Hall. In the earliest days of the Norwich Union the key factor was the entrepreneurial drive of one man, Thomas Bignold, an opportunist who saw the potential for fire and life insurance in a prosperous city of wooden buildings. Bignold's foundation and development of the business were accompanied and ultimately affected by his own troubled temperament, which threatened the stability of the enterprise. However, his son, Samuel, took over and earned the soubriquet 'Father of the City'. Samuel's habit was to rise early, and, after breakfast, ride the 3 miles from his home at Catton Old Hall into Norwich. (Mantle, J., *Norwich Union The First 200 Years*, James & James (Publishers) Ltd, 1997)

NOVEMBER 15TH

1924: On this day Dr Bertram Pollock, Bishop of Norwich, was inadvertently inveigled in what became known as the 'tithe war'. He had extended an invitation to a group of local farmers for dinner at his palace in order to discuss the serious depression in the industry. Unbeknownst to him, a life-long opponent of tithe, Albert Mobbs, was among the guests. Mr Mobbs took the bishop by surprise and ambushed him about the old tithe system (a tithe being 'one tenth' of a farm's produce), which had been converted to cash payments. During the agricultural depression, the tithe burden on farming had become intolerable. The bishop was mildly sympathetic to the cause and the following year rose in the House of Commons declaring, 'The land in England can no longer support all those who look to get their livelihood from it ... there is not enough to go round to satisfy the desires or even the claims of all.' The bishop and Mr Mobbs corresponded for several years but eventually the bishop tired of the subject and declared he could do nothing more as his first loyalty was to the church. The 'tithe war' lasted until 1976. (Mobbs, A.G., *Eighty Years on Suffolk Soil*, unpublished, 1974)

NOVEMBER 16TH

1620: On this day the *Mayflower* arrived in Plymouth Bay. Desire Minter and John Hooke – both from Norwich – were among the passengers seeking a new life in the Americas. Desire was the daughter of William and Sarah (née Willet) Minter and was travelling with the Carver family, for whom she worked together with a child under their care and four servants. The Minters had moved to Leiden (in Holland) where William had died. Desire was about twenty years of age at the time of the crossing but, unusually, she returned to England five years later. She had become ill and died soon afterwards. John and Catherine Carver died early on and Desire was among those who received an acre in the 1623 division of land.

John Hooke of Norwich, aged thirteen, was apprenticed to Isaac Allerton with whom he travelled. His parents John and Alice (née Thompson) Hooke were married at St Peter Mancroft in 1605 and John was born in around 1607. His father, John, died, and Alice remarried. She apprenticed young John to Isaac Allerton of Leiden for a period of twelve years. Isaac took him to America but he died sometime during the first winter. (www.mayflowerhistory.com)

NOVEMBER 17TH

1997: On this day the fastest car in the world brought Norwich to a standstill as thousands flocked to meet the record-breaking Thrust SSC team. More than 9,000 people waited for up to 2 hours at Norwich Airport to see RAF fighter pilot Wing Commander Andy Green and the new legendary supersonic Thrust2 car. Queues stretched for more than half a mile to see the vehicle which made history when it broke the sound barrier the previous month in Nevada's Black Rock Desert. It was powered by two jet engines taken from a Phantom fighter/ bomber aircraft. City Hall officials were forced to close the gates 45 minutes early and turn people away because numbers were so overwhelming. Andy Green thanked the crowds for turning out, 'The response has been quite phenomenal. There is a tremendous amount of enthusiasm here which is great to see.' Andy and the Thrust team spent 7½ hours at the airport signing thousands of autographs. With posters selling for £5, model Thrust cars for £20 and signatures coming for a donation of £5, the day would have gone some way to helping pay back the team's £250,000 debt. (*Eastern Evening News*, 17 November 1997)

November 18th

1878: On this day Philippa Flowerdew started work at Colman's Carrow Works as an industrial nurse, the first ever such appointment to be made. She not only provided first aid but was responsible for delivering food parcels to the sick. The philanthropic Colman family, who had moved their business into Norwich in 1856, took a benevolent interest in the workforce by supplying schooling for employees' children and contributing to the social life of its staff, e.g. Christmas dinner in the granary and staff outings. The company, which by the late 1890s employed 2,000 people, was one of the first to offer a meals service for its workers – 4*d* bought hot meat, vegetable stew and a pint of coffee. Colman's also provided a clothing club and lodgings for working girls, followed by a lending library and a pension fund, although it was also common practice in the 1920s and '30s that women were dismissed when they married. The founder, Jeremiah James Colman, was regarded as the local grandee and something of a patriarch by his workforce, which was employed under conditions that in many respects anticipated the Welfare State. (The Mustard Shop, Royal Arcade, Norwich)

NOVEMBER 19TH

1820: On this day 'an eccentric person', eighty-one-year-old Charles Archer, died in St Andrew's parish. It was his constant practice to be at his post every morning at 4 a.m. with his kettle of hot cocoa and saloop (an infusion of aromatic herbs and ground orchid root). This post, or station was near the Two Necked Swan Inn (also known as The Swan with Two Necks) on the Market Place and he was allowed half a pint of porter each morning for calling up the landlord at 6 a.m., which custom continued for some fourteen years. He drank at that house 2,556 pints, or something more than 319 gallons. He had formerly been in the 12th Regiment of Foot and lost a leg in the memorable siege of Gibraltar; he had been granted a pension which he received for thirty-nine years. But what most affected his mind – next to the misfortune of having his leg shot away – was a circumstance often related by himself to anyone who would listen, namely he had seen a hog snatch up his leg in its mouth and run away with it without his being able to prevent it. (Mackie, C., *Norfolk Annals Vol. I*, 1901)

NOVEMBER 20TH

1881: On this day Edward Meyrick Goulburn, Dean of Norwich, recorded in his diary, 'heard to my great grief that the railway threatens again the invasion of the Close.' Goulburn was a frequent railway traveller but he referred to the proposed Lynn and Fakenham line as 'this horrid railway', since the engineers wanted to run the line through the Cathedral Close and demolish the Ethelbert Gate. For most of 1881 he waged the greatest campaign of his career to stop it. Goulburn had seen the plan showing the proposed line earlier in the year but following representation to the Great Eastern Railway Co. thought he had persuaded the company against it. At the March chapter meeting it was agreed 'to thank GER for their helping us to exclude a railway from the Close.' That, he thought, was the end of the matter. However, in November the scheme was revived and Goulburn was again forced into action. He requested mayor Hunter to 'feel the pulse of the Town Council' about the proposal. After a long and arduous campaign lasting well into 1882, the bill was finally withdrawn. It appeared that the Close had been saved. (Henderson, Noel (ed), *The Goulburn Norwich Diaries*, The Canterbury Press, 1996)

NOVEMBER 21ST

1507: On this day John Bale (1495–1563) entered the Norwich Carmelite convent on his twelfth birthday. He became a zealous Roman Catholic and his career was, to say the least, colourful. Due to his 'earthy' turn of phrase and 'his rude vigour of expression and his want of good taste and moderation' he was known as 'Bilious Bale' by contemporary scholars. Having taken monastic vows he later renounced them in favour of marriage and several children. He walked the religious tightrope by repudiating Catholicism and embracing Protestantism at the Reformation, returning briefly to Queen Mary's Catholicism before settling for Elizabeth I's new Church of England. John was renowned for his controversial preaching, which led to his being arrested on a charge of high treason. He was once shipwrecked, taken by pirates and sold for a ransom. John Quinton, a Norfolk librarian, gave an opinion of Bale's literary efforts, 'A wood-cut of a man in Roman armour but with the cross on his shield and the point of his sword bursting into flame, is hardly likely to have resembled Sir John Oldcastle, except in the same way as Bale resembled a real historian.' (Hannah, I.C., *The Heart of East Anglia*, Heath Cranton & Ouseley, 1910)

NOVEMBER 22ND

1990: On this day staff members at Jarrold's department store togged out in Victorian costumes and offered 15 per cent off their wares. The firm was celebrating 150 years in London Street, through the reigns of nine monarchs and two world wars, and so playing a part in generations of Norwich families. A singing santa brought a dose of festive cheer when he arrived in the evening to turn on the London Street Christmas lights. Surrounded by scores of children, the santa pulled up in a horse-drawn carriage and delighted them with a quick burst of song before taking residence in the children's department. And he was accompanied by an equally popular guest – a giant Teenage Mutant Ninja Turtle. There was also a display of women's clothes through the ages, courtesy of Strangers Hall museum, and a demonstration of an old printing press. In John Jarrold's 1770 notebook were jotted down things that interested him, such as recipes for Indian Pickle, love poems and notable local happenings together with his 'Rules to Make A Good Tradesman', such as, 'Be not too talkative but speak as much as it necessary to recommend your goods and always observe within the Rule of Decency.' (*Eastern Daily Press*, 23 November 1990)

November 23rd

1950: On this day the Assembly House, on Theatre Street, was opened by the Lord Lieutenant of Norfolk, Sir Edmund Bacon. Just after the end of the Second World War, Henry Jesse Sexton, OBE, a leading Norwich shoe manufacturer, bought both the Assembly House and Noverre Rooms. He spent £70,000 on the restoration and furnishing of the beautiful Georgian building, which had been described by the architect, Stephen Rowland Pierce, as being riddled with 'decay, dry rot, beetles, neglect and Blitz.' The house needed underpinning and the central beam in the ceiling was rotten at one end. Henry Sexton formed the H.J. Sexton Norwich Arts Trust and, after the considerable restoration work was completed, presented the Assembly House to the city. Mr Sexton said this was his way of 'putting something back' into the city in which he had prospered. 'As originally built it was reserved for the pleasure and entertainment of the privileged few', he said, 'but it is my wish that in its revival it should be dedicated to the use and enjoyment of the whole community.' (Fower, E., *The Assembly House* (undated); Brooks, P., *Norwich: Stories of a City*, Fort Publishing, 2003)

November 24th

1877: On this day Anna Sewell sold all the rights to her classic book *Black Beauty* to her mother's Norwich publishers Jarrold & Sons for just £40, with no royalty clause. It was published as *Black Beauty: his grooms and companions, the autobiography of a horse*; it has since sold around 30 million copies worldwide and is said to be the sixth bestseller in the English language. The book was written intermittently from 1871–1877, at a time when her health declined and she became housebound. When she was fourteen she fell and injured both ankles while walking home from school and for the rest of her life was unable to walk or stand for any length of time. Her dependence on horse-drawn transportation fostered her respect for the animals, and she wrote, 'I have been confined to the house and to my sofa [but] when I am able, been writing what I think will turn out a little book, its special aim being to induce kindness, sympathy and an understanding treatment of horses.' *Black Beauty* was published in 1877 and Anna lived just long enough to hear of its success. She died at Old Catton in April 1878. (*East Anglian Daily Times*, 2 December 2011)

NOVEMBER 25TH

1829: On this day the Norfolk and Norwich Horticultural Society held its first show at the Swan Inn near St Peter Mancroft. It is thought to be one of the oldest of such provincial societies in the country, traceable in an almost unbroken line to 1631 when the city first held the annual 'Florists' Feasts'. When Thomas Fuller visited Norwich in 1662 he found it to be famous as a city of gardens. He observed that it was the Dutch who first 'advanced the use and reputation of flowers in this city' in which, he said, that houses and trees are equally blended in. Certainly the Dutch passed on their fanatical devotion to the tulip, but it was in the seventeenth century that immigrants from the Low Countries and northern France, or 'Strangers' as they were called, introduced the 'Florists' Feasts', which became important events in the social calendar. Although they were occasions for masques and merrymaking, their main purpose remained the promotion and judging of horticultural competitions. The trade of 'gardener' is recorded in the Register of Norwich Freemen from 1659 onwards. (Priestley, U. & Fenner, A., *Shops and Shopkeepers in Norwich 1660–1730*, University of East Anglia, 1985)

NOVEMBER 26TH

1973: On this day David Sainsbury, grandson of J.J. Sainsbury, founder of the grocery and supermarket firm, made the original endowment of £3 million for building of the Sainsbury Centre in the grounds of the University of East Anglia (UEA), which had opened in 1963. The centre was to be the focus for the new School of Arts and would eventually house a collection of 570 works of art worth about £5 million (in 1976), all donated by the Sainsbury family. The centre's design was a matter of some controversy but was described as 'a remarkably elegant functional building, the equivalent of the early industrial revolution sheds, warehouses, etc.' Its sometime description as 'a sophisticated aircraft hangar' gave rise to rumours that the Russians had detected the centre by spy satellite. Its hangar design and mysterious underground delivery ramp, whose entrance was masked by a wood, aroused their suspicions that it was a missile site and they asked to come and inspect it. Its chief designer, Norman Foster (now Lord Foster), used to arrive at UEA by helicopter and the hangar design foreshadows his later design of Stansted Airport. (Sanderson, M., *The History of the University of East Anglia Norwich*, Hambledon & London, 2002)

November 27th

1846: On this day the Norwich City Council delegated their powers in the matter of fire cover to a Watch Committee consisting of four councillors and an alderman. They in turn were to appoint a fire brigade, under the auspices of the police force. A sergeant and five constables were required to attend all fires in the city with the council fire engine. Six suits of clothing were purchased along with six hats. The men acted as policemen during the day but were required to sleep near the fire station (then the Guildhall) each night. Unfortunately some of the five founding fathers of the brigade did not last long. Sergeant Copeman was dismissed for being intoxicated on duty in 1848, and Mr Underwood and Mr Fairhead were dismissed in January 1849 for inefficiency, and received two weeks' pay with their dismissal notice. In 1851 the police force was reorganised which meant that, in reality, all policemen became firemen and not just the original five. Two years later it was found that only one of the council's three engines was fit for use – the remaining two were beyond repair. (Veriod, B.S., *A History of the Norwich City Fire Brigade*, Bryan S. Veriod, 1986)

NOVEMBER 28TH

1983: On this day the city's British Home Stores (BHS) reopened its doors after a major revamp costing almost £2 million. Shoppers were greeted at the St Stephen's store entrance by the Staffordshire Regiment Band, as Divisional Director Colin Williams cut the blue ribbon to allow shoppers into the store. The store had originally opened twenty years previously, but the revamp swept away the uniform rows of counters and gangways of the past, in favour of 'circular walkways, carpeting and varied groupings of racks, shelves and hangers.' A new restaurant was created at the back of the store alongside the food department, which had a new in-house bakery. The project included the fitting of a new refrigeration plant and ovens as well as large-scale alterations to flooring, ceilings and decor. The main contractors were Wiltshire's but Stanley Dell, head of the development, said many local sub-contractors had been used and that the scheme also meant an increase in the number of people working in the Norwich store. Work had been going on around the clock to finish the store in time for the 9 a.m. opening. Norwich was one of six BHS stores to receive the 'new look' that year. (*Eastern Evening News*, 28 November 1983)

NOVEMBER 29TH

1848: On this day William Cooper wrote to Lord Douro, 'I have just heard and from good authority, that Jermy the Recorder, and his son were last night shot dead by an enraged tenant. This will render the Recordship vacant. Can you under present circumstances at all assist me in obtaining it?' The city was to hear more of the incident over the coming months after James Blomfield Rush was arrested and later hanged for the murder. Meanwhile the post of Recorder did have to be filled, although Lord Douro was not sure that Mr Cooper was the man for the job. He wrote to his friend Samuel Bignold:

> I have declined to interfere for the natural reasons, one is that a Recorder appointment by my intercession would never be considered impartial ... What a dreadful occurrence! In these days when the murder of persons in authority is so common one must take care not to irritate personally, which Jermy had no objection to do. You will never be murdered from anger for people bear a great deal if their blood is not up.

(Bignold, Sir R., *Five Generations of the Bignold Family*, Batsford Ltd, 1948)

NOVEMBER 30TH

1774: On this day, St Andrew's feast day, the Scots Society of Norwich came into being. An assembly of exiled Scots had been celebrating the festival of their patron saint and at the end of the festivities they discovered a surplus of 13*s* 6*d*. One of the company suggested it be laid aside as a 'distress fund' to be at the disposal of 'any poor Scotsman who might come to Norwich in distress ... and need the whole or any part of it.' At this time any Scot (or other 'foreigner') becoming destitute in England was in a sorry plight. The Poor Law bodies found it difficult to support their own poor and rarely provided assistance for 'outsiders'. But it appears that no destitute Scots found their way to Norwich as, when the gentlemen assembled the following year, it was discovered that the fund had not been drawn upon. In 1776 the Scots Society was officially formed; the Earl of Rosebery was governor and Bartlett Gurney were the society's bankers. In 1784, it was decided funds should be used to help strangers in general, not just Scots, and it was renamed the Society of Universal Good-Will. (McCutcheon, E., *Norwich Through the Ages*, The Alastair Press, 1989)

DECEMBER 1ST

1834: On this day twenty-three-year-old Mary Ann Adams, convicted at Norwich Assizes for stealing a purse containing 4 sovereigns, arrived in New South Wales (Australia) aboard the convict barque, *George Hibbert*. She was one of 144 convicts and the journey took almost six months. Her death sentence had been altered to transportation for life, an alternative particularly favoured by the Norwich courts at the time. While awaiting transportation in Norwich Gaol, she made a keepsake token from a worn-down two-pence coin. On it she inscribed, 'When this you see, remember me when I am far away'. The keepsake remains on display at the Norwich Castle Museum to serve as a reminder as she intended. By the time Mary was transported, Britain had a number of Australian settlements which relied on woman like Mary marrying and raising children. As a women, she was outnumbered by male convicts by about 6 to 1, so her presence was important to the new colony. Although the number of crimes punishable by death was reduced in the 1820s, by 1831 on average one person was still executed each week in England and Wales. Transportation therefore saved the lives of many who would otherwise have been hanged. (Norwich Castle Museum)

DECEMBER 2ND

1853: On this day the authoress Amelia Opie died in a house on Castle Meadow; since pulled down, it was known at the time of its destruction as Opie House. Even as a girl she was described as the 'rising genius of that sparkling coterie of literary society once existing in Norwich.' Born in Calvert Street, Amelia was the only child of John Alderson, a prominent Norwich physician. She had a penchant for parties, balls and colourful clothing, all of which she was able to indulge. She married the artist John Opie in 1801, the same year she began her writing career by publishing her first novel, *Father and Daughter*. It was well received and Sir Walter Scott said that he had cried over it 'more than he ever cried over such things.' John died in 1807 and she returned to Colegate to live with her widowed father. She travelled widely, to Paris, Edinburgh, London and Cornwall, but always returned to Norwich. In 1825 she was received into the membership of the Society of Friends, perhaps with the hope of becoming the second Mrs Joseph John Gurney. If so she was disappointed, as he married elsewhere. (Madders, Mrs, *Fletcher's Norwich Handbook*, J. Fletcher, 1857)

December 3rd

1820: On this day the Duke of Wellington became an honorary Freeman of the City of Norwich. A few days earlier he and the Duke of York visited Norwich on their way to Gunton to visit Lord Suffield. The two dukes and their entourage used the Angel Inn for refreshment. They returned on the Sunday and attended service at the cathedral, before retiring once more to the Angel. The corporation had not expected Wellington's visit and assembled in some haste to decide how to mark such an auspicious occasion. The mayor, sheriffs and other civic dignitaries presented themselves at the Angel. The steward read the address and the freedom was duly conferred on both His Royal Highness and His Grace, who courteously acknowledged the honour by asking the corporation to stay for lunch. Wellington passed through Norwich on several occasions and was a very popular figure. In 1819 he had gone through Norwich on his way to Blicking and had been cheered in the streets. In May 1843, the Scots Greys made their regimental headquarters at Norwich, due mainly to the influence of the duke, whose statue is in the Cathedral Close. (Thompson, L.P., *Norwich Inns*, W.E. Harrison & Sons, 1947)

DECEMBER 4TH

1830: On this day the Town Clerk issued a proclamation from the Guildhall on behalf of the city mayor and magistrates that the lawbreaking, 'Swing' rioters (employed in the destruction of threshing machines) would be suitably punished. The authorities considered the public had:

> A paramount duty which they owe to their Sovereign and their Country at this moment of general disturbance, to declare that, whilst in common with the rest of their Fellow Citizens, they are on the one hand ready to do all which sympathy and benevolence can suggest for the relief of distressed operatives in this populous place, so on the other hand it is their full determination to act with the promptitude, decision, and vigour, which circumstances imperatively demand, in prohibiting tumultuous assemblies, and suppressing riotous proceedings, in opposing every kind of open outrage, and actively endeavouring to detect secret attacks, on either Person or Property.

They were anxious that their 'Fellow Citizens' should know that 'persons who are guilty of these lawless proceedings, are liable on conviction to suffer Death, and that the loss incurred by Individuals by the destruction of their Property must be paid by the Public, and will consequently tend to the increase of the County Rate.' (Morson, M., *Norfolk: Mayhem and Murder*, Wharncliffe Books, 2008)

DECEMBER 5TH

1977: On this day it was announced that well-known amateur boxer, John Culyer, had acquired the former Robin Hood public house on Dereham Road, as part of Culyer Sports, a family business founded by John in 1971. After his retirement from being a physical training instructor in the Royal Air Force, John started business in a small shop at No.105 Dereham Road, where he specialised in sports equipment and trophies. At the time the sports market was growing and the new premises was devoted entirely to sports equipment and clothing, with its own fitting rooms and a special section for each sport. The out-of-city site had the advantage of having its own car park. John was a founder member and the first secretary of the Eastern Counties Amateur Boxing Association and also an international referee – he officiated on four occasions at the National Championships at Wembley. He also helped to found the Watton & District Amateur Boxing Club, one of whose champions was Justin Fashanu, who later gave up boxing in favour of football. Fashanu began his career as an apprentice with Norwich City Football Club, turning professional in 1978 and staying with the club until 1981. (*Eastern Evening News*, 5 December 1977)

DECEMBER 6TH

1327: On this day began the tradition of the Boy Bishop, Blomefield records:

> This Boy Bishop ... was a chorister bishop, always chosen by his fellow children on St Nicholas's Day; and on that day above all others, because that saint's Legend says, that while he laid in his cradle, he fasted Wednesday and Friday, and knew the scriptures ... therefore children worship him before all saints.

The young bishop enjoyed a four-day 'episcopy' and he 'was to bear the name and hold the state of a bishop, answerably habited with a crosier or pastoral staff in his hand, and a mitre on his head; and such a one too some had, even richer than the real Bishop's.' Whatever the real Bishop's duties were:

> ... the same was done by this Boy Bishop .. the Mass itself only excepted. He went in solemn procession to the cathedral's high altar, there performing the service of the Holy Innocents ... the main cause of this institution, which was so guarded that nobody, under pain of excommunication, should interrupt or press upon during the procession or any part of the service.

(Blomefield, F., *Topographical History of the County of Norfolk, Volume IV*, 1806)

DECEMBER 7TH

1745: On this day the *Norwich Mercury* carried an advertisement that saw the start of a regular Norwich–London coach service. Philip Sargent and Thomas Youngman advertised:

> There will be a Coach and six able Horses, set out from the Castle Inn in the Market-place, Norwich, for London, to carry Fowles and Presents as usual, on Sunday Morning December the 22nd, which will be there on Christmas Eve; and likewise another on Sunday Morning the 29th Inst to be there on New Year Eve without fail, at the Green Dragon in Bishopsgate Street, London.

Parcels were to be taken to the Dolphin Inn on St Giles or to the Castle Inn in the marketplace. The coaching age had begun and by the following Christmas other operators were advertising a similar service. Robert Tyrrell's coaches set out from the Fleece Inn 'to carry Fowles and Parcels for London'. The Christmas coaches became a familiar sight on the Norwich–London road and are immortalised in Robert Seymour's famous print of 1835, 'The Norwich Coach at Christmas Tide', which shows geese and turkeys festooned from every possible point, and the roof piled high with hampers, with others suspended beneath the coach. (*Norwich Mercury*, 7 December 1745)

DECEMBER 8TH

1910: On this day the *Eastern Daily Press* announced the completion of St John's Roman Catholic cathedral. The newspaper was generous in its praise:

> The Duke of Norfolk has endowed his fellow Roman Catholics in Norwich, and the city in general, with the finest addition which has been made for centuries to the treasury of great English ecclesiastical architecture ... [that is] in a very real way a general public asset, an addition to the great things possessed by East Anglia.

The Duke gave a lunch to 250 invited guests, including city dignitaries and prominent citizens. The eight courses cost 15s a head, including wine with every course, and later a lavish tea, 'including of table appointments, waiters, flowers, etc., cost 2 shillings 6 pence.' Some, of course, regarded the Duke's great building with suspicion. Percy Lubbock, a relation of the Quaker Gurneys of Earlham, said that the building which had replaced the former city goal was little better than its predecessor. 'We scarcely spoke of it, the exotic upstart – we looked and passed; it could by no manner of means be regarded as part of our Norwich, and on the whole we ignored its intrusion.' (*Eastern Daily Press*; Rossi, A., *Norwich Roman Catholic Cathedral*, 1998)

DECEMBER 9TH

1974: On this day Methodist minister and full-time bus driver, Jack Burton, wrote in his journal:

> When, with my wife and children, I was homeless and desperate, a couple in their seventies found an old cottage for us to rent, which they scrubbed and tidied from top to bottom. (This was when I left the security of the manse and first embarked on a 'worker-priest' ministry.) ... I do not forget such kindness. It was beyond description; it was so sweet and good that it made heavy burdens light, and because it was offered freely and naturally and quietly and unconditionally it placed me eternally and gladly in their debt. I buried Herbert in May, and controlled by voice only with difficulty – and then not with complete success ... I made a special journey to visit Edith today. She has missed him terribly. They would have been married sixty years this month.

Cheered and saddened by his visit, he was touched to receive seasonal greetings from 'friends to whom once I ministered: "As we draw near to worship at the manger, we remember you with love and gratitude". Those generous words comforted me. Thus do we minister, and are ministered unto.' (Burton, J., *Transport of Delight*, SCM Press, 1976)

DECEMBER 10TH

1917: On this day Norwich City Football Club went into voluntary liquidation, 'owing to the company being unable to meet its liabilities'. At the Annual General Meeting, the directors' report showed that the policy of 'carrying on' during the war had further increased the indebtedness of the club, bringing the total accumulated losses to over £7,000, and the bank was pressing for payment. The chairman remarked ruefully that, 'it is the first time I have been in the chair and it looks as if it is going to be the last.' It appears that only two matches took place during the 1917–18 season, the first a charity match in October of that year and the second the Norwich Hospital Cup match the following April. The affairs of the club were put on ice and the Nest locked up. However, in February 1919 it was proposed that a new company be formed with a nominal capital of £5,000 and that Norwich City FC be reformed. In March, Major Franklin Buckley was appointed as the new manager and very soon the Nest was looking like its old self and City were back in business. (Davage, M., Eastwood, J. & Platt, K., *Canary Citizens*, Jarrold, 2001)

DECEMBER 11TH

1895: On this day James Hooper wrote one of his regular Walks Round Norwich columns. The weather was:

> … almost as good as any; gauzy mists, remnants of the trailing garments of the night by no means obscure the sun, and, as noontide approaches, the frost gems have well nigh disappeared. Our way to Catton, which is some 2 miles nearer the North Pole than Norwich and is, we are told 'a delightful suburban village' … decorated with many picturesque mansions.

He recounts numerous theories on the origins of 'Catton', citing Blomefield as writing, 'Cat is the name of a river … leading his readers to assume that Catton means the town on the river Cat.'

James concluded that, 'there is little doubt that Catton is so named from the common cat which was very much respected, not to say venerated, by (among others) the old Germans, ancient Britains, and the Scots.' After many more 'cat' observations, and a visit to the church, he headed for home, 'We have done very imperfect justice to Catton, for several pilgrimages might be taken thereto without exhausting its interest; but the lowering December sun warns us that we must take the homewards track.' (James Hooper's Journalism (Scrapbook), Colman Collection, 11F)

DECEMBER 12TH

1899: On this day installation of a new five-manual organ with sixty-four speaking stops and 4,148 pipes in Norwich Cathedral was completed. For many years there had been discussions about building a new cathedral organ. Little had been done to the instrument erected in 1833 and it was hopelessly underpowered to lead the large congregations attending services in the nave. When Frank Bates was appointed organist in 1885 he considered it to be one of the poorest cathedral organs in the country. Following extensive fundraising by the dean, a new organ was built by the local firm Norman Brothers & Beard. The city organist, Dr Edward Bunnett, was invited to give two recitals on the instrument a month after its opening. The significance of the invitation was not lost on the Norwich public who, remembering Bunnett's intimate association with the cathedral many years before, regarded it as a well-deserved compliment to them. The recitals attracted large audiences and the programme included Spohr's trio for boys' voices, 'Jesus, Heavenly Master', an echo of the time when this was sung by Bunnett and two other choristers to Jenny Lind in 1847. (Roast, T., *Dr Edward Bunnett, Eighty Years of making music in Norwich*, Gateway Music, 2007)

DECEMBER 13TH

1424: On this day, the Friday after St Lucy's Day, an indenture tripartite was made between the mayor, aldermen and commons of Norwich, containing constituents for better government of the city. It was made at the Guildhall and afterwards given the royal assent by Henry VI under the broad seal. It proclaimed that the city was lacking 'good and virtuous government ... to the great dishonour of the mayor and aldermen.' To remedy such 'evil', eight ordinances were made, the first requiring that 'the aldermen shall always give good counsel to the mayor, as the aldermen of London do.' They must 'keep secret all matters treated of, until they be shown in common assembly ... on pain of being displaced.' Under a 20s penalty, no alderman could quarrel with his fellows before he had first shown his grievance to the mayor. Aldermen were henceforth required to swear to obey the ordinances. 'So help me God at the holy doom'. The mayor issued a proclamation saying that he, 'commandeth that each man keep the peace ... and that no man disturb or break the aforesaid peace'. (*The History of the City and County of Norwich from the Earliest Accounts to the Present Time*, printed by John Crouse, 1768)

DECEMBER 14TH

1734: On this day a testimonial appeared in the columns of the *Norwich Mercury* given by one of the city minstrels to the efficacy of a patent medicine which was much advertised by William Chase:

> Mr Wiston, one of our City Waits, having got a Cold, was taken with great and tormenting Pains all about him, and took several things which had no Effect; but sending for a Bottle of BATEMAN'S Pectoral Drops to my Shop, took one Dose going to Bed, and found the greatest Relief imaginable in 3 or 4 Hours time. He desir'd me to give this Publick Notice, for the good of others. There are three Doses in a Bottle, and sold by W. Chase in Norwich for 1s.

The Pectoral Drops, it was stated, 'are Diaphoretic, Diuretic, and Cordial, containing in themselves all those three several Qualities, [and is] the Reason why they Effect (with the Blessing of God) so many Cures in raging Colds, Pains in the Limbs, etc.' The main ingredients of the drops were aniseed, camphor and opium so the effects would only be temporary and could be dangerous as the amount of opium varied according to the supplier. (*Norwich Mercury*, 14–21 December 1734)

December 15th

1973: On this day Norwich City Football Club played the first home match under the control of John Bond. It aroused huge interest and over 20,000 fans braved wintry conditions to see how the revitalised Canaries would cope against Bill Shankly's high-flying Liverpool. Ted MacDougall was making his home debut and his former Bournemouth colleagues, Mel Machin and John Benson, were also pulling on the yellow and green shirt for the first time. The game, on a snow-covered pitch, started in sensational fashion when Paul Cheesley cracked in a marvellous goal in the first minute. He blasted a thunderous drive past the advancing England keeper Ray Clemence. It was his first goal in twenty-three city appearances. After months of gloom, this taste of life under Bond was just what the doctor ordered and the roar that greeted the goal must have travelled many miles down the river Wensum. Unfortunately Bill Shankly's men responded positively to the shock and with less than 20 minutes on the clock, Kevin Keegan headed on an Ian Callaghan corner and the slim-line Scot, Peter Cormack, nipped in to beat Keelan from close range. Final score – Norwich 1: Liverpool 1. (Hadgraft, R., *Norwich City: The Modern Era*, Desert Island Books, 2003)

DECEMBER 16TH

1955: On this day the *Eastern Evening News* did a round up of the city's Christmastide events. In Norwich Cathedral around 1,000 children from every secondary school in Norwich attended the annual Carol Service for Schools. At the foot of a large decorated Christmas tree in the west end of the nave the Bishop of Norwich (Dr Percy Herbert), the Lord mayor of Norwich (Dr Ian Dickson), and the Dean (the Very Revd Norman Hook) received from the children gifts which were to be distributed among local children's hospitals, 'One of the most impressive of the toys given was a two-thirds scale model of an electric milk float, produced by pupils of the Wensum View School.' During the service, lessons were read by the Lord mayor, the Dean, Mr L.H. Bush, headmaster of the Wensum View School, and the Bishop. At St Clement's Church Colegate, a nativity play written by the Rector, Revd L.P. Palmer, was performed. After each scene the audience joined in the singing of Christmas carols. At the Norwich Art School, members of the Norfolk and Norwich Art Circle were taking time off Christmas preparations 'to spend a few quiet hours drawing.' (*Eastern Evening News*, 16 December 1955)

DECEMBER 17TH

1815: On this day the distinguished Norwich surgeon, John Green Crosse, operated on a woman who had a large neck tumour. He wrote, 'All those present at this operation seemed to think that it was one of the best that they had ever seen ... as well as if I had been dissecting the subject upon the table.' He admits to sounding 'unsympathetic' but praised the patient, 'The operation was extremely painful to the patient who did not faint but was very chilly and shivering and did not get warm and quiet until an hour after she had been in bed and taken a little wine and water.' Not a man of sentiment he once recorded:

> Marriage is a great step – an era of life. How much depends on the wisdom of the choice and how much more upon one's own conduct after entering upon such an engagement ... it has been said in regard to a wife, 'Before marriage you should look with your eyes wide open, ever after with them half shut' – his own choice he referred to as 'the cheerful and suitable partner of my life'.

(Crosse, M.V., *A Surgeon in the Early Nineteenth Century*, E. & S. Livingstone, 1968)

DECEMBER 18TH

1907: On this day, the usual *Norwich Mercury* football reports were supplemented by comments on the standard of refereeing:

As in the match on the previous Saturday against West Ham the referee [today] came in for a certain amount of 'ragging' from almost all parts of the ground. It can be admitted that there were a number of decisions on both occasions with which we did not agree, but on the other hand it should not be forgotten (1) that the referee has only one pair of eyes, and is not infallible; (2) that he is the man on the spot ... and (3) that he is in sole charge of the game, and has a great deal of power which he may be inclined on some occasions to use against unruly spectators. The Norwich crowd has always had a fine reputation for sportsmanlike behaviour, and we fear that this continual jeering at the referee is a sign of degeneracy. In the long run it is probable that the wrongful offside decisions and fouls overlooked on one side quite balance those on the other, and it is quite certain that the referees who come to Norwich are absolutely impartial.

(*Norwich Mercury*, 18 December 1907)

DECEMBER 19TH

1785: On this day parson James Woodforde took a ride to Norwich. He arrived just after 1 p.m. and 'put up our Horses at the Kings Head and there dined on, a fine piece of boiled Beef and a Saddle of Mutton, etc.' After lunch he saw the:

> ... learned Pigg at the rampant Horse in St Stephens – there was but a small company there but soon got larger. We stayed about an Hour. It was wonderful to see the sagacity of the Animal. It was a Boar Pigg, very thin, quite black with a magic Collar on his Neck. He would spell any word or Number from the Letters and Figures placed before him ... paid for seeing the Pigg one shilling.

He afterwards took a turn around the city before attending a lecture on astronomy at the Assembly Rooms, with which he was 'highly pleased'. His appetite restored, he returned to the Kings Head for 'the best Supper I ever met with at an Inn ... Hashed Fowl, Veal Scollopes, a fine Woodcock, a Couple of Whistling Plovers, a real Teal of the small kind and hot Apple Pye.' (Beresford, J. ed., *The Diary of a Country Parson: James Woodforde, 1758–1802*, Oxford University Press, 1978)

DECEMBER 20TH

1932: On this day a newspaper correspondent wrote:

I wonder if the prospect of a ride in a £5 car conjures up for you visions of a slow, jerky, bumpy altogether ridiculous jaunt – seated much nearer Heaven than one usually is in the cars of today – getting out and pushing up hills ... that, at any rate, was the vision conjured up by an advertisement in the *Daily Press* where secondhand cars were offered from £5 to £1,200 in a year-end Mann Egerton clearance sale. Thinking I'd have a bit of fun, off I went to their showrooms, and asked for a trial run in the £5 car. The car was of good appearance, in fact, a 1925 Fiat two-seater ... it still bore evident signs of initial good quality and I'm sure that a little polishing cream would work wonders. We made a lively start off the car park into Prince of Wales Road, into Riverside Road, and then chugging up the various hills and twists and turns of Gilman Road ... all this time the little car behaved splendidly ... I wondered how its performance would have compared with the £2,100 Rolls Royce!

(Gurney-Read, J., *Trades & Industries of Norwich*, Gliddon Books, 1988)

DECEMBER 21ST

1805: On this day a ball was held at the Assembly Rooms to celebrate the victory of Admiral Horatio Nelson at the Battle of Trafalgar and attended by most of the county's nobility and gentry. The music room was used for supper, the ladies sitting down first and the men at a second session. The present restaurant was used for dancing, though it remains a mystery how 400 guests danced there, but the accounts are explicit enough that it was so. 'The smaller room was appropriated to the ball, in which the arrangements for dancing had been made by roping off a sufficient width on each side of the room.' The musicians were in the galleries over the entrance to the room – the sockets for their candles can still be seen at the top of the balustrade – and dancing continued until 4 a.m. The dances were themed, 'a hundred couples danced arranged in four sets according to Nelson's victories.' Much of the panelling was obscured by transparencies depicting crowns, wheatsheaves, cornucopeias, Britannias, capering sailors and a tablet inscribed 'Nelson lives though dead'. (Stephenson, A., *The Assembly House Norwich*, H.J. Sexton Norwich Arts Trust, undated)

DECEMBER 22ND

1821: On this day the pamphleteer and radical publisher, William Cobbett (1763–1835), attended the Radical Reform Dinner in Norwich where a party of gentlemen dined with him in order to hear his ideas. The *Post* thought that:

> ... our readers will not require from us a list of the toasts drunk, for if any, the sentiments entertained by Mr Cobbett and his friends are too well known to require repetition. Indeed, we have not been told whether Mr Cobbett succeeded in converting the gentlemen assembled to his way of thinking and acting; that is abstaining altogether from drinking any excisable articles, in which case we conclude they would separate early!

Cobbett wrote of Norwich:

> The meat and poultry and vegetable market is beautiful. It is kept in a large open square in the middle, or near so, of the city. The ground is a pretty sharp slope, so that you can see all at once ... the women have a sort of uniform brown great coast, with white aprons and bibs (I think they call them) going from the apron up to the bosom. They equal in neatness (for nothing can surpass) the market women in Philadelphia.

(*Bury and Norwich Post*, 26 December 1821; Cobbett, W., *Rural Rides*, 1830)

December 23rd

1737: On this day John Wesley was in Norwich, invited to preach at the Norwich Tabernacle by James Wheatley, the city's first Methodist preacher. Wesley did not approve of the preacher, 'James Wheatley now repeated his offer of the Tabernacle. But I was in no haste. I wanted to consult my friends, and consider the thing thoroughly.' Eventually Wesley consented, 'I went up and preached to a large congregation without any let or hindrance.' On the Sunday, 'the Tabernacle was thoroughly filled, and mostly with quiet hearers. I saw none who behaved amiss but two soldiers, who struck some that desired them to be silent. But they were seized and carried to the commanding officers, who ordered them to be soundly whipped.' The following day he preached, he thought, to good effect, 'Stony hearts were broke; many mourners comforted; many believers strengthened. Prejudice vanished away; a few only kept their fierceness till the afternoon.' Norwich was suspicious of Wesley and he thought 'her people seemed fickle, perverse, and unstable as water'. In 1758 he wrote, 'It seems the time is come when our labour even in Norwich, will not be in vain'. (Curnock, N. (ed), *The Journal of the Rev. John Wesley*, A.M. Volume IV, Epworth Press, 1938)

DECEMBER 24TH

1645: On this day the mayor of Norwich sent directions to ministers and churchwardens that they were to have neither sermons nor communions in their churches the next day, and that all shops were to be open as usual. For the younger element in the city, the festival of Christmas and the gaieties of Guild Day existed only in the memories of their elders. In the past, life in Norwich had not lacked colour and enjoyment, even for the humblest citizen. Guild Days were celebrated with pageantry and sideshows, the streets adorned with garlands and streamers, Snap and Dick Fool raising laughter all along the route. There were stage-plays, shows of tumblers and freaks, and the Florists' Feasts with their songs and masques. Christmas was kept with the traditional mingling of gaiety and religious observance. All this had been swept away but many still secretly recalled the seasonal pre-Puritan festivities. Puritan clergy, though, did their best to discourage such backward glances. At St Peter Mancroft, the vociferous John Carter assailed the corporation for laxity and indulgence. The rule of the godly, he proclaimed, should be far more severe. (Ketton-Cremer, R.W., *Norfolk in the Civil War: A Portrait of a Society in Conflict*, Giddon Books, 1985)

DECEMBER 25TH

1121: On this day Henry I celebrated Christmas in the castle chapel, in all likelihood the first King of England to have visited the city. The castle was designed to be a provincial Royal Palace, the centre of control, defence and administration, rather than a fortification. Work began on the stone keep in 1095 on instruction from William (Rufus) II, son of William the Conqueror. Following Rufus' death it was continued by his brother, Henry I, and completed in 1121. Henry and his courtiers celebrated its completion at a 'crown-wearing feast' on Christmas Day. As well as the castle, he also wanted to inspect the Benedictine Priory for which he had granted Herbert de Losinga a decree on Christmas Day 1100, to set up 'in the church ... monks there who shall be irremovable.' Building the priory and castle involved considerable destruction of the Anglo-Saxon town, as intended by William the Conqueror, whose grant of property to Bishop Herfast in 1075 is recorded in the Domesday Book. Henry's visit to Norwich in 1121 conferred distinction on the city, while at the same time making it abundantly clear that the Norman rulers were here to stay. (Norfolk Museums & Archaeological Services, Castle Exhibition)

DECEMBER 26TH

1634: On this day the Bishop of Norwich, Richard Corbett, gave notice to the Walloon congregation 'in the most peremptory tones' that they must quit their chapel 'before Whitsuntide.' Ever since the great immigration from the Low Countries, in 1567, the Walloons in Norwich had been allowed by successive bishops to use the chapel attached to the palace for their own worship. When they first arrived, in Bishop Parkhurst's time, they found it 'more like a dovehouse than a church, full of muck and ordure, the roof decayed and the windows broken.' They repaired it at considerable expense, so that the bishops had begun to avail themselves of it again 'for baptising their children, ordaining English ministers, and other uses at their pleasure.' Bishop Richard, influenced by Archbishop Laud's desire for 'ecclesiastical conformity throughout the land', told the Walloons, 'Your discipline, I know, cares not much for a consecrated place, and any other room in Norwich that hath but breadth and length may serve your turn as well as a chapel ... Depart, and hire some other place for your irregular meetings.' (Ketton-Cremer, R.W., *Norfolk in the Civil War: A Portrait of a Society in Conflict*, The Lavenham Press, 1985)

DECEMBER 27TH

1963: On this day, Mary Barnard recorded that Norwich was in the grip of a 'Big Freeze' and that the icy weather would go down in history 'in the annals of Eaton End.' It had begun just before Christmas and 'we thought it just a cold snap, but since then it has mercilessly gone ON and ON.' She later wrote:

> It is now in its fourth week. Most of the time we just freeze ... We shovel snow, we light paraffin stoves because we have no anthracite (nobody has had, for three weeks). We are without water because the mains are frozen below ground and we are therefore thrown back on archaic forms of heating unused by us for years, like paraffin, logs and occasionally a hay box ... We [still] have a gas stove that works but no water to heat on it ... I have fed eleven people most of the holidays in spite of insuperable difficulties, and am now expert at making and freezing a mousse in half-an-hour (for we have no fridge).

Christmas lasted roughly a fortnight and it was to be mid-January before any real relief came. (Barnard, M., *Diary of an Optimist*, The Larks Press, 1995)

December 28th

1829: On this day the Home Secretary, Robert Peel, responded to local magistrates' alarm over increasing lawlessness in the city, in particular the shooting of cloth manufacturer William Springall, which the *Norfolk Chronicle* called, 'an outrage so unenglishman like.' Peel issued a statement that read:

> Whereas it hath been humbly represented unto the King, that, about half-past Ten o'clock on the night of Tuesday, the 22nd instant, a large number of Persons attacked the house of WILLIAM SPRINGALL in the Boatswain's Call Yard ... in the city of Norwich ... and with great violence broke open the said House ... several Men entered therein one of whom FIRED a PISTOL at the said William Springall, and seriously wounded him ... afterwards some of them Cut the Work of Seven Looms in the said House and committed other Acts of Violence.

The Home Secretary offered a pardon to any gang member who gave information leading to the 'apprehending and bringing to justice' of the gunman, and a further reward of £100 for information about his accomplice 'so that he, she, or them, may be apprehended and convicted thereof.' The reward was to be paid by the City Treasurer but there is no evidence that the culprit was apprehended. (Morson, M., *Norfolk: Mayhem and Murder*, Wharncliffe Books, 2008)

DECEMBER 29TH

1868: On this day pawnbroker's assistant, William Sheward of No.7 Tabernacle Street (now Bishopgate), left his common-law wife and their three children and departed for London. This short, elderly, well-dressed man presented himself at Walworth police station, South London. He confessed to such a diabolical crime that Inspector James Davis thought he must be either drunk or mad. Sheward subsequently dictated his statement, 'I, William Sheward of Norwich, charge myself with the wilful murder of my wife.' It had happened over eighteen years previously at their home in Norwich on 14 June 1849. Reports of his terrible crime caused horror throughout the country, it having all the ingredients which sold popular newspapers: cold-blooded murder, sex, butchery, bankruptcy, and finally capital punishment. William and Martha had constantly rowed about money and on the fatal day, Sheward grabbed a razor and slashed her throat. He compounded his crime by butchering her body and distributing it around the city. Sheward was returned to Norwich and stood trial for murder. A month later the black flag was hoisted over the prison gate, signalling to the large crowd outside that the executioner had accomplished his task. (Howat, P., *Tales of Old Norfolk*, Countryside Books, 1991)

DECEMBER 30TH

1822: On this day one of the most noteworthy recorded cases of horse-drawn coach drivers racing against each other occurred when the Norwich Times and the Norwich Day coaches both left London at 5.30 a.m. The Times was driven by John Thorogood, who not only had the reputation of being a crack coach driver but was also a proprietor of the coach company. The route from London to Norwich was then a distance of 116 miles, and both coaches raced along at breakneck speed, neither stopping to change horses or to pick up or drop passengers over the last 25 miles. In spite of Thorogood's reputation, the Day was first to arrive in Norwich at 4.45 p.m., 10 minutes ahead of the Times, the driver of the Day setting up a new record of 11 hours 15 minutes. Rivalry between coach companies was fierce and drivers of rival coaches plying the same route invariably competed to be the first to arrive at a destination. When John Thorogood finally retired in 1825 he had travelled several thousands of miles and had seen the cities of London and Norwich daily. (Richings, D., & Rudderham, R., *Strange Tales of East Anglia*, S.B. Publications, 1998)

DECEMBER 31ST

1868: On this day the Dean of Norwich, Edward Meyrick Goulburn, attended church and afterwards went for a walk on to Mousehold. Long walks were part of his daily routine, often 5 or 6 miles, during which he covered every road and path leading out of Norwich to Eaton, Earlham, Costessey, Sprowston, Rackheath, Thorpe and Lakenham. He had a particular fascination for the twelfth-century site of the martyrdom of St William of Norwich, and for the fifteenth-century Lollards' Pit. Whenever possible he took his visitors on a walk which included these sites, always preferring company to solitude – friends, relatives, his Canons, the Precentor, the Chapter Clerk, visiting preachers, anyone who would go. Frequently they were occasions for business or theological discussion, and for his colleagues in the cathedral they were a more relaxed way of working out a problem, or discussing a plan, than sitting across a table from each other. If he did have to go alone, he took a book, or *The Times*, and could be seen going along reading, or meditating on his next sermon, as well as greeting friends and acquaintances and stopping for a chat. (Henderson, S.J. Noel (Ed), *The Goulburn Norwich Diaries*, The Canterbury Press, 1966)